Building on Bion: Branches

The International Library of Group Analysis

Edited by Malcolm Pines, Institute of Group Analysis, London

The aim of this series is to represent innovative work in group psychotherapy, particularly but not exclusively group analysis. Group analysis, taught and practised widely in Europe, derives from the work of SH Foulkes.

INTERNATIONAL LIBRARY OF GROUP ANALYSIS 21

Building on Bion: Branches

Contemporary Developments and Applications of Bion's Contributions to Theory and Practice

Edited by Robert M. Lipgar and Malcolm Pines

Jessica Kingsley Publishers
London and New York

First published in the United Kingdom in 2003
by Jessica Kingsley Publishers Ltd
116 Pentonville Road
London N1 9JB, England
and
29 West 35th Street, 10th fl.
New York, NY 10001-2299, USA

www.jkp.com

Copyright © 2003 Jessica Kingsley Publishers

Library of Congress Cataloging in Publication Data
A CIP catalog record for this book is available from the Library of Congress

British Library Cataloguing in Publication Data
A CIP catalogue record for this book is available from the British Library

ISBN 1 84310 711 2

Printed and Bound in Great Britain by
Athenaeum Press, Gateshead, Tyne and Wear

Contents

Part I: Working with Groups

Part II: Application – Putting Bion's Ideas to Work

Part III: Bion as Pioneer in Thinking, Learning and Transmitting Knowledge

Introduction

Bion, the Navigator of the Deep and Formless Infinite

Overview

James S. Grotstein

Bion's (1961a) 'A Psycho-analytic theory of thinking,' which represented an epistemological harvest of his findings on schizophrenic thought disorder, became the bedrock and launching pad for his future explorations in mental functioning. Interestingly, he published an updated version of his *Experiences in Groups* in the same year, from which fact we can glean that he was involved with epistemology from the psychoanalytic point of view and was probably attempting to integrate his findings and conclusions there with his ideas about groups. These efforts would converge in a reformulation of the group process with his concept of the 'messiah' or 'genius' in *Attention and Interpretation* (Bion 1970).

In the meanwhile, however, his application of psychoanalytic concepts to groups, particularly splitting and projective identification, found their way from the original small group to larger mid-sized groups and to the large groups, the last of which came to be known as the 'Tavistock Group.' Mark Ettin (Chapter 1) describes the differences between these groups. He makes the following statement: 'The Tavistock Group...more readily stimulates a *group unconscious* process by inducing members to associate to the shared predicament at the level of primary (basic assumptive) as well as secondary (work group) processes... The median group on the other hand seeks to cultivate the *group's mind*, that is, rational, relational, and collective collaboration through dialogue and brain storming.' This is but a single sample of how he uniquely compares the respective groups. Gerhard Wilke (Chapter 2) takes up the issue of the alleged prejudice that the large group has become associated more with destructiveness than with creativeness and focuses on the conductor role. Sher (Chapter 3) integrates Bion's ideas about individual and group psychology and candidly reveals his own personal – and all too lonely – experiences as a conference director. His experiences beautifully illustrate how confusing it is for a group director to distinguish between (a) projective identification emerging solely from group members with no reality behind them, and (b) projective identifications into the assumed reality of the director's behavior. Jeffrey Roth (Chapter 4) uniquely discusses Alcoholics Anonymous as a 'pharmacological treatment' in its own right and discusses it as a successful work group.

Between 1962 and 1970 a series of short and dense but profound books came out that were slowly but surely to change the way psychoanalysts, at first only Kleinians but later other psychoanalysts as well, would regard how they practice. The title of each of these works is holographic in so far as each could represent the entirety of what he wrote during that time and represent his signature works: *Learning from Experience* (1962), *Elements of Psycho-Analysis* (1963), *Transformations* (1965), and *Attention and Interpretation* (1970). Perhaps one might also add *Two Papers: The Grid and the Caesura* (1977b). In the meanwhile Bion had moved from London to Los Angeles (1965) and began working on his monumental three-volume monograph, *A Memoir of the Future* (1975, 1977a, 1979). *Cogitations* (1992), his private notebook, was published posthumously.

Bion had been distressed over the great controversy between Anna Freud and her followers and Melanie Klein and her followers. He came of age analytically during the peak of that conflict. He thought that the controversy could have been ameliorated had there been a scientific language that would support a greater degree of accuracy in clinical observations and formulations. Consequently, one sees a propensity in his earlier works here to mathematize psychoanalysis into 'functions,' 'factors,' and the like. For instance, he states: 'Suppose I see the man walking. I may say that his walk is a function of his personality and that I find, after investigation, that the factors of this function are his love for a girl and his envy of her friend' (Bion 1961, p. ix). Bion was to pursue his mathematical zeal (he was a polymath) up through *Transformations*, following which other propensities emerge, those of philosophy and mysticism. Throughout all his subsequent works, however, one witnesses the tight discipline of his reasoning. Bion is the consummate ratiocinist. He always thinks binocularly, perhaps we might now say with an admirable balance between his 'right-hemisphere' and 'left-hemisphere,' i.e., between his soaring 'imaginative conjectures' and 'wild thoughts' and his common sense and ability to correlate.

Highlights from *Learning from Experience*

Because of the density and complexity of Bion's works I shall limit myself here to brief highlights from his principal works. What I shall allude to can be thought of as small islands in a vast archipelago that is connected by a vast land mass on the ocean floor.

After explaining his rationale for using mathematical terms, such as functions and factors, Bion delves into a discussion of alpha function,[1] an idea he had come upon when he realized that schizophrenics, as infants, were deprived of the experience of having a mother who was willing and able to tolerate (contain) her infant's experiences of dread. He revised the term 'alpha-function' (in *Cogitations* 1992 where he refers to it as 'dream-work alpha') which was 'intentionally, devoid of meaning' (p.3). He goes on to say:

> Since the object of this meaningless term is to provide psycho-analytic investigation with a counterpart of the mathematical variable, an unknown that can be invested with a value when its use helped to determine what that value is, it is important that it should not be prematurely used to convey meanings, for the premature meanings may be precisely those that is it essential to exclude. (Bion 1962, p.3)

From this citation we can glean Bion's attempt at scientific and mathematical rigour. 'Alpha-function' is a useful term because it lacks associations with other entities; therefore it avoids becoming saturated as an idea. This thinking on his part is the forerunner of his later statement 'Abandon memory and desire.' Hanna Biran (Chapter 5) discusses alpha-function and attacks on linking from the group perspective in the context of consulting to a large group organization. She demonstrates the effect of alpha function with experiences relevant and even particular to the organization context to which she was consulting.

Attention and notation

In Chapter 2 Bion (1962) refers to Freud's (1911) work, 'Two principles of mental functioning,' in which the latter separates the reality principle from the pleasure principle and alludes to consciousness as being the sense-organ responsible for psychic qualities. This sense-organ subserves the function of *attention*. The function of *notation* was added in order for memory-traces to be laid down. 'Notation and the deposition of results of attention are also phenomena to be investigated by the aid of the theory of alpha-function' (Bion 1962, p5). Here we see the beginnings of a theory of thinking and also the forerunner of the Grid. In terms of the group one could hypothesize that the group, with its leader, constitutes a grid that is to process 'wild thoughts,' think about them, and follow through on all their possible meanings and abstractions. Robert Hinshelwood (in Volume 1) applies these ideas to the group process.

The alimentary model

In discussing thinking, Bion was interested in how we know what we know, how thoughts become thoughts to be thought about. Being influenced by Klein, he chose the model or metaphor of the alimentary canal, i.e. where food is *in*gested and then *di*gested into its irreducible building blocks, e.g. amino acids, sugars, fatty acids, i.e. elementary thoughts. He suggests that the raw data (beta elements) that are to be 'ingested' and 'digested' require alpha-function in order to be broken down into alpha-elements that are suitable for notation in dreaming.[2] He then states:

> As alpha-function makes the sense impressions of the emotional experience available for conscious and dream-thought the patient who cannot dream cannot go to sleep and cannot wake up. (Bion 1962, p.7).

Of additional importance here is his designation, 'sense impressions of emotional experience.' Bion's whole oeuvre is about emotions as thoughts! In the meanwhile, however, he is laying down the fundamentals for a theory of emotional thinking in which 'thoughts,' also known as beta-elements or 'thoughts without a thinker,' are initially unmentalized. They require or, more accurately, await a thinker to think them. The first of these 'thinkers' is alpha-function, which 'alpha-bet(a)izes' the beta-elements into alpha-elements, that thereafter become qualified, mentalized thoughts. Without alpha-function the beta-elements can only be handled by evacuation or premature action via projective identification.[3] Bion then states that attacks against alpha-function, say by envy or hate, destroy the possibility for the patient to have contact with himself or others. The group correlate of this is that the group members, facing a crisis, may fuse into a concrete unity and aggregate (see Earl Hopper, Volume 1), and then massively project into the leader, thus eventuating an incohesion (anarchy), the group equivalent of psychosis.

The contact-barrier and the beta-screen

Bion then broadened the role of alpha-function and of alpha-elements into the establishment of a *contact barrier* between consciousness and unconsciousness, one that allows repression, rather than projective identification, to take priority. This contact barrier allows for the selective passage of elements from the unconscious and consciousness to travel in either direction. In psychotics, however, another barrier takes place, a 'beta-screen,' i.e. a ring of beta elements that is porous to information traveling between what would otherwise be consciousness and the unconscious (since in psychosis the distinction no longer exists owing to the absence of a contact barrier of alpha-elements). Consciousness is projected into the analyst, and the patient is held captive by the beta-screen and cannot receive or process interpretations. The group – and intergroups within a larger social system – equivalent of a beta ring – can currently be seen in terrorist organizations.

Alpha-function and thinking

Bion continues to develop his alimentary model of thinking by referring to the necessity for the infant to tolerate frustration long enough to be able to encode his/her raw sense impressions into alpha-thoughts. In the meanwhile, the infant's mother must employ *her* alpha-function to accept, tolerate, and 'translate' (into meaning) her infant's raw sense impressions. Bion believes that ultimately the infant introjects his/her mother's alpha-function as his/her own and becomes a 'thinker' once (s)he can project his/her 'wild thoughts' into this now internalized maternal container. (While agreeing with Bion in the essentials of this process, it is my belief that the capacity for alpha-function is an inherent given, a Kantian a priori category that is incipient in the infant and needs maternal reinforcement for development.) By constructing the model of alpha-function and containment, Bion altered Freud's (1911) hypothesis of the primacy of the pleasure principle over the reality principle in infancy by suggesting that the infant is projecting its reality as well as its unpleasure into mother; therefore the reality principle and the pleasure principle are coeval.[4]

In Chapter 12, as Bion develops his concept of the container and the containing function, he introduces the term 'maternal reverie' to designate the state of mind she must be in to employ her alpha-function. He then states:

> [A] 'need for the breast'...is a feeling that is equated with a 'bad breast.' This bad breast has to be exchanged for a good breast. An infant capable of tolerating frustration can permit itself to have a sense of reality, to be dominated by the reality principle. If its intolerance of frustration reaches beyond a certain degree omnipotent mechanisms come into operation, notably projective identification. This might still be regarded as realistic, in that it suggests awareness of the value of a capacity for thought as a means of softening frustration when the reality principle is dominant. But it depends for its efficacy on the existence of the mother's capacity for reverie... We have thus approached a mental life unmapped by the theories elaborated for the understanding of neurosis. (Bion 1962, p.37)

Here Bion is setting forth the basic requirements for thinking to take place. The infant (the infantile portion of the personality) must be able to tolerate frustration (frustrating feeling-thoughts), i.e. the experience of containing a 'bad breast,' long enough in order to allow for the circumstance of mother's return, or, in lieu of that, the ability of the infant's own alpha-function to remind him that she *will* return.

L, H and K links

Bion extracts the idea of the libidinal and aggressive instincts from Freud and the epistemophilic instinct from Klein to conceive of L (love), H (hate), and K (knowledge) as the irreducible links between self and objects. In short, they constitute the basis of object-relations and constitute *his* version of Freud's (and Klein's) instinctual drives. He also ingeniously conceived of their negative counterparts, –L, –H, and –K. Groups can either be involved constructively with K links along with balanced L and H (normal ambivalence) or destructively with –K links (attacking reality) along with imbalances or splitting between L and H or even using –H and –L linkages with one another, i.e. indifference, passive-aggressiveness, and/or disingenuous fellowship.

Abstraction

Bion assigns the function of abstraction to alpha-function. Abstraction has two meanings. One is the breakdown of a substance or idea into its component elements. The other is proceeding in the direction that is the obverse of the concrete. Abstraction is a common denominator in the operation of metaphor. Ultimately, abstraction will describe the increasing levels of sophistication of thoughts, proceeding vertically downward on his Grid. One working group function would be that of being able to think about the tasks at hand by abstracting the significant elements that are common to each enterprise and being able to make conclusions (constant conjunctions) about them, i.e. to theorize about them.

The 'selected fact'

Here Bion first employs the concept of the 'selected fact,' which he borrowed from Poincaré, the mathematician. It is destined to become an essential element in his theory of technique. Put simply, the mother's or the analyst's use of alpha-function in a state of reverie amounts to their use of their tolerance of their own frustration long enough so that, through their unconscious alpha-function, they can ultimately detect the hidden order or coherence to the hitherto chaotic utterances (also thanks to abstraction). It amounts to 'listening with the third ear.' The group leader must patiently listen for the selected fact to emerge so that he can effectively interpret the group's anxiety.

Elements of Psycho-Analysis

In this work Bion is interested in formalising a scientific deductive system for application to psychoanalysis. He states:

> For the purposes for which I want them the elements of psycho-analysis must have the following characteristics: 1. They must be capable of representing a realization that they were originally used to describe. 2. They must be capable of articulation with other similar elements. 3. When so articulated they should form a scientific deductive system capable of representing a realisation suppose one existed… (Bion 1963, pp. 2–3)

After establishing his desire to make psychoanalysis scientifically based,[5] Bion proceeds to list some of the scientific elements: ♀ ♂ as container and contained, which he links with projective identification; 'PS/D,' which he associates with the selected fact (from the chaos of P–S to the certainty of D); the L, H, and K links between psychoanalytic objects ('Any objects linked are to be assumed to be affected by each other' [*ibid.* p.3]); and R (for reason), and I (for idea). He states:

> By α-function I mean that function by which sense impressions are trans-formed into elements capable of storage for use in dreams and other thoughts. R is to represent a function that is intended to serve the passions, whatever they may be, by leading to their dominance in the world of reality. By passions I mean all that is comprised in L, H, K. R is associated with I in so far as I is used to bridge the gap between an impulse and its fulfilment. R insures that it is bridged to some purpose other than the modification of frustration during the temporal pause. (*ibid.* p.4)

The above is a beautiful summary of Bion's theory of thinking.

He then goes on to elucidate psychoanalytic elements and psychoanalytic objects. He states:

> I shall consider an object sensible to psycho-analytic scrutiny if, and only if, it fulfils conditions analogous to the conditions that are fulfilled when a physical object's presence is confirmed by the evidence of two or more senses… The problem is to determine just how far we can go in accepting deductions from sensa as having, in the field of psycho-analysis, the same validity as sensa have in physics or philosophy. (*ibid.* p.10)

He goes on to describe 'common sense' and 'correlation' as confirmations in reality of the judgements of our sensa. Finally, he states:

> Psycho-analytic elements and the objects derived from them have the following dimensions: 1. Extension in the domain of sense. 2. Extension in the domain of myth. 3. Extension in the domain of passion. (*ibid.* p.11)

The psycho-analytic object is the task of the analysis for the analyst to detect in the material of the moment. It must be apprehended in its sensual form (i.e. smell, sight, hearing, etc.), in its existence as a phantasy (myth), and in its emotional qualities. Bion then goes on to say:

> Awareness of passion is not dependent on sense. For senses to be active only one mind is necessary: passion is evidence that two minds are linked and that there cannot possibly be fewer than two minds if passion is present. (*ibid.* p.13)

Then, after discussing the need for the analyst to achieve detachment with his/her analysand, he discusses the analyst's introspection after detachment. He elaborates the following categories:

1. Definition.

2. 'Statements representing the realization in such a way that the analyst's anxiety that the situation is unknown and correspondingly dangerous to him is denied by an interpretation intended to prove to himself and the patient that this is not so...'

3. Statements that are representations of present and past realizations, i.e. notations.

4. Statements representing a scientific deductive system in so far as such a system can be expressed in ordinary conversational English, i.e. attention.

5. The function of the theoretical formulations in this category are interpretations being used with an intention to illuminate material, that would otherwise remain obscure, in order to help the patient to release still further material...

6. Functions of interpretations that fall in this category...are analogous to actions... (*ibid* pp.18–20)

Here Bion is categorizing the intent, conscious or unconscious, of interpretations and correlating them with the Grid.

Subsequently, Bion lays out the relationship between alpha-function and alpha-elements on one hand and pre-conceptions[6] on the other. Alpha-function not only processes the sensory data of emotional experience. It also processes the evolution of inherent preconceptions as they mate with their realizations in external experience – to become conceptions, and with more abstraction, concepts. He then states:

> I propose provisionally to represent the apparatus for thinking by the sign ♀♂. The material...out of which this apparatus is manufactured is *I*. The material with which this apparatus is designed to deal, is *I*. *I* develops a capacity for any one of its aspects to assume indifferently the functions ♀♂ to any other one of its aspects ♀ or ♂. We must now consider *I* in its ♀♂ operation, an operation usually spoken of in ordinary conversation as thinking. From the point of view of meaning thinking depends on the successful introjection of the good breast that is originally responsible for the performance of α-function. (*ibid.* pp.31–32)

I understand this difficult passage to mean that ♀♂ is Bion's way of stating that the mind is fundamentally a container and that I, ideas, can be attributed either to ♀ or ♂. Put another way, I came first as beta-elements or 'thoughts (ideas) without a thinker' looking for ♀♂ to think them. Subsequently, ♀♂ thinks alpha-bet(a)-ized I.

The grid

Bion then discusses many aspects of his Grid. When asked what prompted him to devise the Grid, he would unfailingly answer that he wanted to find a way that members of differing psychoanalytic schools could discuss ideas from a common point of view. When asked when he used the Grid, he would answer, 'in the evening when thinking about a session, never during the session. I don't believe either answer.' When one examines the Grid closely, one first realizes that the horizontal columns deal with the progression or sophistication of the process of *thinking*, whereas the vertical columns deal with the evolution of levels of abstraction of *thoughts*. When one puts them together, one begins to realize that *the Grid is a polar-coordinated way of representing normal thinking about thoughts, and as such, charts the way we think about patients' associations, and our thoughts about these associations as well as our own — during the analytic session, not just following it.* This principle applies to group processes as well. The group leader can avail himself of the Grid to channel the variegated voices speaking within the group into a coherent pattern of collective meaning, as Hanna Biran (Chapter 5) seeks to explicate.

Reversible perspective

Bion refers to the phenomenon of reversible perspective in psychotic thinking. It is a formidable defense that is due to extreme mental pain. It manifests itself by the patient's alternating the perspective of the context in which the analyst interprets to him. The latter's *figure* (as in figure/ground) becomes the former's *ground*. Once during a rainy day, I interpreted to a schizophrenic that he seemed tearful about something that had happened to him. He responded that he didn't mind the rain. He likes rain, he said. Later, Bion extracted from this mechanism the healthy idea of shifting perspectives in order to achieve binocular vision.

Transformations

In *Elements of Psycho-Analysis* Bion sought to establish a new, unique scientific vocabulary to approach his epistemological foray into the workings of the mind. In *Transformations* we find yet another unique contribution to the psychoanalytic literature, one which follows in line with his alimentary model for thinking, but also one which puts into effect the new formulations from his previous work. Ideas, like food, must undergo transformative changes before they can be stored for further use. Moreover, it is important that the essential ingredients of the food or thought remain invariant in the transformation even though other aspects may have undergone radical changes. Bion states:

> By analogy with the artist and the mathematician I propose that the work of the psycho-analyst should be regarded as transformation of a realization (the actual psycho-analytic experience) into an interpretation or series of interpretations. Two concepts have been introduced, transformation and invariance. The book will be devoted to these concepts and their application to the problems of psycho-analytic practice. (Bion 1965, p.6)

And indeed, that is what the book is about. Psychoanalysis and group processes as well employ the relationship between transformation and invariance in the following way: the frame or setting of the analytic or group work constitutes one class of invariants, whereas the emotions that transpire there undergo transformations, the end result of which is that the irreducible element of the emotions becomes another invariant. The way the emotions are expressed may be the variable.

The point of transition in Bion's thinking between deterministic science and 'mystical science'

After introducing such recondite mathematical terms as 'T1pa,' 'T2pa, T1pβ, and T2pβ' (where, in the first example, the initial real experience, α, of the patient is undergoing a transformation (T) to p (patient) β (transformed experience) and T2 represents a second series of transformations, Bion then states that the element to be transformed is initially a real experience, O, which he associates with Kant's thing-in-itself or noumenon, i.e. unknowable. Bion states:

> In practice this means that I shall regard only those aspects of the patient's behaviour which are significant as representing his view of O… From the analytic treatment as a whole I hope to discover from the invariants in this

material what O is, what he *does* to transform O (that is to say, the nature of T (patient) a) and, consequently, the nature of T (patient). This last point is the *set* of transformations, to which his particular transformation (T patient) is to be assigned. (*ibid.* p.15)

In other words, in deciphering the patient's transformation of O, we learn about the patient. The analyst must pay close attention to the analysand's material to detect his experience (approximation) of O, how the analysand transforms his emotional experience of O (in his free associations), and what the invariant is that persists in the associations. The other point of significance here is Bion's introduction of 'O,' which is to have a significant impact on his subsequent work and enter the mystical. All this time he has taken unusual pains to introduce formal mathematical and (linear) scientific logic to psychoanalysis. Now he is entering the realm of nonlinear science or 'emotional science,' as he will call it, and he is invoking Immanuel Kant in support of his views.

After presenting a clinical illustration, Bion states:

The first question is, What is O (patient), or, to express it in more conversational terms, what was the patient talking *about*? One answer is that he was talking about the week-end break. Let us examine this… Such a solution cannot be arrived at by any ordinary view of his statements. To re-state the question and answer in terms of transformation theory: O (analyst), the patient's statements, have been transformed by me, my mental processes being represented by T (analyst) α, to form a view, T (analyst) β, from which I deduce that T (patient) = the week-end break. Or rather that I have assumed that week-end break, O, exists, and that the phenomena associated with O by the patient is something I denote by T (patient). (*ibid.* p.17)

My 'translation' of these series of transformations is as follows: The week-end break is the adaptive context and signifier of 'O,' the 'thing-in-itself,' the analytic object that exists in the patient's mind, is an as yet unmentalized beta^7-element. The patient relates his associations to the analyst, who then, thanks to his reverie and containment, 'becomes' O and transforms his experience of O into alpha-elements. What Bion is emphasizing here is the difference between the patient's experience of O and the analyst's experience of the patient's and his own O in response. This principle, from a psychoanalytic point of view, applies to the relationship between the leader and the group as well.

Bion goes on to define differing kinds of transformations: 'rigid-motion transformations,' 'projective transformations,' and 'transformations in hallucinosis.' The first designates that kind of transference conception held by classical and other analysts and is characterized by Freud's (1915) statement that transference is a *displacement* of past object cathexes. What is to be understood by this, according to Bion, is that that kind of transference designates an intactness of the object or the object-relations situation so that there is little distortion in the comparison between the past and the present. In geometric terms, Bion thinks of the verisimilitude of the transference as a 'rigid-motion,' that is, the phenomenon has been transferred from one locale to another with little change.

Projective transformation is Bion's way of representing the transformation that occurs when projective identification, rather than displacement, occurs. In projective identification the projected identity significantly alters the subject's perception of the object. One aspect of projective transformations is the achievement of the confusional state, i.e. fusion with the object, in order to become unaware of mental pain, O. Another is the evacuation of mental pain itself into an object, in either case an avoidance of recognition of one's state of mind. A third is using protective transformations as a prelude to enactments.

Transformations in hallucinosis are frankly psychotic and represent, initially, the patient's attempt to achieve the trouble-free state. Subsequently, the objects whose existence had become distorted in the patient's flight to hallucinosis then return as persecutory hallucinations. Bion states:

> In rigid motion transformations the invariants establish the relationship with O. But in projective transformations the differences between Op [the O of the patient][8] and Oa [the O of the analyst] do not permit a process of arguing back from Tp and Taβ to Op and Oa as it can be done in rigid motion transformations. The crux lies in the nature of Op in projective transformations. Op is apparently the stimulus: yet it has qualities which seem to be appropriate to Kant's primary quality. The difficulty becomes less formidable if Op in projective transformation is a psychic reality and has the same capacity for initiating a train of mental events as is possessed by an event of external reality such as a break in the routine of sessions. A feeling of dread might be such an internal psychic quality. (*ibid.* pp.31–32)

This dense series of statements can perhaps become more understandable if we consider that patients who use rigid motion transformations have symbol (alpha-) function and can therefore lend themselves to a communication with the analyst, who thereupon can experience a consensual feeling about the patient's O. With the patient using projective transformations, however, their

O is closer to Kant's thing-in-itself because of the lack of symbolic function (alpha-function). Further, T represents the phenomenal counterpart to noumenal O.

Bion goes on:

> The psychoanalyst tries to help the patient to transform that part of an emotional experience of which he is unconscious into an emotional experience if which he is conscious. If he does this he helps the patient to achieve private knowledge... [T]he psychoanalyst must transform *his* private experience of psycho-analysis so that it becomes a public experience... [N]o one can ever know what happens in the analytic session, the thing-in-itself, O; we can only speak of what the analyst or patient *feels* happens, his emotional experience, that which I denote by T. (*ibid.* pp.31–33)

This passage summarizes Bion's conception of transformations. O, the patient's unconscious raw experience, must be transformed[9] so that it becomes the patient's private knowledge about himself, but in so far as the series of transformations conducted by the analyst were operative as well, the patient's experience of O has now become *publicated*, according to Bion.

The point and the line

Even though Bion is moving steadily into O, he has not yet forfeited his geometric model. He states:

> The point has appeared clinically as dot or dots, spot or spots ('spots' in or before the eyes is a fairly common phenomenon). I have described the point or line as an object indistinguishable from the place where the breast or penis was. Owing to the difficulty of being sure what the patient is experiencing I resort to a variety of descriptions, each of which is unsatisfactory. The spot, for example, seems to be part conscience, part breast, part faeces, destroyed, non-existent yet present, cruel and malignant. The inadequacy of description or categorization as thought at all has led me to the term $\forall$-element as a method of representing it. The spoken word seems significant only because it is invisible and intangible; the visual image is significant because it is inaudible. Every word represents what it is not – a 'no-thing', to be distinguished from 'nothing'. (*ibid.* pp.78–79)

In the above citation Bion is establishing one of the most important canons of his epistemological theory. What must be added to the above is the quality of being able to tolerate frustration. The infant who is able to tolerate frustration is able to tolerate the absence of the breast as a 'nothing,' whereas the infant who cannot tolerate frustration attacks his image of the breast, and this attacked image deteriorates into the 'no-thing' as a concrete phantom-object that represents what he has done to the breast and its transformation into a conscience. The faeces represent the mode of attack. The concrete 'no-thing' becomes a phantasmally real object that falsely fills the space for thought, thereby preventing any possibility of real thoughts emerging.

Godhead and O

The remainder of the book focuses on Bion's revolutionary conception of O. Though Bion seems to have become highly revered by London Kleinians for his work in psychosis and in his formulations of container–contained and intersubjective projective identification, no mention is made of his conception of O and its link with 'godhead,' which represents Bion's departure from linear science into 'mystical' or 'emotional science.'

O is his term for the Absolute Truth about an Ultimate Reality that exists beyond the senses and the images that the senses create. It corresponds in many ways to Lacan's (1966) 'Register of the Real.' It is indescribable, ineffable, inscrutable. One can only 'become' it.[10] Bion associates O also with life as it is, the psychoanalytic object, infinity, noumena, things-in-themselves, chaos, and 'godhead.' 'Godhead' is interesting. Bion was well read in Christian and Jewish mysticism. In particular, he referred to Meister Eckhart's distinction between the immanent 'God' within us and the 'Godhead' of essence that is independent of humans. This is a distinction that goes all the way back to Plato, who distinguished between the god of essence and god, the creator of the world, the *demiurge*. Bion reverses Eckhart's distinction and places 'godhead' (small 'g') immanently within man as O. I think that Bion is conflating O's infinite nature with animism to create 'godhead.' Clinically speaking, however, O behaves as if it *were* God, until we transform our experience of it into mundane, earthly terms.

The ultimate significance of 'O,' once it is conflated with Matte-Blanco's (1975, 1981, 1988) theory that infinite sets and bi-logic characterize the unconscious, is that 'O' constitutes the ultimate repressed, not the drives. Paulo Sandler, Claudio Neri, and Victor Schermer (Volume 1) and Lia Pistener de Cortiñas and Jacqueline Colombier (Chapters 8 and 9 in this volume) take up the issue of 'O' in reference to the group.

Transformations was to become yet a new turning point in Bion's quest for the Holy Grail of his psychoanalytic foray into epistemology. One can observe his gradual disengagement from mathematical and 'scientific' models to one that can be characterized as *mystical*. Thereafter, Bion will speak of 'mystical science,' and will spend his efforts in clarifying 'transformations in – and from – O.'

Attention and interpretation

Bion begins by referring to the *'Language of Achievement,'* a notion he borrowed from Keats having to do with tolerating frustration rather than ending one's frustration by jumping to conclusions. As one has been able to see thus far, the ability to tolerate frustration is ground zero in Bion's episteme. The idea of language, however, leads to a discussion of the dilemma of whether language leads to, or misleads away from, truth. Bion thereupon discusses the psychology of the liar. Bion is less interested in the liar[11], however, than in the attempt to acquire the Language of Achievement to achieve intimate contact with truth. (See Lia Pistiner de Cortiñas (Chapter 8) on this issue.) He states:

> It is too often forgotten that the gift of speech, so centrally employed, has been elaborated as much for the purpose of concealing thought by dissimulation and lying as for the purpose of elucidating or communicating thought. Therefore, the Language of Achievement, if it is to be employed for elucidating the truth, must be recognized as deriving not only from sensuous experience but also from impulses and dispositions far from those ordinarily associated with scientific discussion. Freud…felt the need to isolate himself – insulate himself? – from the group in order to work. This would mean insulating ourselves against the very material we should study. (Bion 1966, p.3)

In this citation we see a new Bion, one who has made the tolerance of frustration central to his theory of thinking about O and has now begun to add a different dimension to psychoanalytic listening, one, ironically, that dates back to Freud himself. Bion now calls it learning the Language of Achievement. What I believe he means by this is as follows: in order to qualify to become a 'Man of Achievement,' the subject must be able to tolerate frustration and doubt long enough for the selected fact of truth to emerge. The result would be the 'Language of Achievement.' The subject who cannot wait because he cannot tolerate doubt or frustration allows falsehood to fill the gap; thus, he becomes the falsifier or liar. The application of this principle to group processes is all too obvious.

Soon Bion will come out with his clarion call to *abandon memory and desire*[12] (and understanding and preconceptions as well). In short, the patient's language is not the Language of Achievement. It is the language of deception, i.e. defensive. Bion believes that the analyst must eschew what I would call 'left-hemispheric' listening for 'right-hemispheric' listening – by *listening to oneself listening to the patient*. In other words, the analyst must 'cast a beam of intense darkness' into the analytic session (not listen to the patient, in effect) so as to be able to look (really, listen) within himself as to how he, the analyst, is unconsciously receiving and transforming the patient's experience of O – and matching it up with his own O, prior to transforming it into K for the patient. Robert French and Peter Simpson (Chapter 6) effectively capture this aspect of Bion's ideas about 'learning through not knowing' – or even more specifically, through 'Unknowing,' and thereby allowing oneself direct exposure to Truth.

Later, Bion returns to his theory of groups but in a new way. In the chapter 'The mystic and the Group' he elaborates on an idea that the group, both the individuals and the establishment, need a genius or mystic to save them. He states:

> The group needs to preserve its coherence and identity; efforts to do so are manifested in conventions, laws, culture, and language. It also needs the exceptional individual and therefore needs to make provision for the exceptional individual... The exceptional individual may be variously described as a genius, a messiah, a mystic... In this it is evident that the character of the group...cannot be excluded from the facts of the evolution of the mystic in a group. The disruptive force of the mystical nihilist, or of the mystic whose impact on a particular group is of a disruptive or nihilist character, extends to and depends on the Language of Achievement, be it expressed in action, speech, writing, or aesthetic. (Bion 1966 pp. 63–64)

In other words, depending on whether the group's need depends on truth or falsehood, the mystic thus summoned takes his unconscious cue and responds accordingly. Claudio Neri (Volume 1) takes up the issue of the genius in his concept of the 'genius loci,' which is an attribute initially of the leader of the work group but rotates between members of the group. The function of the genius loci is to maintain group identity and assure the affective continuity of the group in moments of crisis and change. The genius loci 'regulates syncretic sociality and works through the connection between the affective life and rational life of the group.'

Lia Pistiner de Cortiñas (Chapter 8) develops some ideas that Bion carried over from group to individual psychoanalysis. One was that Bion emphasized that psychoanalysis is a science of *relationships* rather than of objects or persons. A second was that the methods for observing and gauging these relationships were through the instruments of binocular vision, use of different vertices (points of reference), use of reversible perspectives, and others. A third was the issue of mental growth and development through the acceptance of truth rather than the procedure of making the unconscious conscious, as is the case in the Freudian and Kleinian techniques.

Jacqueline Colombier (Chapter 9) uniquely and dramatically compares Glenn Gould's lyrical, aesthetic techniques of composition with Wilfred Bion. She makes the statement that Gould and Bion treat the voice horizontally and vertically to serve their respective projects. She uses this instrument in approaching Bion's *Memoirs of the Future*.

Steven Brown (Chapter 10) discusses the seeming paradox of Bion the scientist and polymath and Bion the mystic. In other words, how could he rationalize his all-abiding interests in science, physics, and mathematics with his realizations about the utter ineffability of the mind? Brown thereupon discusses a virtual *doppelgänger* of Bion's, William Stephenson, a scientist who had had a Kleinian analysis and who, like Bion, stood on the razor's edge between the two domains.

There is much more in Bion's work to unravel, and my briefest of summaries hardly does justice to it. If nothing else I hope I have inspired the reader to read or to reread these texts, as well as Bion's other works, particularly *Cogitations* (1992) and *A Memoir of the Future* (1975, 1977a, 1979), as perhaps the most profound and far-reaching attempts to explore the mind to date. Bion was truly a genius and mystic. Someone once said that Bion was 'miles behind his face.' While that might have been true, it is also true that he was face-to-face with Truth virtually all his life, paid a price for it, and left his experience as a legacy for us. But let me try to synopsize his legacy: Bion bequeathed to us the most profound and far-reaching epistemological, onto-logical and phenomenological model of the unconscious to date. He tran-scended Freud with his ground-breaking conception of Transformations in and from O. He relegated the drives to a lesser hierarchy and installed the absolute truth about ultimate reality, along with the truth instinct, as the major dilemma that mankind has to deal with. Bion was both a mystic and a visionary; he saw through the images of disguise that blind our mortal sight.

References

Bion, W. R. (1961a) 'A psycho-analytic theory of thinking.' *International Journal of Psycho-Analysis* 43, 306–310.

Bion, W. R. (1961b) *Experiences in Groups*. London: Tavistock.

Bion, W. R. (1962) *Learning From Experience*. London: Heinemann.

Bion, W. R. (1963) *Elements of Psycho-Analysis*. London: Heinemann.

Bion, W. R. (1965) *Transformations*. London: Heinemann.

Bion, W. R. (1966) 'Catastrophic change.' The Bulletin of the British Psycho-Analytic Society, No. 5.

Bion, W. R. (1970) *Attention and Interpretation*.

Bion, W. R. (1975) *A Memoir of the Future. Book I: The Dream*. Rio de Janeiro, Brazil: Imago Press.

Bion, W. R. (1977a) *A Memoir of the Future. Book II: The Past Presented*. Brazil: Imago Editora.

Bion, W. R. (1977b) *Two Papers: The Grid and the Caesura*. Ed. Jayme Salomao. Rio de Janeiro: Imago Editora, Ltd.

Bion, W. R. (1979) *A Memoir of the Future. Book III: The Dawn of Oblivion*. Perthshire: Clunie Press.

Bion, W. R. (1992) *Cogitations*. London: Karnac Books.

de Bianchedi, E. T. (1993) 'Lies and falsities.' *Journal of Melanie Klein and Object Relations 11*, 30–46.

Freud, S. (1911) 'Formulations of the two principles of mental functioning.' *Standard Edition 12*, 213–226. London: Hogarth Press, 1958.

Freud, S. (1941[1915]) 'Observations on transference-love. (Further recommendations on the technique of psycho-analysis, III.)' In: *Remembering, Repeating, and Working-Through*. London: Hogarth Press, pp. 157–171.

Lacan, J. (1966) *Écrits: 1949–1960*. Trans. A. Sheridan. New York: W. W. Norton, 1977.

Matte Blanco, I. (1975) *The Unconscious as Infinite Sets*. London: Duckworth Press.

Matte-Blanco, I. (1981) 'Reflecting with Bion.' In *Do I Dare Disturb the Universe? A Memorial to Wilfred R. Bion*. Ed. J. S. Grotstein. Beverly Hills: Caesura Press, 1981, pp.489–528.

Matte Blanco, I. (1988) *Thinking, Feeling, and Being: Clinical Reflections on the Fundamental Antinomy of Human Beings*. London/New York: Tavistock and Routledge.

Endnotes

1.   Bion sought terms such as 'alpha,' 'beta,' etc. because they were unencumbered with used meaning. He was seeking to create a special terminology or language that, by its lack of saturation, would be more versatile for expression and more appealing to professionals.

2.   Here Bion was prescient. We now know that REM sleep and dreaming facilitate memory.

3.   It occurs to me that the function of the group leader is to supply his/her alpha-function to the beta-elements emerging from the group members to give proper interpretations about truth, on one hand, and to be the agent of repression

for those ideas which the group is not yet ready to hear, i.e. considerations of timing and dosage.

4.   It is my belief that Freud's pleasure principle, since it subserves the lie to the Truth, constitutes Column 2 on Bion's Grid.

5.   It should also be pointed out that Bion had another motive in his unique way of expressing himself, to he was hoping to reduce the mis-communications and frustrating theoretical conflicts amongst his fellow analysts. Furthermore, he believed that the scientific method was the best tool we had to resolve conflicting views of reality.

6.   See Brown's (this volume) contribution in which he deals with Bion's concepts of pre-conception and realisation.

7.   The 'beta' of 'beta-element' should not be confused with the sequence of transformations from 'α' (the beginning) to 'β' (the end or result).

8.   Brackets are mine.

9.   This does not mean that O becomes transformed. Only the patient's experience of O becomes transformed. Similarly, the unconscious can never become conscious; only our experiences of it can be become conscious.

10.   Although I am not sure, I have an idea that, by 'become,' Bion means the way it was used by Plato, i.e. 'that which is is always becoming' – but not arriving!

11.   I infer from Bion, though he didn't actually state so, that the liar, like the psychotic, is closer to the truth that has to be avoided. Normal people and neurotics employ falsehoods (de Bianchedi, 1993).

12.   Bion explains his dictum, 'Abandon memory and desire,' by linking their role to the verdict of the senses. I think this idea is better understood if we consider that knowledge, memory, desire, understanding, preconceptions, etc., are revealed in sensory images. Bion seeks to transcend the image to approach Reality-in-itself, without disguise.

Part I

Working with Groups

1

Bion's Legacy to Median and Large Groups

Mark F. Ettin

I. Introduction to median and large group wrk

Toward a methodology of large-group leadership

> The term 'group therapy' can have two meanings. It can refer to the treatment of individuals assembled for special therapeutic sessions, or it can refer to the planned endeavor to develop in a group the forces that lead to a smoothly running co-operative endeavor. (Bion 1961, with John Rickman, p.II)

A variety of microcosmic experiential, laboratory group methods have been applied to study, simulate, or potentially solve macrocosmic societal problems. This paper compares, contrasts and integrates two of these technologies, the median group approach adapted from group analytic practice (de Maré, Piper and Thompson 1991; de Maré 1989, 1994a, 1994b) and the Tavistock large group method inspired by W. R. Bion (1961) as adapted in A. K. Rice group relations conferences (Kreeger 1975; Turquet 1975). A three-and-a-half day median group experience will be described from the author's participant–observer position to provide data for this analysis.

It is conceded that this narrative is but one of many possible social constructions of reality. The character of that workshop and the conduct of its formal leader may also be unique to time, place and style of intervention. Notwithstanding these qualifications, it is suggested that the time has come to sketch the geography of median and large groups and outline a practice methodology of large-group leadership that can be applied within and across theoretical approaches in both clinical (group analysis) and psychoeducational (group relations) settings. The rich data of the experiential workshop and like experiences is conducive to formulating general propositions about the work of median and large groups. Propositions presented in this paper reflect on a group's organizational structure, leadership, member–leader interface, subgrouping tendencies, thematic development and evolving culture.

This paper is presented in three parts: I. An introduction to the parameters of median and large group work; II. The exposition of a median group experience; and III. A critical comparison of models. The seminal work of Wilfred R. Bion informs this effort.

Wilfred Bion and self-study groups

> The apparent difference between group psychology and individual psychology is an illusion produced by the fact that the group provides an intelligible field of study for certain aspects of individual psychology, and in so doing brings into prominence phenomena that appear alien to an observer unaccustomed to using the group. (Bion 1961, p.134)

> The explanation of certain phenomena must be sought in the matrix of the group and not in the individuals that make up the group. (*ibid.* pp.132–133)

Wilfred Bion (1961), a pioneer in the study of group dynamics, received his basic training in the British military during World War II and later at the Tavistock Clinic in London. He assumed an anthropological stance when 'taking groups' and 'leading them' in a nondirective fashion. While in group, Bion eschewed the familiar, hierarchical command structure of the military or medical model that his patients expected him to assume. Rather, he sat back and observed how members, deprived of 'expected structure' and 'usual leadership', comported themselves as a social body, with respect to their task and in relationship to him as consultant. Psychoanalytically inspired and scientifically minded, Bion's group-as-a-whole formulations often included specification of the data that supported his hypotheses.

Bion's groups were in essence self-study groups, where members might come to understand collective dynamics and explore common tensions. By participating freely, members could also learn about how each contributed to a group's dynamics, including the roles they volunteered for or were induced to play. Through his experiences in groups, Bion discovered some of the natural tendencies of group life, under conditions of felt dependency, paucity of formal structure and limited or circumscribed leadership. His studies shed light on what it means to be a group, that is, how an unrelated assortment of people come together through conscious collaboration or unconscious collusion.

A full cultural understanding of any 'group event' – it might be added – cannot be arrived at without comparing and contrasting what various participants to the process notice, feel, think and do about it. In the aftermath of Bion's experiences in groups, the A. K. Rice Institute (AKRI), based in the US, has sought to establish a more collaborative (Gustafson and Cooper 1985) and less heroic (Noumair 1999) institutional culture, with members invited to share in the process of learning from experience (as Bion's 1962, book suggests). To do so implies that members in group relations conferences strike an anthropological pose, driven by curiosity and unhampered by memory or desire that would reduce what is now knowable to one's preexisting mental or social constructions. That is, the membership is invited to share the formal leaders' participant–observer position. For example, Shapiro and Carr (1991), two leading contributors to A. K. Rice work in the US, suggest that the meaning of group realities needs to be negotiated by the members. This requires that each participant adopt an 'interpretive stance,' by speaking about their experiences in and of the group, while avowing their particular contributions to the group's construction. Similarities and contrasts about what is happening (in each member's view) and how they are participating (in the experiences being described) are the phenomena that yield shared understandings. Even if members are silent, the internal processing of interactional and intersubjective experience can provide critical data and the personal insight necessary for members (as participant–observers) to formulate collective constructions of shared, whole-group or sociocultural events. This process in an AKRI 'working conference' demonstrates in operational essence what is meant by a 'social construction of reality' (Sampson 1993).

Bion's legacy to groups extends psychoanalysis of individuals to psychoanalysis of groups, whether small, median or large. For Bion believed that man is a social animal – frightened by, and ever-battling with and against, his own groupishness. Group life is arguably the natural venue to study individuals' social inheritance.

Some comparisons between a Tavistock large group set-up and midsize or median group analysis

> It is possible for a clinician to turn attention to the structure of a group and to the forces operating in that structure without losing touch with his patient. (Bion 1961, with Rickman, p.25)

A relatively unstructured large group event is an important part of Tavistock and A. K. Rice conferences (Rice 1965; Turquet 1975; Main 1975). Participation in an A. K. Rice large group includes the whole of the membership (usually between 40 and 60 persons). Three or four consultants, selected by the conference director out of a consultant staff of approximately nine, take up a consultative role. The ratio of members to leaders is approximately 15–20 to 1. A median group described in diary by de Maré, Piper and Thompson (1991) had a membership of 41, ranged as low as 21, with a mean attendance of 30. Two conveners were present, which would approximate the same member–leader ratio (15 to 1) as in a Tavistock large group. It might be noted that the typical size of a psychoeducational group common in clinical practice – usually facilitated by one leader – is twelve to fifteen participants (Ettin 1999).

The size of the group as a process determinant

The size of a group is an important factor that changes the dynamics and demand characteristics within the group matrix. De Maré *et al.* (1991) suggest that 20 members is an ideal number for a median group (although it can take in more). Rice, writing about his early experiences with Tavistock conferences, indicated that 'the smallest group that we have so far used for the large group is twenty, the largest fifty (Rice 1975, p.106). Miller (1985) reported that large groups were composed of forty to eighty members with up to four consultants. Foulkes suggested that in group-analytic practice large groups have at least 30 members 'but more likely between 50 and 100 or even 120' (Foulkes 1975, p.52). In a recent group-analytic conference in Copenhagen (1996), the large group included 450 members with one formal leader. All of the authors cited above acknowledge that the size of a group has a significant effect on its dynamics and on the experience of its members and leaders. Group size, theoretical orientation and leadership style are interdependent variables.

With this conclusion in mind, a proposition about large group size is offered and followed up with a brief description and initial data about the median group that forms the experiential basis for this report. This includes the author's subjective reaction to the match between this group's size and the number of conveners and the impact of this on the proceedings. More detailed reports about the median group's process and content will follow later in Part II of the paper.

Proposition 1. The less personal and interpersonal a large group becomes, the more members (and leaders) are confronted with the group-as-a-mystery, which comes alive according to what participants project into it.

   (a) As the degree of personal contact diminishes in a group, the more the influence of the group's largeness or strangeness can be felt.

   (b) Members may cognitively simplify their experiences of the large group in order to grasp it.

   (c) As the degree of personal contact is limited by the size or paucity of structure of a group, the more impersonal, imposing, and uniform the group may appear to its members.

   (d) The emotions that adhere to the large group tend to be strongly felt and result in the split of good and bad attributions, especially if its complexity is unattended or unappreciated.

The median group that will be the basis for discussion in this paper, had 30 participants and one convener (as formal leader). It appeared to be short on leadership and a covert wish of this member, throughout the experience, was that a second convener be present. A logical choice would have been the person (Sarah) who brought an esteemed group analyst (Simon) to the US and also invited the workshop participants to a prestigious American university with which she was affiliated. Sarah participated ostensibly as a member, although sometimes she acted as if responsible for the experience as a whole when addressing the administrative and functional needs of the group. Her role, as it was taken up, was similar to that of the director of administration of an A. K. Rice conference, with the significant difference that Sarah also sat in the median group as a fully-participating member.

The group set-up and what it pulls for

> In groups of which I am the psychiatrist I am the most obvious person, by
> virtue of my position, in whom to invest the right to establish rules of
> procedure. I take advantage of this position to establish no rules of
> procedure and to put forward no agenda. (Bion 1961, p.77)

A typical median group was described by de Maré *et al.* (1991). It met for
thirty-six sessions weekly over eleven months. The median group chronicled
here met as an experiential training group for twelve sessions over four days.
This time frame roughly parallels that of an extended-weekend A. K. Rice
conference, although an AKRI conference has fewer large group meetings
and other group events interspersed and may (or may not) be residential with
members living on site.

A median group sits in a large circle so that members can see and talk to
(or at least at) one another. The Tavistock large group is most often seated in a
spiral or 'cyclone' formation (in contrast to the original concentric circle
motif; Lipgar 2000). Some members are figuratively in the eye of the storm
and others keep (or are kept) at the periphery, where they are less likely to
influence, be swept up, blown away or participate fully in the centrality of the
experience. The median group seating is more conducive to dialogue. Chairs
are arranged to provide a face-to-face horizontal leveling of the experience.
The Tavistock seating arrangement, depending on one's position in the spiral,
may or may not allow a member to see the person to whom they are speaking
(or the person speaking to them). Voices come from behind as well as from the
side and front. In the Tavistock set-up, the group as a whole is more structur-
ally strung out and socially disembodied.

The Tavistock seating arrangement elicits more primitive psychological
processes that include rampant projections, resultant projective identifications, and existential anxiety that is often persecutory in nature (Klein 1992).
The group flow is usually less coherent than in the median group (which is
more topical, however charged with feeling). In the Tavistock set-up, people
seldom talk to or answer one another, but frequently speak in soliloquy,
addressing 'the group' (Ettin 2000a), that is, the membership-at-large or the
consultant staff as a leadership team. As a result, part-processes are scattered
about, sometimes to be relocated in the group itself and sometimes in specific
members, subgroups or consultants.

The understanding and recollection of these psychic contents benefit
from interpretive formulations offered by consultants (and sometimes by
members), about the whole of the group or the various parts that persons or

partisan subgroups represent for it. Bion comments – though not specifically about the large group – on how to access this material and when to interpret it:

> In group treatment many interpretations, and among the most important, have to be made on the strength of the analyst's own emotional reactions. It is my belief that these reactions are dependent on the fact that the analyst is at the receiving end of what Melanie Klein (1946) has called projective identification. (Bion 1961, p.149)

> I judge the occasion to be ripe for an interpretation when the interpretation would seem both obvious and unobserved. (Bion 1961, p.143)

Interventions can be figurative (metaphorical and symbolic) or literal (consultative and interpretive – with supporting data cited and linked to phenomenological experiences) as the consultant remarks on how the group members are using the leadership (the consultants), each other and the group as a whole. In the median group, by contrast, it is easier to understand what is said and who is saying it, whether or not one agrees with the sentiments being expressed or can find a direct way to link with or respond to them. These differences are largely due to differential group size, aims, theories and practices as they are mirrored by the group structure and physical (seating) arrangements as well as the consultancy stance and orientation to that role (which is different from that of the median group's convener/conductor).

The responsibilities and prerogatives of leadership

> We are not concerned to give individual treatment in public, but to draw attention to the actual experiences of the group, and…the way in which the group and the individual deal with the individual. (Bion 1961, p.80)

In a group – like the one being described – where agenda or procedures are left unstructured, the group's first operational structure (whether explicitly or implicitly communicated) is provided by the presence and expectations of formal leadership. Members, if they have nothing else in common, are more or less 'joined' with the leader, in this case the 'convener' who brought them all together. A pertinent question is: what is the median group leader's role once the group is convened? Certainly the leader does not have to be autocratic; such a stance would be antithetical to the democratization of the group process and attenuate the leadership potential of members. The leader can, however, function as a consultant in the participant–observer, consultant–analyst mode (Lipgar 1994). That stance would acknowledge a formal leader's acceptance of personal and professional authority within the context of the group. Constructive attention to a group's emotional currents and emergent trends would be required.

The formal leader (whether convener, conductor or consultant) can offer schooled and experience-sensitive consultations to help the membership understand their collective experience, encourage them to participate in it and address impediments to doing so. Members maintain an observing ego (especially when not directly involved in a particular interaction or dialogue) and can be encouraged to consult to their own unique or shared experiences. This metaprocessing, if premature or excessive, however, may take members out of the participant mode, thereby robbing the process of its spontaneity. The role of the consultant (in Bionic and Foulkesian traditions) is to be in (participant) and out of (observer) the experience simultaneously. This is accomplished by using the data of one's own experience for insight into the process and formulations about the contributing context for outsight into the group's dynamics (de Maré *et al.* 1991).

Under-supervised, the membership is likely to be more cautious or more reckless. With an absence of a formal leadership function, chaos and collusion is more likely than coherence and collaboration. The formal leadership need not direct the process forcibly and thereby over-control or otherwise interfere with free-floating discussion (Foulkes 1964). He or she can, rather, operate from behind (Anthony 1991), so that the group can set its own agenda, come to cultural understandings and explore subgroup identifications when following and processing its own course. The possibility of emergent dynamics and organizational configurations being self-reflective and productive increases exponentially when someone capable is at the tiller, someone whose role it is to attend to group process and emergent culture.

Proposition 2. It is very difficult to go from insight (into individual and family dynamics) to outsight (about whole-group or sociocultural processes) without oversight by someone given the authority to:

(a) consult to the group process, so that underlying dynamic currents do not operate unattended to, confound or derail the group from its task;

(b) identify current themes and motifs, so that members realize the common reference points around which they are building their chain of associations;

(c) clarify or deconstruct the issues that underlie conflicts activated in the group as a whole, so that the membership does not become polarized and engage in destructive splitting or scapegoating;

(d) contextualize the experiences in the room, as a bridge from one member (or subgroup) to another and from one theme to the next;

(e) explore the acontextual (universal) motifs and common (existential) dilemmas that have been activated by the here-and-now of the group, so that members can appreciate how they are responding to prototypical human struggles.

II. Clinical exposition of this median group

What is happening and where is the median group going?

Many techniques are in daily use for the investigation of work-group function. For investigation of basic assumption phenomena, I consider psycho-analysis, or some extension of technique derived directly from it, to be essential. (Bion 1961, p.154)

The psychiatrist should find interpretations that give the group insight into what is going on; to bring the ba and W into contact. (Bion 1961, p.126)

This median group (which will now be described in more detail) was difficult to track. It lacked articulation. Much went on, including the telling of poignant personal stories, some wonderful member-generated insights and outsights, an illuminating cross-cultural perspective provided by the 'foreign' members, the evocation of group symbols (such as a swan strangled by the refuse of technology, a decapitated leader whose head wound up on the top of an adjacent building) and group dreams (a perpetually circling train with two missing cars that reflected the group's preoccupation with two missing members).

Unfortunately, the meanings or implications of these individual revelations, personal stories and group symbols were not explored in any depth. Cultural productions (like group dreams or group-reflective metaphors) can be woven together into a fabric (as a socially-construed, coherent narrative) that would cover (or uncover) the common denominator of shared or intersubjective experiences. Without this happening, it was very difficult to identify 'what' was being worked on or learned. The process felt fragmented and the group appeared to channel its anxiety into manic bouts of participation.

Each member's entry into the group as a potential contributor was quickly followed by another and another, with little linking of associations or time allowed for 'contemplative silence' (Hinshelwood 1994). The various remarks did not often inform the process, but rather punctuated or interrupted it. Various members became angry or distraught when the group seemingly did not hear or could not work with what they contributed. Yet, these insults to the integrity of the enterprise and communal value of participants' contributions did not appear wholly personal. They were rather symptomatic of 'disabling cultural norms' (Whitaker and Lieberman, 1964) and the unanalyzed group forces that drove them. Turquet (1975) observed a similar process in an A. K. Rice large group setting:

> Many an I.M. [individual member] statement is actively ignored; not only does it not elicit a response but it is cut off at source, ending there in space, treated as a non-event, with the result that much of the discussion is discontinuous, or disjointed and non-syntactical, remaining idiosyncratic to the individual opening speaker...there being no sense of following on...no forwarding. (Turquet 1975, p.105)

WHO WOULD SPEAK AND WHO WILL LISTEN?

In this median group, the various contributions of the members were very competitive. The membership as a whole was rarely silent or introspective. Participants seemed to believe that, given the size of the group, its verbosity, and the obvious intelligence of the members, one had to be quick and clever about getting something in edgewise. This had a scattering effect that seemed antithetical to the intended 'brain-storming' that median group theory recommends. Many contributions felt egocentric rather than group-centered or culturally targeted. Some members never 'got it' and continued to personalize the proceedings in a way that inevitably led to misunderstandings, narcissistic injuries and the perpetuation of familial dynamics.

Few members were given (though some tried to take up) the consultative role and interpretive stance, by identifying the group's chief concerns, common group tensions (Ezriel 1950), tentative cultural compromises, material arrangements, or ongoing accommodations. By-and-large, individuals (alone or affiliated in subgroups) were not authorized to consult to the group (although some felt that they were). Potentially useful contributions were not always recognized, let alone followed, for what they represented to and for the group. The group seemed in need of a town crier with a clear and resonant voice that could be heard and heeded.

There were a few notable exceptions to the group's inattention, in its response to the more poetic and integrating contributions of Estella and Nadia (two of the group's more articulate members from overseas). The group seemed to listen more intently and give more credence to the words of its 'foreign' members. This was evidenced by the fact that they were invited to speak, not interrupted, that a respectful (and rare) silence often followed their contributions, and that other members were able to link with these contributions in ways that affected the flow of associations. Perhaps members from 'overseas' or from foreign countries were less frequently viewed as objects of competition and as a result were allowed some prominence. They may also have represented an idealized version of Simon (a foreigner and an invited leader and close disciple of de Maré), and thus shared in the group's positive transference.

Proposition 3. It is hard for a group to 'make up its mind' and come to consensus about the collective experience, or know if it is on or off task, without the kind of guidance and mirroring provided by formal leadership. Consultation can lend the membership the confidence to hold together by offering viable hypotheses, as group-centered reflections that focus on and contextualize specific collective processes in order to represent or transform them.

Proposition 4. Following a group relations perspective, the group as a whole must deal with the nature of authority as vested in the ascribed leader – the convener in the case of a median group – before authority can be effectively assumed by or dispersed among the members at large (whatever the leader's preferred style).

  (a) The group must differentiate between the legitimate role of the convener and the potential roles of members – however much these may overlap – in order fully to authorize members to speak to and for the group. This is necessary if members are to interact creatively, thereby fostering a collaborative effort that supports listening as well as speaking, and spirited dialogue in addition to periods of silent reflection.

(b) If the formal leader does not assume his or her proper authority, and the group does not deal with the role vacuum (including their feelings toward the convener for not sufficiently taking up a consultative role), then the members will struggle unnecessarily to find the center of their experience and vie for leadership in a competitive rather than a cooperative manner.

(c) Under these conditions, the group will not develop maximally, utilize its participants' resources, come to contextual understandings, or otherwise approach its organizational potential.

(d) While the presence of competent leaders may not (and cannot) do away with primitive and aggressive large-group dynamics, it can further the possibility that members will modulate and contain accompanying affects within the group matrix, thereby allowing the dynamics to be channeled or worked more fully *in situ*, as is evident in Bion's (1961) work-group mentality.

WHO WILL SAVE THE GROUP AND WHAT WILL MEMBERS BELIEVE IN?

The leader need not be identified with any individual in the group; it need not be a person at all but may be identified with an idea or an inanimate object. In a dependent group the place of the leader may be filled by the history of the group…making a record of its meetings. The record then becomes a 'bible' to which appeal is made… The group resorts to bible-making when threatened with an idea the acceptance of which would entail development on the part of the individuals comprising the group. (Bion 1961, p. 155)

The membership knew about the de Maré's median model (more or less) through the pre-workshop dissemination of materials. His inspiration came from the self-governance practices in Athens, the Greek city-state, as it was two millennia ago. Public meetings of the populace were convened in amphitheater settings to discuss and resolve issues of the day. Every citizen could conceivably have a say or otherwise participate in the 'Greek chorus' that gave voice, direction and impetus to collective decisions. The central organizing idea for de Maré's (1994a, 1994b) median group experience was the notion of *koinonia*, that is, impersonal fellowship arrived at by working from hateful exchanges toward loving dialogues. The following of this sequence was purported eventually to move the group process away from familial dynamics and 'kin' relations toward the development of cultural dynamics and 'kith' relations. Participants did not, however, know how to proceed in any practical or linear way. Struggles ensued initially, as members attempted to find (or invent) conflicts so that they could be used to energize and later transform interactions in the direction that de Maré would recommend and Simon might approve. This attempt to please the leader resulted in what Bion (1961) referred to as budding dependency culture.

The ensuing experience could in actuality be likened to a people following a bible. The book *Koinonia* (de Maré *et al.* 1991) was written with inspiration, thoughtfulness, some hyperbole and notable erudition. Hypnotic phrases that recurred throughout the text were echoed in the early group discussion and served as group prayers or mantras. De Maré (as chief scribe) and Simon (as his prophet) could easily be cast as saviors who would provide members with salvation and assure the group's continued existence, if only they were heard and followed. The group ethos that actually prevailed was that Simon would not (or was not allowed to) lead.

Proposition 5. In the presence or absence of functional leadership, a group may organize itself around a central idea as an *a priori* organizing principle. The body of ideas, *in toto*, serves as a 'group bible' or secular manifesto that commands a following.

(a) Large group dynamics can manifest in or be formulated as mytho-religious tendencies (Slater 1966).

(b) By activating members' deep hopes and fears, the microcosm of the large or median group reflects on humanity's macrocosmic need to believe in the omnipresence and omnipotence of otherworldly forces and forms, whether benign or malevolent.

In a group relations context, Lawrence (1991) has written about the revelatory function of groups (in contrast to the need for salvation). His method assumes a group-centered rather than a leader-centered approach, wherein epiphanies arise from within the membership through the presentation of shared experiences, such as socially inspired dreams, fantasies and associations (Lawrence and Armstrong 1998; Ettin 2000a). This is in contrast to leader indoctrination, preaching or prophesy.

HERETICAL SENTIMENTS

> Any leader is ignored by the group when his behavior or characteristics fall
> outside the limits set by the prevalent basic assumption. Further, the leader
> must be held by the same 'faith' that holds the group – not to awaken the
> group's faith but because the attitude of the group and leader alike are
> functions of the active basic assumption. (Bion 1961, p.171)

Since the leadership of other reported median groups demonstrated a greater
frequency and range of interventions (including interpretations), it must be
wondered why Simon acted differently in the present group. Did the
membership prevent him from taking up his proper authority? And if so, why?
Every now and again Simon would be resurrected to give parables (about his
experiences) or prophesy about where the group was supposed to be going.
This was an awkward process that often felt artificial, based perhaps on a compulsively driven need of the members for direction (Ba dependence). While
the mission seemed messianic, some members demonstrated a lack of faith.

An experienced group member (Michael), as non-believer, angrily
reported feeling alienated and alone (Ba flight). He criticized the membership
for its naive acceptance and outright encouragement of Simon's abdication of
the leadership function (Ba fight). This outburst (however true it rang)
suggested a split Michael created to handle his anxiety – between his
'good-and-right thoughts' and the 'bad-and-wrong group consensus.'
Michael now demanded the floor and begged to be heard. He suggested that
the group could not tolerate a leader (whether him or Simon), as it longed to
level the process and banish all signs of hierarchy or differentiation of role (as
Simon declared that the group must), even if this led to a basic assumption
culture that induced 'fusion and confusion' (Hopper 1997). Bion clarifies the
process: 'I suggest that what the group really wants to know is my motives for
being present, and, since these have not been discovered, they are not satisfied
with any substitute' (Bion 1961, p.33).

Still, Michael provoked the group by suggesting that 'the emperor had no
clothes.' Some members took this to be an especially blatant accusation that
Simon was incompetent. Michael clarified that what he meant to imply was
that Simon would not accept the cloak of leadership (at least in the way in
which Michael would drape it around him). Michael reported respect for
Simon's experiences with groups, enjoyment of his monologues, and delight
in his person, viewing Simon as a well-chiseled character with precious
experience to share. He also recognized Simon as sage, a position he had
earned through experience, life work and age. This was true even as Michael

mourned (depressive position) what he perceived to be Simon's abdication and disavowal of the consultative role, evident in his refraining from following and commenting on the to-and-fro, here-and-now process of the median group experience. Simon's presence was missed, especially at times when the group became stuck or misled. For the most part, the group remained focused more on Simon's person than his role. Bion's (1961) observation is relevant:

> However irrelevant it may appear to be to the purpose of the meeting, the preoccupation with...my personality certainly seemed to obtrude itself, unwelcome though that might be to the group and to myself. (p.31)

In reality, Michael's anger was not primarily at Simon. It was at the group as a whole for not challenging their formal leader to give more and for rejecting what he did attempt to provide (counterdependence). The group's consensual norm fostered lowered expectations and ignored the convener's potentially useful comments, as they were offered early in the median experience. Members began to lose patience with Simon's intellectualisms and with his spirited forays into the past or future – to the virtual neglect of the present. The membership seemed to resolve, by silent consensus, to ignore or censure him. Early on, Simon spoke of feeling silenced and acknowledged his own withdrawal with apparent resignation. This removed stance gave way paradoxically to a period of uncharacteristic engagement.

Member–leader interface

WHAT MUST A GROUP DO TO PROTECT ITS INTEGRITY AND WHO WILL BE FORCED OUT AS IT ATTEMPTS TO EXCLUDE DIFFERENCES?

> What happens if I use this idea of group attitude to the individual as a basis of interpretation? (Bion 1961, pp.43–44)

This group found its 'scapegoat leader' (Beck 1981) in Jacob, the member most reactive to the proposal of collective standards to which members were expected to comply. Jacob seemed to find fault with any agreement the group would make and, in fact, abhorred the very idea of group decision-making. He resisted or otherwise fought against any manifestation of 'groupness' and thereby became the spokesperson for anti-group sentiments (Nitsun 1996) and a 'me-ness' basic assumptive culture (Lawrence, Bain and Gould 1996). If Jacob could be silenced (since he would not be won over), a collective illusion could be maintained that goodwill, consensus, and equal access to power were enough to provide all the direction that the group would need. This utopian fantasy (Gibbard and Hartman 1973) was entertained, despite the fact that a committee as a whole rarely functions very well. When a group selects 'a bench rather than a chair' it is usually because of some resistance or organizational problem with authority that is not acknowledged or worked through.

Philip, the most inscrutable member, was induced (and readily demonstrated his valence) to act as the group assassin when he viciously and relentlessly attacked Jacob, in a self-proclaimed attempt to silence him. Jacob, in turn, committed symbolic suicide (as Simon labeled it), by not showing up for the next morning's session. Jacob admitted (after returning for the afternoon session), that he did this to punish the group for his being censured. When he was absent, Dorothy continued the scapegoating process by 'acting in' her own (and the membership's) sadistic tendencies, blaming Jacob (in his absence) exclusively for the group's difficulties and attributing malevolent intentions to him without recognizing these traits in herself.

The interaction between Jacob and Philip, and Jacob's subsequent withdrawal, was clearly a manifestation of the group's fight–flight culture (Bion 1961). With Jacob missing, Simon joined the group 'as if' he was a member. He cast Philip (as a second scapegoat) in the role of devil, thereby condemning and banishing him from the heavenly circle of the median group's good graces. The membership seemed ambivalent about Simon using his power in this way and became split around the condemnation and defense of Philip (and of Simon).

The group struggled to decide whether it (and especially Philip) had murdered Jacob or whether he committed (figurative or literal) suicide. This dynamic and the psychological meaning of these events for the group as a whole were never acknowledged or processed. The membership seemed content to proceed without expecting much from Simon until the end of the workshop, when rage at him surfaced and he was demonized in a particularly virulent manner, with accusations that he was anti-Semitic. This happened despite the fact that Jacob (whom Simon vehemently defended) was Jewish.

Simon added to the confusion and fed the group's resentment by periodically claiming the right to respond as an ordinary member. This position rang false and seemed irresponsible. He was not as careful as he might have been to specify or clarify what he meant at these times. Despite claims to the contrary, Simon retained his power to inflict or relieve pain by his attentions (or inattentions) to individual members. A similar issue had come up in the last session of another median group described in diary by de Maré, Piper and Thompson (1991), when a member claimed to be injured by de Maré. Then and there, de

Maré acknowledged his special position by admitting that 'of all the people in the group, he, by the nature of his status as convener, could hurt people most in a primitive, primal-horde type of response' (p.249).

Proposition 6. The God-head figure (as idealized leader) and the Devil-tailed figure (as demonized leader) are inevitably paired. They are identified together according to the intimate relationship between heaven and hell, good and evil, and creation and destruction (Miles 1995).

(a) A group that follows an elevated and idealized leader is capable of the promise and excesses that accrue to messianic movements and sectarian societies. The membership can come together through the strength of its ties to the beloved leader and the ideal that he or she represents (Freud, 1922/1967). Members may trade their individuality to be part of a single-minded, incestuous, cult-like, in-group or primal horde. The psychosocial and sociocultural conditions that support group fusionary tendencies also elicit personal identity diffusion (Hopper 1997).

(b) A group with a demonized leader will have members who fight among themselves and fragment as a result of internal tensions that are acted in or acted out. Individual members may be persecuted or purged in the service of the leader's maintaining control of the group.

Proposition 7. An unreflective (or unanalyzed) group that splits apart, as a result of projections and attributions of good and bad or other paired oppositions, can become consumed by differences and not able to contain, analyze or integrate its polarities.

(a) The members of a polarized group may find it difficult to maintain their personal integrity, reach for wholeness or become differentiated, since doing so requires avowing and taking responsibility for one's own splits, contradictions and paradoxes.

(b) In polarized groups, members' discrepant reactions may be suppressed, denied, displaced in role reversals, or vehemently acted out through pervasive (or perverse) reaction formations.

THE POWER AND FRAGILITY OF MEMBERSHIP

> Only if individuals come sufficiently close to one another is it possible to give an interpretation without shouting it; equally it is necessary for all members of the group to witness the evidence on which interpretations are based. (Bion 1961, p.168)

There is an old group adage that states: 'If one member of a group tells you that you are a horse, they are obviously crazy and can be ignored. If two members tell you that you are a horse, it's likely a conspiracy that should be defended against. If three members tell you that you are a horse (though it may be a projective identification), you had better buy a saddle!'

Proposition 8. Members serve as agents for the group's dynamics by inter-acting within the matrix when assuming necessary roles, giving voice to collective concerns or manifesting current trends (whether progressive or regressive, adaptive or defensive).

  (a) Members evidence (at least) a four-fold identity when representing: (1) self, (2) a partisan or subgroup position, (3) the group as a whole, or (4) society-at-large.

Proposition 9. Members join in a 'group moment' (or movement) and are recruited to do so according to their 'valence' (Bion 1961), that is, the tendency to experience certain emotions, practice particular behaviors, voice specific ideas, or take up critical positions that the group needs represented.

  (a) The pressure (to feel, act or change) put on a member by a group can be the result of inter-member agreement or consensus reached by data collection and reality testing. This is called feedback.

  (b) The pressure put on a member by a group can be the result of intragroup and intersubjective forces manifest as projective identifications. That is, when members disavow their own feelings and beliefs or work their own issues through a hot-seated member, this is called scapegoating.

  (c) A change from projective identification driven by irrational forces to reality testing based on rational analysis requires the exchange of attributions for data and the willingness of members to explore and avow their own position with regard to ascendant beliefs and resonant feelings.

Proposition 10. Members who do not join, form or identify with a subgroup may find themselves alienated from the group as a whole and withdrawn from the process.

Proposition 11. Members who take up an impossible or unspeakable position, however representative it may be, are in danger of being censured by the group. This constitutes a collective attempt to banish certain issues or defend against particular feelings.

Proposition 12. Critical to the members' and the group's survival is the willingness and ability to reintegrate scapegoated or censured members and reclaim split-off parts or disavowed positions. This entails the exploration of the 'other side' of oneself and a range of extant group positions, complexities, contradictions and paradoxes contained in various group cultures (Ettin 2000a).

Subgroups

THE PARTISANSHIP AND PURPOSE OF SUBGROUPING

> I speak of the group coming together as a group. When a group has come together in this way, it has become something as real and as much a part of human life as a family. (Bion 1961, p.69)

Forsyth (1990) suggests that: 'Groups not only have a pervasive influence on our lives, but they are the fundamental components of society. In a sense each of us belongs not to society at large but to groups that are embedded in society.' Agazarian (1989, 1992) makes the important distinction between functional subgroups and stereotype subgroups. Functional subgroups serve to contain a whole group's (or society's) differences until the time when they can be integrated within the group as a whole (or society-at-large). Stereotype subgroups, in contrast, are estranged or formed in opposition to the group as a whole. They may become extreme, inflexible and split-off, thereby exerting a fragmenting effect on the group. It is possible to enter a dialogue with the membership of a functional subgroup. It is much more difficult (if at all possible) to engage constructively with the views of stereotype subgroups, since they rigidly hold (whether willingly or unwillingly) the whole group's unwanted aspects or polarized positions. Subgroups can be stereotyped by the group as a whole, when too exclusively identifying them with certain positive or negative attributes, beliefs, values or actions. Stereotype subgroups are often feared (as a threat to the status quo), discounted (made irrelevant), marginalized (ostracized, rendered insignificant or extreme), quarantined (consigned to a ghetto), extruded (banished, purged) or 'cleansed,' ('sanitized' or 'killed off').

Proposition 13. Emergent subgroups represent the whole group's diversity, alternative goals, competing strategies and divergent identifications.

Proposition 14. Some subgroups are demographic by nature, with their membership determined *a priori* (that is, before the group experience), and some subgroups result from identifications formed and positions taken during the course of the group.

(a) It is rarely possible to change one's subgroup if it is based on biological determinants (i.e. race, gender, age, ethnicity).

(b) It is possible to make one's biological or demographic subgroup identification less salient by becoming more identified by one's functional subgroup alliances which reflect one's positions within the larger group. (e.g. in the US people of color can choose to be known as Republicans).

(c) Demographic subgroups based on religion, nationality, status, class or economics allow for the possibility of change within an open system, through marriage, mobility, traversing of permeable boundaries, conversion or social transposition.

Proposition 15. Functional subgroups emerge as a result of the whole-group interaction, as members take positions in response to common group tensions (Ezriel 1950) and form alliances around alternative solutions to shared problems.

Proposition 16. Subgrouping is an important part of group development to the extent that the group as a whole can identify and explore the parts of the process that are being expressed by or housed in a particular subgroup. The operative question becomes: 'What is this subgroup representing, holding, or expressing for the group as a whole?'

Proposition 17. When subgroups are identified, but their special contribution to the process is not explored, they are often split off or alternatively enlisted to meet the defensive needs of the group. In the latter case, subgroups are more likely than not to become vague, amorphous, divisive or stereotypic.

Proposition 18. When subgroups are identified in light of the meaning they hold for the whole group, then their members can be better contained and their energy and values are more available to the group as a whole and to the membership-at-large.

WHO WILL BE JOINED AND WHAT WILL A GROUP BE FOR OR AGAINST?

Subgroup identifications were a big part of the median group selected for discussion in this paper. The several subgroups that emerged will be acknowledged according to their membership attributions, the positions they took with respect to whole group's tensions, and their functional or stereotypical roles and constraints. Some participants held membership in more than one subgroup (whether willingly or unwillingly, knowingly or unknowingly).

(a) *The Local Group Psychotherapy Society* subgroup, or 'the Eight,' as they were named, were referred to throughout the experience. The members of this group informally represented the organization that co-sponsored the workshop. The composition of this subgroup or the number of members, however, was never clear even to those who were thought to be a part of it. It served as a stereotype subgroup that seemed to represent insider status. 'The Eight' had few self-avowed members and held no authority relevant the median group's functioning. Thus it served a defensive purpose of distracting the group from its task in times of high tension. The embedded organizational hostility in the room that felt unmanageable could be put into the amorphous eight.

This subgroup could also have represented the whole group's wish and search to identify the hidden leadership pool or responsible cadre among the membership. A normal succession issue became more critical, given Simon's views and behaviors, which served to limit the convener role. 'The Eight' also represented the membership's ambivalence about taking up its proper authority. This subgroup was both envied and despised (as two different sides of the same idealization), so much so that no one would openly declare themselves to be a member of it, let alone its leader.

(b) *The Shadow Eight*, as a secret in-group, gathered at Sarah's house for dinner on the second night of the workshop. Six members who had an intimate connection to Simon or Sarah, or a significant part in the evolution of this workshop, met with them by special invitation. It is hypothesized that 'the Shadow Eight' comprised the real insiders who were hidden behind the 'the Eight,' as it was conjured up during the sessions.

Presumably, uninvited median group members were not consciously aware of the dinner party either before or after it was held, let alone who attended it. It is suggested, however, that the membership-at-large intuited the existence of this group of eight and found a stand-in for it during the workshop proper. Since the membership had no direct knowledge of or access to the Shadow Eight, it reified the loose grouping of members ('the Eight') of the Local Group Society. Since the Shadow Eight was unidentifiable, so was its proxy.

(c) *The Foreigners* comprised an important subgroup in the workshop since they were identified with Simon as a visitor from afar. This geographic subgroup was more recognizable and well-defined than the previous two, despite its internal diversity. It seemed to hold enthusiasm about the experience, and gratefulness at being able to participate. It was also endowed with a certain wisdom and perspective on the process that could only be represented at a distance. Three members of 'the Shadow Eight' were foreigners.

It was less threatening for the American contingent, who made up the overwhelming majority of the membership, to listen and take heed from members of the foreign subgroup – who were actually invited to speak – than from other Americans. It is hypothesized that this pattern represented a need for some distance from the process, and a wish for an outside perspective and wider cultural frame. The special place given to this subgroup resulted from the linking of foreignness with benign intent, reduced competition, and special insight. Since they were not viewed as competitors, the foreigners were, in effect, written off as well as written in. The recognition of the foreign subgroup may have been less dangerous than exploring the functional differences (that which was foreign) among the membership at large.

(d) *The Psychoanalysts'* subgroup was as amorphous or more, than 'the Eight.' In reality, there were few, if any, psychoanalysts in the median group (as it was composed), although there was a large representation of psychotherapists. The denotation 'psychoanalyst' encompassed all those in the larger group who were psychologically-minded or would bring a psychodynamic or group dynamic perspective to the proceedings. The whole group seemed to fear and resent any tendency to 'analyze' the group as a whole or one another as individuals. It is unclear what the fear was about since the membership did not 'unpack' what this mythical group was 'holding' for it. No one claimed membership in this subgroup, though the lurking idea of its presence was maintained and warded off throughout. Perhaps Simon was thought to be a member of the psychoanalysts or, in essence, its leader – although if asked he might have disavowed this identification (Pines 2000). If Simon was considered a leader-member of this subgroup, than he (above anyone else) needed to be constrained by the group as a whole, whose members feared being the object of exposure and analysis.

(e)   *The Physicists' or Dialogue* subgroup seemed to function to keep the whole group honest and suppress the 'psychoanalysts' subgroup.' This subgroup represented a body of experience that reflected an alternative methodology (the dialogue group) developed by the renowned physicist, David Bohm (1996), for questioning deeply held assumptions about culture, meaning and identity. Bohm, an analysand of de Maré's, was later exposed to de Maré's ideas about sociotherapy and subsequently convened agenda-less groups of 15 to 40 persons that operated in an anarchistic and democratic fashion with little structural leadership or formal facilitation.

Members of this dialogue subgroup, unlike 'the Eight,' readily and proudly claimed allegiance to it. They represented the near side of the split between 'science' and 'subjectivity.' The membership, that included at least two physicists, only seemed interested in personal experience as it provided data for dialogue – not as it forged connections with other persons. They derived some surplus power (in the group as a whole) from the shared assumption (which the membership-at-large never questioned) that their queries and challenges were scientifically anchored and motivated by objectivity. Perhaps the group as a whole needed to maintain a belief that catering to its rationality would protect it from its irrationality. After all, the median model prizes 'thinking,' above all else. The workshop members were invited and, no doubt, self-selected due to an attraction to the idea of rationally thinking-through the group process.

(f)   *The Elders,* a biological subgroup present throughout, came to prominence in the meeting where Arthur (a charming though somewhat cantankerous psychiatrist) and Cynthia (a pioneer in Trigant Burrow's early American experiment with large experiential groups) flanked Simon, as a sort of Praetorian guard. Arthur seemed to represent traditional group methods and Cynthia was characterized admiringly (by the women) as 'fearless and courageous' in her introspection and ability to articulate her insights. Simon sometimes behaved like an elder statesman (or a grandfather), when telling stories about the history and various incarnations of the median group method.

The Elders represented a wealth of experience that the group alternately welcomed and rejected. This may also have been tied to the issue of generational succession, which was not explored in any depth during the sessions. Presumably, it was too dangerous to talk directly about competitive strivings and wishes for control over the proceedings. It was easier to act them out. The 'fathers' and 'mothers,' as the ascendant generation, may have been too busy establishing their own claims to power and position in the group to listen much to the stories and ruminations of their elders. This was unfortunate, since to change the implications or avert the reenactments of history, one must first acknowledge, study and understand them.

(g) *The Conceptualizers* responded less personally and more thoughtfully to the group process. They offered many of the member consultations to the group process. They were willing to go beyond available data, thereby differentiating themselves from the physicists' subgroup. At times their contributions were illuminating and at other times they were 'heady,' top-heavy, and impersonal.

(h) *The Feelers* acted in counter-pose to Simon's emphasis on thinking and as a counterbalance to the conceptualizers. A few self-selected members seemed to carry the group's feeling. They were sensitive to individuals' needs and responsive to the narcissistic injuries of others. Their contributions throughout the workshop kept the group in touch with its humanity, even if the expressions of caring (and protestations against injustice) seemed, at times, to be excessive or dramatic.

(i)   *The Singletons and Silents* (or members who didn't yet claim a place in society) were a subgroup in category only. They were joined in that they did not vocalize much during the twelve sessions. Each member may have empathized with a particular subgroup without actually declaring himself or herself or joining it. It is hypothesized that the members of this subgroup had much to say that would have clarified the process, since they held the unique and, in this group, seldom-prized position of listeners.

(j) *The Women*, as a demographic subgroup, began to declare and define themselves toward the conclusion of the workshop. This group of heretofore quiet women transformed themselves into a functional subgroup when they found their voice. Several spoke up about their wish and intention to exercise power and influence in alternative ways to those being utilized in the group to date. They also declared how difficult it was to do so in 'this' group. 'The Women' spoke for the silent contingent (which also included some men) who would not, or could not, join in the competition or accept (what they believed to be) the resulting patriarchal culture. This reaction is consistent with Burack's observation that feminists 'remain ambivalent about leadership, which is seen to connote power and masculinity in addition to complicating issues of equality' (Burack 1997, p.28).

In their open and non-defensive manner of speaking and in what they had to say, 'the Women' modeled an alternative style of leadership and communication that was more egalitarian and relationship-sensitive. Since their subgroup never gained ascendance, 'the Women' functioned more as a soft-spoken protest group than a leadership contingent. That their attempts to influence the group discourse were tentative may mirror extant sociopolitical conditions and dynamics still evident in the foundation matrix. Cohn suggests that: 'If as women clinicians and thinkers, we germinate ideas that are particular to the female experience, we have to struggle to regard our insights as serious and important, to find the words to articulate our concepts and to provide emphasis to promote our thoughts (Cohn 1998, p.121). That did not happen in this median group.

The prevalence of whole group and subgroup themes

A short list of pertinent themes that configured in this median group will now be elaborated.

(a) *Status* concerns were evident in the whole group's returning to the theme of the Group of Eight throughout the experience. The setting of the group meetings, at a prestigious university's School of Government (surrounded by slums), certainly enhanced the awareness of a privileged inside and a disadvantaged outside.

(b) *Class* was brought up by Anthony, a man from a lower middle-class, blue-collar background. Although he mentioned class inequities on a number of occasions, the group did not seem to engage this theme with any conviction or investment. Nor did any members identify directly with Anthony and form a subgroup around him, though several with similar backgrounds might have done so. Somehow his presentation did not resonate for the membership. Anthony did some good work (for himself) with Arthur, but this had more to do with the status theme. In essence, Anthony was asking: 'Will you accept me into the establishment?' 'Do you see me as having what it takes to make it?' The issue appeared to be more a personal concern (perhaps about achievement/under-achievement) than a collective preoccupation with class distinctions. Another reason why this theme was not joined by the membership might have been because of our select population and prevailing competitiveness. No one else was ready to identify him or herself as an underdog.

(c) *Freedom versus constraint* manifest in aversion to analysis, a wish for 'laissez-faire leadership' (Lewin, Lippitt and White 1939) and a prohibition against constraining rules of engagement. To be analytic was dangerous, since it implied that members might not be freely choosing their actions, but rather acting in accordance with hidden or unconscious motivations. In this median group, that perspective was politically incorrect. Those who took up the role of analyst could be and sometimes were ignored, or worse, effectively dismissed. Arthur, for example, assumed the role of 'task leader' (Beck 1981) and standard bearer early in the group, by insisting that the membership adhere to standard group process norms (time boundaries, ban on eating during sessions, etc.). He was admonished by various members (especially Jacob) for his effort; his suggestions were responded to as unhelpful, pedantic, and stifling to personal freedom.

(d) *Prejudice* came into the group with the introduction of the issue of anti–Semitism. A turning point occurred when it was revealed, in Jacob's absence, that his family had a holocaust background. This revelation put Jacob's distrust of group dynamics and collective decision-making into perspective. Around this time, and as a reaction formation, the group projected onto Hilda the persecutory position and attributes of 'the German.' She did not accept this projection. Anti-Semitism was later housed in Simon, who denied it, though in a way that was unconvincing to some of the members. The theme of racial prejudice came to the foreground of the group's attention soon thereafter.

WILL THE GROUP'S DIFFERENCES KEEP IT APART AND IN PERPETUAL CONFLICT?

> Group culture is a function of the conflict between the individual's desire and the group mentality. (Bion 1961, p.66)

The possibility of racial prejudice was initially introduced when Cynthia, the group's elder female, spoke of her fear of intruders (presumably from the black neighborhoods that bordered her home). She proclaimed her right to have her space and property defended by 'the key-holder' (perhaps a symbol of access to privilege and locking in the good and safe life).

Later in the session, Cynthia became quite distressed about the significance of her feelings and came in touch with how the group interpreted her fears and responded to her in light of them. A larger issue was raised concerning what is gained and what is sacrificed as members and whole communities arm and segregate themselves through fear (often quite justified) of their neighbors, who undoubtedly have less access (and don't hold the key) to material wealth and personal safety.

The group's interaction with Nancy, the lone black person in the group, brought this theme into clearer focus by adding a human dimension. It was an interesting phenomenon (or epiphenomenon) that Nancy (a black woman) and Jacob (a Jewish man), a seemingly odd couple, maintained a close and personal outside relationship that predated the median experience – which they brought into the group without hesitation or shame. The group seemed matter-of-factly to accept their obvious care and affection for one another without question. Did this mean that the group could readily accept (that is, they expected) the pairing of scapegoating with race? Or, perhaps this pairing of traditional underdogs was a way for the group as a whole to undo the 'murdering' that the membership felt it was committing.

Nancy was eloquent in her heart-felt and personal description of her experience of being black and the splits that entailed – identification with people of color juxtaposed with the wish to transcend her subgroup through acceptance into the mainstream culture (i.e. out of the 'hood' and into the headquarters of corporate America). Nancy became an 'emotional leader' (Beck 1981) when describing the danger that she lived with, that culminated in the violent death of a nuclear family member. This disclosure saddened and paradoxically soothed the group. Her resolve and striving was to create a better place for herself, without repressing formative experience or denying background and heritage. Nancy's struggles highlighted the complexities of crossing racial and cultural barriers – that is, maintaining personal integrity and primary group identity, while opening up to others, integrating differences or joining subgroups that are different from one's own. The group considered the challenge of coming together, despite (and even because of) its differences. Could they – by prizing diversity while still finding enough in common – support integration and avoid segregation of members with different backgrounds, nationalities, religious affiliations, racial heritages or other subgroup identities? The membership considered how societies (including this median group) might find alternatives to the violence (whether physical, emotional or verbal) that would marginalize or extrude persons or parts of 'the other' (and of oneself) that were different, frightening, seemingly inferior, or otherwise unacceptable. They came to realize how drastic solutions disintegrate or demoralize a group, as in the case of Jacob's and Philip's demonization and dismissals.

This median group could certainly empathize with Nancy, given her stark, though fair-minded, account that was communicated through sadness and sincerity rather than through rage or destructiveness (to property or persons). In the group, at this time, it seemed impossible to maintain racial prejudice. Surely the result might have been different if more people of color were present and if alternate spokespersons expressed themselves through anger, envy, disdain, blame or entitlement.

Reverse prejudice may have been practiced through the idealization of the 'foreign' subgroup, composed of different nationalities, who were kept at a distance, albeit in a more benign fashion. Would this too have changed given more time, exposure, representation or diversity?

THE EVOLUTION OF GROUP CULTURE

> I employ the phrase 'culture of the group' in an extremely loose manner; I include in it the structure that the group achieves at any given moment, the occupations it pursues and the organization it adapts. (Bion 1961, p.55.)

By his own admission, Bion presented a limited definition of group culture. In common usage, the concept of culture implies both a process and a product. A cultural process involves the evolution of a collective venture, marked by the sharing of information, associations, dialogue and meaning-making. This enterprise creates a sense of shared purpose, however different members' backgrounds, differentiated their particular aims, and whatever specific tasks the group takes to be its legitimate work. The products of culture-building include: shared history, group norms, common language, collective representations, transformative rituals, group myths and cultural symbols. These products of the process lend a group its sense of integrity and continuity and thereby contribute to its organizational structure and the meaning it holds for its members. Group identity is furthered when members willingly engage in group-building and the evolution of a culture to mirror it. By doing so, the membership invents (or borrows from the larger society in which it is embedded) contextual forms that amplify the experience and ritual enactments that enliven it.

Proposition 19. The large group process continually oscillates between paired oppositions whether: chaos and coherence, dependence and counterdependence, independence and interdependence, fight and flight, cohesion and fragmentation, closeness and distance, similarities and differences or individual and group reflections (to name a few). It is this tension that creates the 'space between' and the dialectic that fills a group with emotion and provides the raw material necessary for cultural invention.

Proposition 20. The large (or median) group leader takes up a significant position, and serves as role model in the culture building and articulation process when:

  (a) pointing out the relevance for the group as a whole of member and subgroup contributions;

  (b) identifying emergent processes as they take shape and group-reflective products as they take form; and

  (c) referring back to the group's cultural articulations in times of crisis and opportunity, thereby acknowledging a shared history while fostering institutional memory and encouraging further transformations.

Proposition 21. The cultural level can be accessed through logos (word, dialogue, idea, knowledge, reasoned argument, linear development, logical search pattern, meaning-making, etc.). It can also be approached through mythos (mental or pictorial image, novel configuration, figurative language, collective representation, metaphor, paradox, illusion, allusion, myth, group dream, symbolic reckoning, artistic form) (Ettin, 1994, 1999, 2000a).

MYTHIC SYMBOLS GENERATED BY THIS MEDIAN GROUP

Melanie Klein (1930) has stressed the importance of symbol formation in the development of the individual... The work group understands that particular use of symbols which is involved in communication; the basic-assumption group does not. (Bion 1961, p. 135)

One of the striking things about a group is that, despite the influence of the basic assumption, it is the Work group that triumphs in the long run. Freud himself appears to consider [this]...notably when he discusses the part the group plays in the production of language, folk song, folklore, etc. (Bion 1961, p.135)

This median group reached below the surface of experience to create symbolic forms and recreate mythic stories. The myth arose (as eloquently stated by Nadia) that the workshop society was healed upon Jacob's return, and with the reconciliation between him and Dorothy (Jacob's second most vocal critic after Philip) as king and queen. This was clearly a 'pairing assumption' that involved the group's preoccupation with two members whose coming together would, in fantasy, reincorporate marginalized members and unite them, thereby assuring the whole group's continued existence and ultimate survival. In reality, neither Jacob nor Dorothy, apart or together, were ordained or followed as would be a monarch or royal pair. Nor did they acknowledge any responsibility to act on the group's behalf, as is required of royalty (noblesse oblige). Nevertheless, the group expunged some of its guilt when tacitly supporting two potential casualties, as they joined in a curative ritual engagement.

Brent introduced the biblical allusion of Abraham sacrificing Isaac to amplify the killing interaction between Simon (as messianic father) and Philip (as sacrificial son). The group soon thereafter became preoccupied with the destructive power of hate. Michael, in counterpoint, expressed his terror of the destructive power of love (of ideas, ideals, missions) and suggested that most wars were waged in the name of some passionate identity with one's people or one's cause that led to (or, at least served as a 'justification' for) hating, fighting, persecuting or killing others. He speculated further that Simon's cutting remarks to Philip were made in the hopes of preserving his (and the group's) faith in *koinonia*, through the sacrifice of a member, in this case a prodigal son.

In Kabbalistic fashion, this median group's preoccupation with the number eight had a numinous, mystical quality to it. Eight is one-fourth of the original composition of this median group, the size of a normal small group, and the percentage of the membership that might make up the ruling class of a society. The search for the Group of Eight, evident throughout the workshop, had the character of a ritual Grail quest (perhaps in the hopes of gaining salvation and winning back its lost innocence). The group may also have been trying to conjure up its wholeness. The number four (in this case doubled) is a symbol for completion. Was the group trying to find the source of infinite wisdom through dialogue by continually returning to 'the Eight' (a number associated with infinity)?

III. Comparison of models

A difference in task, purpose and vision

> Early in 1948 the Professional Committee of the Tavistock Clinic asked me to take therapeutic groups, employing my own technique… It was disconcerting to me that the Committee seemed to believe that patients could be cured in such groups as these. (Bion 1961, p.29)

> I cannot forget that when I first attempted to put such methods into operation the experiment was terminated by my removal in fact from my post. (Bion 1961, p.35)

Nitsun refers to Foulkesian group analysis and Bionic group relations as 'two highly divergent approaches to groups in England' (Nitsun 2000, p.460). A difference in purpose, task and perhaps vision characterizes these models (Ettin, Cohen and Fidler 1997). Alderfer and Klein suggest that Bion's work and 'the Tavistock tradition [are] associated with a relatively pessimistic view of human nature' (Alderfer and Klein 1978, p.20). Nitsun (2000) agrees with this assessment and adds that Foulkes treated the group experience as reparative and restorative and thereby accented its constructive features (despite the acknowledgement of unconscious processes operating at the projective and primordial levels of analysis – Foulkes 1964). In contrast, Bion viewed the group experience as regressive and conflictual and thereby attended primarily to its destructive and disintegrative potentials. Bion himself expressed feelings of frustration with group work and futility about the possibility of treating members in this milieu (in contrast to the psychoanalysis of individuals). With respect to groups, he said: 'It seems impossible to achieve precision by interpretation, for even when the formulation of an interpretation is satisfying there seems small reason to suppose it reaches its destination' (Bion 1961, p.114).

The impersonal set-up of a Tavistock large group engages the spirit of Wotan, the Germanic God of war, poetry, knowledge and wisdom. It also summons the power of Thanatos, the Greek God of destruction (Nitsun 2000). The pursuit of knowledge must be hard fought, and ever so fleeting, due to destructive and disintegrative qualities of the large group-as-a-primal-horde (Freud 1922/1967). De Maré's work with median groups is based in Foulkesian (1964) group analysis that represents a more optimistic position, one in which Eros, the Greek God of love, is called upon to touch the group's fate. Hate is to be transformed into cooperative engagement through dialogue, the search for common cultures and the acceptance of difference.

Paradoxically, Bion – who is known mostly for his work with small groups – may have developed a methodology that taps large-group dynamics, since his technique fosters the anonymity of individual members by focusing almost exclusively on the group-as-a-whole as a superordinate system. In contrast, Foulkes' emphasis on communication and linking between members in a dynamic matrix – whether in small, median or large groups – may have been an attempt to carry over small, familial dynamics to larger group settings.

Shields (2001) maps the differences between group analytic and group relations models respectively onto Winnicott's distinction between the 'environmental mother' and 'object mother'. That is, a 'good-enough' 'like-me' group functions symbolically as a nurturant environmental mother that holds members together so that they might mature as individuals and develop collectively. The group as an object mother, instead, exposes members to the frustrations of the 'not-me' and 'not-like-me' world with the inherent difficulties that arise when dealing with 'the other.' That is, a virulent, aggressive or unempathic group functions symbolically as a devouring or abandoning mother. Hinshelwood (1999) attempts to contain these differences in the overarching challenge to 'study the problems of holding together caring and hating.' (p.485). The Tavistock large group – that is designed to permit the examination of psychosocial splits and psychotic anxieties (Lipgar 2000; Skolnick 2000) – may iatrogenically create or amplify these dynamics if the the group as a 'good-enough' environmental mother is not fostered and maintained. Examination and learning cannot take place unless members of the large group team function together as competent consultants, responsible for and accountable to provide management as well as interpretive functions. The median group – that is designed to transform hate and personal estrangement into cooperative endeavor – may discourage or under analyze extant conflicts by favoring thinking over feeling. Unless its leader consults to and intervenes in the identification and working through of covert agendas and common tensions, reason may not prevail over emotionality, and impersonal fellowship may remain a prisoner of the acting in or acting out of hurtful and harmful affects.

MAKING LARGE GROUPS SMALLER

In both group relations and group analysis, members attempt to ground themselves and render the group more familiar and manageable by identifying with others through subgroup affiliations. The large group is too big and the complexity of interaction too convoluted to allow individuals, dyads or familial facsimiles to be the basic unit of structural organization. Issues of race, gender, religion, nationality, class and status, with attendant emotions of envy, jealousy, hate, prejudice and even love, are called forth.

Dysphoric affects, destructive behaviors and disorganized thinking are often located in those members or subgroups that demonstrate a proclivity (valence) or can be induced to experience themselves (and others) uniformly in accordance with stereotypical psychosocial attributions. This large-group dynamic can have a wounding effect on the personal recipient or subgroup receptacle of a whole-group's differences and tensions, with a result being alienation, persecution, loss of affiliation or linkage with self and others. Recent work, that extends beyond Bion, examines why it is so hard for individuals in groups to learn from experience (Hoggert 1998) or tolerate work- (Cano 1998), political- (Biran 1998) or clinical groups (Skolnick 1998) or the organizational dynamics that so often confound or infuriate those who are a part of them (Lawrence and Armstrong 1998).

Members in this median group suffered narcissistic injuries when the whole group fragmented around differences. This led to temporary casualties (dropouts, scapegoats). Seemingly, however, the median process is not as turbulent and potentially destructive to personal integrity as the Tavistock experience can be. Nor is it intended to or designed specifically to provide opportunities for learning about the multiple forces influencing complex relationships between self, role and group as they arise in milieu. That is, the technology of the median group does not foster as deep a resonance with the unconscious level of the collective psyche. Nor do median groups focus specifically on how stereotypes or mythic constructions are assigned to certain ethnic, racial or demographically-defined groups, and at what cost. Steiner and Beukema (2000) suggest an extension of practice, when adapting median- or dialogue-group methods specifically to address contentious issues within and between societal- and identity-level groups.

THE DEPTH OF MEDIAN AND TAVISTOCK LARGE GROUPS

> Basic assumptions help to give form and meaning to the complex and chaotic emotional state that the group unfolds to the investigating participant. (Bion 1961, p.16)

> Group mentality is the unanimous expression of the will of the group, contributed to by the individual in ways of which he is unaware, influencing him disagreeably whenever he thinks or behaves in a manner at variance with the basic assumptions. It is thus a machinery of intercommunication that is designed to ensure that group life is in accordance with basic assumptions. (Bion 1961, p.65)

The Tavistock group (Bion 1961) more readily stimulates a group's unconscious processes by inducing members to associate to the shared predicament at the level of primary (basic assumptive) as well as secondary (work group) processes. The aim is to explore overt and covert dynamics that include members' responsibility for group-as-a-whole trends. Experience with and study of the relationship between leadership and authority is available in the interface between staff and members, who function reciprocally (and sometimes interchangeably) as leaders and followers (Rioch 1975). This entails the analysis of the 'group-in-the-mind' of its members (and formal leaders). Bion (1961) suggested that the so called 'group mind' is composed of the anonymous pooling of members' contributions. Ettin (2001) considers this 'synthetic unconscious' process to comprise an important part of the deep structure of group life and the proper object of a group relations analysis.

The median group, on the other hand, seeks to cultivate the group's mind, that is, rational, relational, and collective collaboration through dialogue and 'brain-storming.' An awareness of cultural and thematic trends that arise in public discourse is intended (de Maré et al. 1991). The goal is sociocultural and the means for accomplishing it is clinical and sociopolitical. The aim of the Tavistock method, in contrast, is to provide opportunities to learn about group relations (Banet and Hayden 1977) and only incidentally to improve them. The goal is psychoeducational and the means is personal participation. Ettin (1997), citing the work Rioch (1975), points out the tension and potential conflicts between a climate of care and a climate of learning.

CONSULTING TO A MEDIAN GROUP EXPERIENCE

> Groups...in Freud's view, approximate to neurotic patterns of behavior, whereas in my view they would approximate to the patterns of psychotic behavior... I very much doubt if any real therapy could result unless these psychotic patterns were laid bare...no matter what group. (Bion 1961 p.181)

The median group described in this paper never felt quite as 'crazy' or creative as a Tavistock large group, though it was sometimes startling, often frustrating, and frequently difficult to locate the work. In times of conflict, the median group felt more neurotic than psychotic. Various members personalized the experience and sometimes lost patience with the process. This attenuation of irrational and unconscious processes may have been because of de Maré's (1994) emphasis, and Simon's concentration (as convener), on 'thinking' and the communication of one's thoughts and feelings. Despite some narcissistic injuries, no one seemed to lose their mind (at least, not for long). Bion (1962) also emphasized thinking – the translation of preverbal and proto-mental experiences or other undigested mental contents (beta elements) into (alpha elements), 'words, dreams, expressions of feeling, and dialogue' (Biran 1998, p.93).

Perhaps another way to contrast a group-analytic median experience with a group relations large-group experience is that the former operates at the level of formulable thoughts and feelings (along with preconceptions or prejudicial affects) and attempts to bring them out in dialogue. The latter often operates at the level of nameless dread connected to the terror of the unknown, unthought known (Bollas 1987) or the irritation caused below the surface by psychic splinters in one's own, others' and the group's experience that cannot yet be absorbed or extruded. The difference is between a culture of inquiry (Pines 1998) and a more primitive (or proto-mental) group mentality concerned with psychosocial survival and defense against psychotic anxieties.

> The sphere of proto-mental events cannot be understood by reference to the individual alone, and the intelligible field of study…is the individuals met together in a group…for proto-mental phenomena are a function of the group and must therefore be studied in the group. (Bion 1961, p.102)

The median group would seem to hold more promise for addressing and possibly resolving real-life issues between people and subgroups. This is likely due to smaller group size, the method's avowed aims of fostering impersonal fellowship, and a leadership stance that pulls for dialogue and rational encounter. At the same time, the learning that one intuits from Bion's observations and theories or from participation in a large group-relations experience might lead one to join with Bion's insight that true and lasting resolutions are not possible without dipping deeply into the reservoirs that provide the unconscious source and psychotic core of our collective strivings and group-to-group struggles. The Tavistock method, that so powerfully exposes unconscious dynamics, does not specifically take as its task the use or taming of these same forces. This may happen, however, as an epiphenomenon or byproduct of rendering the unconscious conscious. Extant dynamics can also be affected indirectly when discovering the contextual significance of personal behaviors or subgroup positions or new knowledge about the deep meaning of sociocultural facts and political forces that the group is representing or recapitulating (Hopper 1996).

Bringing people together in groups

> If the psychiatrist can manage boldly to use the group instead of spending his time more or less unconsciously apologizing for its presence, he will find that the immediate difficulties produced are more than neutralized by the advantages of a proper use of his medium. (Bion 1961, p.81)

It is hypothesized that much of group aggression is generated by self-love (or group-love), which is valued over acceptance of 'otherness' and the appreciation of diversity. Thygesen (1992) considers diversity to be just as much a curative factor in group analysis as is cohesion. Do the ends justify the means, as the human group draws boundaries around intimate affiliations in ways that promote identification with ever smaller segments of humanity? Dialogue can all too easily deteriorate into monologue, rhetoric, or vicious harangue. Love can all too quickly turn itself into hate and a politics of inclusion/exclusion.

The group as a cultural object (Jacobson 1989; Ettin 1994, 1995, 1996) can have the harsh and unforgiving qualities of a large unarticulated mass. It can also breed familiarity through participation in making up something meaningful together that is bigger and more portentous than the self in isolation, aggregation or massification (Hopper 1997; Ettin 2000b). Members can take back from the cultural endeavor a deeper appreciation of group life and a more comprehensive self-understanding. When doing so, group evolution and member development proceed simultaneously.

Patrick de Maré's attempts to move people from hate to love, impersonal fellowship and common interest through dialogue in median groups is to be commended. His is a just cause rightly joined. As participants reflected on their experiences in this median group, various members compared it with other collective modalities that bring people together to study or resolve large (or small) group conflicts. The shared hope was that members, as prominent group leaders in various human endeavors and representatives of particular communities, would refine methods and hone skills so that they might better affect psychological, social and cultural (not only political) solutions to the many problems that face individuals and the groups they compose (Ettin 1993).

The two approaches considered in this chapter, group analysis (and the median group) and group relations (and the Tavistock large group) represent parts of a continuum that encompasses neurotic and psychotic anxieties, optimistic and pessimistic world views, and convener and consultant positions. Wilfred Bion's experiences in small groups and their extrapolation to median and large groups have continuing value and resonance for what is a developing field of study. In group, love and hate of self and others, of 'me' and 'not-me,' is the backdrop for unfolding group dyamics. Studying resultant processes in experiential settings can expose and in some cases transform the politics of everyday life.

References

Agazarian, Y. (1989) 'Group-as-a-whole systems theory and practice.' *Group, 13* (3 and 4), pp.131–154.

Agazarian, Y. (1992) 'Contemporary theories of group psychotherapy: A systems approach to the group-as-a-whole. *International Journal of Group Psychotherapy 42,* 2, 177–204.

Alderfer, C. and Klein, E. (1978) 'Affect, leadership, and organizational boundaries.' *Journal of Personality and Social Systems 1,* 3, 19–33.

Anthony, E. J. (1991) 'The dilemma of therapeutic leadership: The leader who does not lead.' In S. Tuttman (ed) *Psychoanalytic Group Theory and Therapy*. Madison CT: International Universities Press.

Banet, A. and Hayden, C. (1977) 'A Tavistock primer.' In (1977) *Handbook for Group Facilitators* (pp.155–167). San Diego, CA: University Associates.

Burack, C. (1997) 'Black feminist thought as leadership theory.' In L. Estabrook (ed) *Leadership as Legacy: Transformation at the Turn of the Millennium.* Jupiter, FL: A. K. Rice Institute.

Beck, A. (1981) 'The study of group phase development and emergent leadership.' *Group 5*, 4, 48–54.

Bion, W. R. (1961) *Experiences in Groups and Other Papers*. New York: Basic Books.

Bion, W. R. (1962) *Learning from Experience*. New York: Basic Books.

Biran, H. (1998) 'An attempt to apply Bion's alpha- and beta-elements to processes in society at large.' In P. Bion Talamo, F. Borgogno and S. Merciai (eds) *Bion's Legacy to Groups*. London: Karnac Books.

Bohm, D. (1996) *On Dialogue*. London: Routledge.

Bollas, C. (1987) *The Shadow of the Object*. New York: Columbia University Press.

Cano, D. (1998) 'Oneness and me-ness in the baG?' In P. Bion Talamo, F. Borgogno and S. Merciai (eds) *Bion's Legacy to Groups*. London: Karnac Books.

Cohen, B.D., Ettin, M.F. and Fidler, J.W. (2002) *Group Psychotherapy and Political Reality: A Two-way Mirror.* Madison, CT: International Universities Press.

Cohn, B. (1998) Guest editor's introduction to special issue: 'Women in Group.' *Group 22*, 3, 121–127.

de Maré, P. (1989) 'The history of large group phenomena in relation to group analytic psychotherapy: The story of the median group.' *Group 13*, 3 and 4, 173–197.

de Maré, P. (1994a) 'The median group and the psyche.' In D. Brown and L. Zinkin (eds) *The Psyche and the Social World*. London: Routledge.

de Maré, P. (1994b) *The Median Group: Kith, Kin, Koinonia.*

de Maré, P., Piper, R. and Thompson, S. (1991) *Koinonia: From Hate through Dialogue to Culture in the Large Group.* London: Karnac Books.

Ettin, M. (1993) 'Links between group process and social, political and cultural issues.' In H. Kaplan and B. Sadock (eds) *Comprehensive Group Psychotherapy.* Third edition. Baltimore, MD: Williams and Wilkins.

Ettin, M. (1994) 'Symbolic representations and the components of a group-as-a-whole model.' *International Journal of Group Psychotherapy 44*, 2, 209–231.

Ettin, M. (1995) 'The spirit of Jungian group psychotherapy: From taboo to totem.' *International Journal of Group Psychotherapy 45*, 4, 449–470.

Ettin, M. (1996) 'Do you know where your group is? Development of a group-as-a-whole compass. Part I.' *Group 20*, 1, 57–90.

Ettin, M. (1997) 'A comparison of the leadership of small groups in the group psychotherapy and group relations traditions.' In L. Estabrook (ed) *Proceedings of the Twelfth Scientific Meeting of the A. K. Rice Institute.* Jupiter, Fl: A. K. Rice Institute.

Ettin, M. (1999) *Foundations and Applications of Group Psychotherapy: A Sphere of Influence.* London: Jessica Kingsley Publishers.

Ettin, M. (2000a) 'From identified patient to identifiable group: The alchemy of the group as a whole.' *International Journal of Group Psychotherapy 50*, 2, 137–162.

Ettin, M. (2000b) 'Fostering a "group ethos": Truth or dare.' *Group 24*, (2 & 3), 229–240.

Ettin, M. (2001) 'The deep structure of group life: Unconscious dimensions.' *Group 25*, 4, 253–298.

Ettin, M., Cohen, B. and Fidler, J. (1997) 'Group-as-a-whole theory viewed in its twentieth-century context.' *Group Dynamics 1*, 4, 329–340.

Ezriel, H. (1950) 'A psychoanalytic approach to group treatment.' *British Journal of Medical Psychology 23*, 59–74.

Foulkes, S. H (1964) *Therapeutic Group Analysis.* New York: International Universities Press.

Foulkes, S. H. (1975) 'Problems of the large group from a group-analytic point of view.' In L. Kreeger (ed) *The Large Group.* London: Karnac.

Forsyth, D. R. (1990) *Group Dynamics.* Pacific Grove, CA: Brooks/Cole Publishing Co.

Freud, S. (1967) *Group Psychology and the Analysis of the Ego.* New York: Liveright. (Original work published in 1922.)

Gibbard, G. and Hartman, J. (1973) 'The significance of utopian fantasies in small groups.' *International Journal of Group Psychotherapy 23*, 125–147.

Gustafson, J. and Cooper, L. (1985) 'Collaboration in small groups: Theory and technique for the study of small group processes.' In A. Colman and M. Geller (eds) *Group Relations Reader 2* (pp.139–150). Washington, DC: A. K. Rice Institute.

Hinshelwood, R. (1994) 'Attack on reflective space: Containing primitive emotional states.' In V. Schermer and M. Pines (eds) *Ring of Fire: Primitive Affects and Object Relations in Group Psychotherapy.* London: Routledge.

Hinshelwood, R.D. (1999) 'How Foulkesian was Bion?' *Group Analysis 32*, 4, 469–488.

Hoggert, P. (1998) 'The internal establishment.' In. P. Bion Talamo, F. Borgogno and S. Merciai (eds) *Bion's Legacy to Groups.* London: Karnac Books.

Hopper, E. (1989) *Aggregation/Massification and Fission (Fragmentation) Fusion: A Fourth Basic Assumption?* For the VIII International Conference of the IAGP, Amsterdam.

Hopper, E. (1996) 'The social unconscious in clinical work.' *Group 20*, 1, 7–42.

Hopper, E. (1997) 'Traumatic experience in the unconscious life of groups: A fourth basic assumption.' *Group Analysis 30*, 4, 439–470.

Jacobson, L. (1989) 'The group as an object in the cultural field.' *International Journal of Group Psychotherapy 39*, 4, 475–497.

Klein, E. B. (1992) 'Contributions from social systems theory.' In R. Klein, H. Bernard, and D. Singer (eds) *Handbook of Contemporary Group Psychotherapy.* Madison, CT: International Universities Press.

Klein, E.B. (1993) 'Large groups in treatment and training settings.' *Group 17*, 4, 198–209.

Kreeger, L. (ed.) (1975) *The Large Group: Dynamics and Therapy.* London: Karnac Books.

Lawrence, W. G. (1991) 'Won from the void and formless infinite: Experiences in social dreaming.' *Free Associations 2* (Part 2, No. 22), 254–266.

Lawrence, W. G. (1998) *Social Dreaming @ Work.* London: Karnac Books.

Lawrence, W. G. and Armstrong, D. (1998) 'Destructiveness and creativity in organizational life: Experiencing the psychotic edge.' In P. Bion Talamo, F. Borgogno and S. Merciai (eds) *Bion's Legacy to Groups.* London: Karnac Books.

Lawrence, W. G., Bain, A. and Gould, L. (1996) 'The fifth basic assumption.' *Free Associations 6*, 1, 28–55.

Lewin, K., Lippitt, R., and White, R. K. (1939) 'Patterns of aggressive behavior in experimentally-created "social climates".' *Journal of Social Psychology 10*, 271–299.

Lipgar. R. (1994) 'The problem with group psychotherapy.' *Voices 30*, 2, 18–24.

Lipgar, R. (2000) Personal communication.

Main, T. (1975) 'Some psychodynamics of large groups.' In L. Kreeger (ed) *The Large Group: Dynamics and Therapy*. London: Karnac Books.

Miles, J. (1995) *God: A Biography*. New York: Vintage Books.

Miller, E. (1985) 'Organizational development and industrial democracy: A case study.' In A. Colman and M. Geller (eds) *Group Relations Reader 2*. Washington DC: The A. K. Rice Institute.

Nitsun, M. (1996) *The Anti-group*. London: Routledge.

Nitsun, M. (2000) 'The future of the group.' *International Journal of Group Psychotherapy 50*, 4, 455–472.

Noumair, D. (1999) Personal communication.

Pines, M. (1975) 'Overview.' In L. Kreeger (ed) The Large Group (pp.291–311). London: Karnac Books.

Pines, M. (1998) 'The self as a group: The group as a self.' In I. Harwood and M. Pines (eds) *Self-experiences in Group*. London: Jessica Kingsley Publishers.

Pines, M. (2000) Personal communication.

Rice, A. K. (1965) *Learning for Leadership*. London: Tavistock Publications.

Rice, A. K. (1975) 'The basis of conference design.' In A. Colman and W. Bexton (eds) *Group Relations Reader 1*. Washington, DC: A. K. Rice Institute.

Rioch, M. (1975) 'Group relations: Rationale and technique.' In A. Colman and W. H. Bexton (eds) *Group relations Reader 1*. Washington, DC: A. K. Rice Institute.

Sampson, E. (1993) 'Identity politics: Challenges to psychology's understanding.' *American Psychologist 48*, 12, 1219–1230.

Schlachet, P. (1989) 'The concept of group space.' *International Journal of Group Psychotherapy 36*, 1, 33–53.

Shapiro, E. R. and Carr, A. W. (1991) *Lost in Familiar Places: Creating New Connections Between the Individual and Society*. New Haven, CT: Yale University Press.

Shields, W. (2001) 'The subjective experience of the self in the large group: Two models for study.' *International Journal of Group Psychotherapy 51*, 2, 205–223.

Skolnick, M. (1998) 'Schizophrenia from a group perspective.' In P. Bion Talamo, F. Borgogno and S. Merciai (eds) *Bion's Legacy to Groups*. London: Karnac Books.

Skolnick, M. (2000) 'Microcosm-macrocosm.' *Group 24*, 2, 133–145.

Slater, P. (1966) *Microcosm: Structural, Psychological and Religious Evolution in Groups*. New York: John Wiley & Sons.

Steiner, P. and Beukema, S. (2000) 'Dialogue groups in the 21st century: An extension of practice.' *Group 24*, 1, 75–92.

Thygesen (1992) '"Diversity" as a group-specific therapeutic factor in group-analytic psychotherapy.' *Group Analysis 25*, 1, 75–86.

Turquet, P. (1975) 'Threats to identity in the large group.' In L. Kreeger (ed) *The Large Group. Dynamics and Therapy*. London: Karnac Books.

Turquet, P. (1985) 'Leadership: The individual and the group.' In A. Colman and M. Geller (eds) *Group Relations Reader 2* (pp. 71–88). Washington, DC: A.K. Rice Institute.

Whitaker, D. and Lieberman, M. (1964) *Psychotherapy Through the Group Process*. Chicago: Aldine.

2

The Large Group and its Conductor

Gerhard Wilke

Introduction

In the group analytic literature on the large group as used in educational, training and organisational settings there are two omissions which need to be confronted: one is theoretical, the other empirical. Too little has been written about the role and style of the large group conductor and we have scant case material derived from the large group setting. The blank pages are no accident, they have a dynamic meaning within the 'social foundation matrix' of the group analytic movement in post-war Europe. The omissions mirror the ambivalence of the founding father of group analysis towards the large group and are reflected in the different approaches adopted by the disciple generation of large group conductors who pay more homage to Bion than to Foulkes. The intention behind my contribution is to show that writers on the large group have dwelled too much on the destructive and neglected the creative forces of the large group and that we could benefit from a return to group analytic ideas on the conductor role.

I will attempt to construct what the sociologist Max Weber called an 'ideal type' of the large group conducting role in the first two sections and in the third one analyse a large group which met daily with over 400 members at the 1996 Group Analytic Symposium on Destruction and Desire in Copenhagen (Weber 1930). The ideal type will mirror the conductor role as it has emerged in practice and theory during the generation succeeding the founding father of group analysis. I then move on to my thinking on the large group and its role. It will become apparent that I draw heavily on Foulkes's ideas on the small group, on elements in Bion's work on thinking, on certain ideas from social science and philosophy.

Section I

The heirs of Foulkes

Lionel Kreeger implies in his introduction to the *The Large Group* that this type of group space always resembles a psychotic mind, and he perceives the conductor as St George and the large group itself as the dragon (Kreeger 1975). From personal experience I know that his practice as a conductor is very containing at the beginning and the end of each large group. As a participant, it feels as if he is trying to create a safe environment which can serve as a reference point, a benchmark for the attacks on rational dialogue which ensue as soon as the free associative process begins. In the middle phase of a group his stance feels more classically analytic and abstinent. Kreeger seems to end up thinking in the in-between space of a developing large group, like a Kleinian rather than a Foulksian in that he is pessimistic about the therapeutic and rational outcomes of this type of work. Like Bion he is very concerned with how the group and its need for projective cohesion threaten the integrity of the individual mind within the container of the large group. The best we can hope for, he implies, is an insight into the experience of a disturbed mind and momentary reflections in the depressive position – if you like, thoughts, in defence against fragmentation, but not thinking.

Nevertheless, Kreeger develops the elements of a group analytic style of conducting and states that an unmodified form of intervention by the analyst is not workable in the large group. Kreeger concludes from his experience that conducting a large group is very demanding and exhausting work because the conductor is subject to enormous projections whilst needing to concentrate on holding, modelling and enabling the deepening and widening of the communication. He advises the conductor to intervene in order to build a group culture, foster a communal tradition, and help those forces in the large group which struggle for meaning and sense. I internalised this holding and containing style and adopted Kreeger's strong emphasis on starting and ending the group in order to set a boundary in my own practice. Kreeger has been my inner working model of a conducting figure in large groups but I want to take the debate beyond what I know from him.

Social anthropologists like van Gennep have pointed out that groups suffer from an outbreak of moral panic and social disorientation when they touch the in-between space and time boundary of normality and abnormality and have to master something unfamiliar (van Gennep 1960). In the in-between world of a large group its members temporarily lose a sense of being in an ordered and integrated symbolic universe. At such moments, ritual acts help to recreate a sense of order and social familiarity through the sense of reassurance they provide. The conductor of the large group performs a rite of passage when he makes a comment, or enables subgroups to speak and take up a position in the pull and push between progression and regression in the bounded chaos which represents the large group. A little more active participation by the conductor, the master of ceremonies, does no harm.

Why this is especially important at the very beginning and the early phase of the large group was recently explored by Norman Vella (Vella 1999). He revisited Freud's writing on groups and implied that the group does not exist at the beginning. It is, like the primal horde in *Totem and Tabu*, the sole object of satisfaction of the conductor, the all-knowing and denying father, the all-giving and consuming primitive mother. In response, the group gangs up on the conductor to kill him off or it projects poisonous feelings and thoughts into the body of the group to prevent the construction of a matrix. In this situation group development depends on the conductor's use of self in an as yet potential network of relationships, and he has to be active enough to build up a culture which can contain the mental image of the group.

Malcom Pines has pointed out that Bion neglected the capacity for development and psychic improvement contained in the group because he was concerned with arriving at deeper and philosophical insights about the genesis of thinking and social and psychological truths (Pines 1998). In contrast, Foulkes conceptualised specific group factors like mirroring, resonance and re-socialisation as healing and homeostatic for the individual within the group, be it large or small. The starting point and the focus of each thinker is different and yet they have an invisible meeting point where they can complement each other. They can help us think more creatively about the role of the analyst in the large group setting. We need Bion to understand the drives in the large group towards destructiveness and the propensity of the group to lose the connections between its members when they attempt to communicate. Bion, Turquet and Kernberg all stress the attack on thinking and linking which is indeed very striking in both the large group setting and social processes which set such patterns of interaction free. However, we also need to integrate Foulkes's ideas on groups and their capacity for health and communication on several levels simultaneously, not just in projectively merged basic assumption positions. We can use Foulkes's ideas on communication and group leadership in order to enable the modern large group conductor to break out of the mental prison of conceptualising the relationship between group conductor and the group as a projected one-to-one scene. A group therapist in the Bion tradition focuses more on the way in which individual wishes get frustrated because of the group's higher needs. What makes a conducting style group analytic is the fact that the individual's mentality remains just as important as group fantasies and group culture. As a group analyst in the Foulksian tradition Kreeger perceives the function and purpose of the group process as a way of enhancing the ego strength of the individual. He carries out his work of interpreting, describing and modelling subject to the matrix and dramatises, with the group, an analytical and democratic mind-set. As Denis Brown has put it: 'Bion's relative neglect of the group's ego functions and its work task, and his failure to discuss where and how it is achieved, are made good by Foulkes's central concept of the *matrix* as the place in which group communications are made, distortions are corrected and group culture develops. It is in the matrix that interpersonal problems come to be located and where the individual can question his boundaries and re-establish his identity.' (Brown 1985).

Pat de Maré in his book *Koinonia* urges us to use large groups to encourage thinking and dialogue between differing subgroups who can, through their exchanges, prevent warlike scenarios and enhance a civilising process (de Maré *et al.* 1991). He claims that the large group frustrates the satisfaction of libidinal needs and thereby causes hate. This resentment finds a channel for expression in subgroups which are containing enough to hold the hate and turn it into the desire to think and speak. Through a face-to-face dialogue between the subgroups within a large group, hate is transformed into frustration, which in turn is the precondition for using thoughts to tolerate frustration and develop thinking and linking. This theory is very much based on Bion's theory of thinking and learning from experience and claims that large group processes, if tolerated over a span of developmental time, can enhance the capacity of each of its members to be a more engaged and consensus-seeking citizen (Bion 1962).

De Maré argues that the large group has the capacity for generating enormous emotions which can get out of hand but he also believes that it is a sensitive thinking space in which regressive and progressive forces interact and coexist in a push-and-pull relationship. The task of the conductor is to replace mindlessness with connectedness, which he describes as the ability for fellowship. The role of the conductor remains fairly underdeveloped in his book and one is left with the impression that we are dealing with another version of the juxtaposition between analyst and group in an imagined dyadic relationship which mirrors the work of Freud on mass-psychology and ego-development. In addition, de Maré develops his theory from the vantage point of the late and more humane Bion and ignores the basic assumption theory. Only the positive and civilised parts of Bion's work on thinking are brought to bear by de Maré in his analysis of the large group process. Bion's attempts to explore how all new ideas, developed by what he calls mystics and geniuses, are subjected to attacks and attempts at rejection are ignored. The large group conductor is for him a kind of mystic.

In my view we must go beyond de Maré's implied idealisations of the conductor's interventions in the large group and consider how his ideas are often seen as threatening to the current order of the group. Only by acknowledging the negative reception of the conductor's contributions to the group can we begin to perceive and make sense of the forms of resistance against them. Bion pointed out that the task of any leader in a group context is to hold the new ideas whilst they are transferred from those that originate them, whom Bion sees as out of the ordinary, to those that need to accept and integrate them, whom he saw as ordinary. Three ways in which ideas are defended against in a group are identified by Bion: expulsion, dogmatisation, idealisation (Foulkes 1986) .The task of the conductor is to hold these ideas until they can be contained within the group boundary and to do so in the full knowledge of having his own thoughts idealised, expelled or turned into expedient laws.

De Maré assumes that subgroups will inevitably form in a large group and that they have a basic propensity to establish sufficient consensual ground between them to accept and tolerate new ideas which will help the group to renew itself and move beyond a regressive pull. He underestimates the importance of Bion's insights into the way borderline members in the group will attack the experience of dialogue and thinking in order to avoid the digestion and integration of a new experience, a new thought. It is equally important for the large group conductor to be aware of the propensity of schizoid members to attack any linking to prevent thinking, subgroup formation and individuation. The conductor of the large group must not only foster the formation of 'healthy' subgroups which are capable of civilising dialogue but he must also hold fragmented thoughts. In addition, it is important that the conductor generates new thoughts in the role of mystic or genius which break the familiar mould, and hands them over to the commoners in the group so that they can be accepted and integrated as part of the individual learning and group culture-building process. Thinking and dialogue in a group or a relationship depends, according to Bion, on an internalised parental couple. The conductor of the large group must attempt to function as an 'as if' couple with him being the father and the group the mother.

De Maré does not embrace Bion's thinking this far. According to him rational and civilised action is possible in a large group and he sustains the hope that aggressive energy can, through a holding environment and a containing style of leadership, be transformed into learning and an adjustment of the internal object relations world or super-ego function. 'Ego-training in action', which is the aim of all forms of group analysis, is not just possible in the safe environment of the small group but also in the hostile arena of the large group. The main reason why this should be so is the fact that we, as group beings, haven't just evolved the capacity for dealing with and creating complex inter-psychic processes which lead us into social conflict and war under certain conditions, but we have also evolved the capacity for social order and co-operative social and communicative relationships. The capacity to re-create order, to go on overcoming obstacles, to engage in dialogue, to sustain a face-to-face encounter in a 'massified' context, is as worthy of exploration as is the propensity to destroy such rational structures. What has occurred between Kreeger and de Maré is perhaps less a split but a polarisation at either end of a spectrum ranging from an optimistic to a pessimistic view of the large group process. It is the task of the current generation of group conductors to integrate not just Bion and Foulkes but also de Maré and Kreeger in their approach to the conductor's role.

It seems to me that Bion, like Max Weber, set out to gain a deeper understanding of the capacity of thoughts to shape and maintain but also to change and destroy institutionalised structures of order. Max Weber traced the success of Christian Puritanism, rational bureaucracy and representative democracy in transforming social institutions and collective states of mind over time. Bion explored how new ideas threaten the comfortable mental structures of the familiar world. He showed that the first reaction to a new idea, an attempt to say something different, is one of defence: driving the threatening thought out of the known universe. De Maré is primarily concerned with the creation and re-creation of benevolent thoughts and actions in and through the large group and he overly defends against the malevolent forces at work which Bion was so in touch with. In my thinking and conducting work I explore their interdependence in a shared context which is shaped partially by what is happening in the here and now of the large group, and to a significant extent by what is transferred into this setting from the 'foundation matrix' of culture and history through the 'social unconscious'.

Joseph Shaked is loyal to Freud and defines large groups as versions of a mass (Freud 1972). In the large group, members re-experience the archaic mother who threatens to 'incorporate' her children and consequently they regress into a dyadic relationship to both the group and the conductor. In recognition of Freud, Shaked argues that the individual member of a large group projects the ego on to an idealised group or leader construct. Both leader and group are alternately idealised and denigrated and group members relate to each other and the outside world as part-objects with a propensity to split and blame. He goes on to argue that a large group rarely 'progresses' out of the basic assumption positions outlined by Bion and is resistant to becoming a work group. His work overlaps with Bion's as both remain loyal to the central thesis in mass psychology and ego-development and imply that small and large groups always remain leader-fixated and that the 'classical posture' of the analyst provokes this form of dramatisation in a conscious and desirable way (Lorenzer 1995). To Shaked the conductor always remains the central focus and counterpoint of the group: he is the father who gets grudgingly accepted but must always be fought. In this sense the large group provides empirical proof of the Freudian thesis that a society needs leadership and a shared ideology which binds people together and acts as a boundary to the outside world.

Ideally, Shaked argues, the large group conductor works to help the group separate from omnipotent fantasies, magical solutions and idealisations. Shaked proposes that the aim of the large group is similar to the unconscious task of democracy: the integration of death and disorder in everyday life and the separation from the family and the acceptance of the social system. Within the Freudian mass-psychology paradigm he ends up arguing that the large group conductor must always retain the classical stance of an individual analyst; he sits in the group 'as if' he is behind the couch and as if the group is one merged individual. This classical posture transferred from the individual to the large group setting helps to produce very primitive forms of acting out and complex 'scenic dramatisations' in need of translation (Foulkes 1990).

The dyadic paradigm Shaked thinks in is compatible with Bion's work on basic assumptions but does not heed the lessons of the work on thinking and containment. His real achievement is that he shows how it is perfectly possible to go on working in the Freudian tradition as a large group conductor. Nevertheless, his thinking has a pre-Foulkesian ring to it. Foulkes goes beyond Freud in his thinking about the relationship between conductor and group, and adheres to Freud's theory of the personality to make sense of the different parts of the group. His communication theory overcame the limitations of the original Freudian model of reducing psychological interactions to a one-to-one scene. By adopting a matrix model of the mind Foulkes implied that each member is a nodal point in a transpersonal network and that each contribution in a group is connected with psychic problems which are located at the individual, the subgroup and the group-as-a-whole level (Nitsun 1996). It follows that the conductor is freed up to intervene on all these levels and can ensure that the communication flow takes a horizontal, vertical and external direction.

The conductor needs to free himself from being the master of the group and become its servant and co-facilitator because it is impossible to comprehend more than a fraction of the complex exchanges at all these levels in a group. A group analytic conducting style brings more trust into the group and to the task of conducting by resisting the basic assumption, implicit in Bion's and Shaked's thinking, that an individual will become more pathological on entering a group. All cultures need rituals and leaders to structure the transition from one social and cultural time and space period to another; so does a large group during the development of a single session or over a number of days. The group analyst leading such a group must consider being a master of ceremonies as well as occupying the role of analyst and translator. Kreeger doesn't pay enough attention to the conductor as a transitional object and translator; de Maré assumes that there is a 'natural' tendency to move from hate to dialogue through structural transpositions without much evidence of the conductor as an active analytical subject in the process; Shaked takes up an orthodox Freudian stance and enters a dyadic relationship with the group and focuses on the transference to the conductor. The constituent elements of the group matrix are blocked out of the field of vision. What distinguishes these three authors from a group analytic conception of the large group is their need to stay loyal to Freud's idea that mass-psychology can be reduced to a two-person psychology. None of them takes Foulkes's ideas about the group and its conductor – working on the group as a whole, the subgroup, the individual and the social foundation matrix level simultaneously – seriously enough.

Section II

The restoration of Foulkes to the large group

Foulkes said that the large group could be approached in a group analytic way but he wrote just one article on the subject, which leaves us none the wiser about a Foulkesian way of conducting such groups. We have to turn Nitsun's argument about the negative Bionian and positive Foulkesian group tradition, in his book *The Anti-Group,* on its head (Nitsun 1996). If Foulkes's pro-group perspective has been too dominant in group analytic thinking about the small group, the anti-group perspective of Bion has been too influential in relation to the large group. Whilst Nitsun says that group analysts need to own the destructive side of groups to reach a more integrated view of small group phenomena, it is clear to me that group analysts have neglected the creative potential of large groups, abandoning the task of understanding the dynamics of such groups to Klein's followers. Bion's work on basic assumptions, augmented by his later work on thought formation and learning from experience, provides the best framework for understanding both the regressive and progressive pulls in a large group. But the orthodox conducting style associated with this Post-Freudian paradigm and its emphasis on abstinence and group-as-a-whole interventions, which all of Foulkes's disciples seem to have adopted, needs to be replaced with a flexible, containing and 'civilising' conducting style which is in line with his ideas on the role of the group conductor and modern conceptions of the analytic encounter.

Perhaps Foulkes's refusal to engage with the large group is related to the fact that he developed a positive view of small groups even though he experienced the massification of the mob and its submission to a psychopathic leader in the Third Reich. Foulkes had to emigrate owing to the threat posed by a large group that had lost its mind. The impact of this experience becomes visible when one reads all the references in Foulkes relating to the term 'conductor'. His thinking in relation to the role aims to avoid talk about the leader or the power such a person can gain over a dependent group. It is at this point that the use of Foulkesian conducting principles have to be integrated with the insights of Bion about the fear of annihilation and massification which is typical of the early phases of large group development. Ironically, it is also at this early point in the life of the large group that the conductor has to go beyond both Foulkes and Bion in the way he intervenes verbally and acts out a modelling function.

Those members of the large group who carry a need for the re-enactment of symptoms of severe cultural and historical trauma and those who fear erasure because they lost a loved object prematurely and therefore experience attachment as fusion will, according to Earl Hopper, develop a valency for the fourth basic assumption of Incohesion: Aggregation/Massification or I:A/M. Hopper proposes that group analysts use the word 'personification' instead of 'valency' and argues that the people in a group who come to personify the fear of fission and fragmentation will bring an atmosphere of 'merger hunger' and 'contact shunning' into the group, and he shows that this has implications for the conducting style (Hopper 1997). He argues that the conductor needs to become more 'transparent', 'supportive' and active enough to use the basic assumption processes to help the group function as a work group. The conductor helps the group in this position develop sufficient levels of safety that traumatic re-enactments can slowly be translated into a verbal dialogue.

The one person who has written empirically about the dynamic development of a large group and the behaviour of the group analytic conductor within such a group is Robin Skynner (Skynner 1974). He analyses a large staff group at the Maudsley Hospital in London and concludes that the conductor has to abandon the classical abstinent stance in the large group and treat it like a small group with deprived and severely disturbed patients. In both small and large group settings the conductor must, according to Skynner, retain classical analytic thinking but adopt a more active and interactive posture. Disturbed patients re-experience deprivation in the face of an abstinent analyst. By becoming more active and involved the conductor can help a group avoid a complete re-enactment of a 'basic fault scenario' (Balint 1968) and strengthen those members who are 'grown up enough' to enter a working alliance with the conductor and the imagined group sufficently to weave a matrix which can hold the more disturbed members adequately to allow for the development of a dialectical interaction between regressing and progressing members and subgroups.

Skynner deals with a hole in Foulksian thinking because he is arguing that large groups tend, like borderline patients, to want to stay in a state of dyadic fusion or pre-Oedipal conflict. The conductor therefore has to work hard at making himself available as a father figure and focus in the early stages of the group's development not just on creating a matrix which can serve as an environmental mother but on being a location point within that matrix which can be related to as what I would call a 'patrix'. Skynner himself goes so far as to suggest that the group analyst make himself available as a scapegoat in order to help the group form a basic culture out of the guilt associated with the attempted patricide of the conductor and poisoning of the body of the group. In a toned-down version of this argument for an active stance in the group conductor role Halton has pointed out that:

> one cannot assume that people who come together from a sense of distress and a conscious desire for help are, *ipso facto,* able to reach the necessary depth of experience and insight with the minimal help that is offered by Bion and Foulkes. Experience suggests that one has to be interpretively active, particularly in relation to persecutory anxieties which often arise at the beginnings of a group, but also sometimes for long periods, in which more aggressive and psychotic anxieties become excessive and barely tolerable. Often the object that can best contain these anxieties is the therapist (Foulkes 1986a). (Halton 1999)

Both the Winnicottian and Kohutian agendas point to the analyst having to be and model an ideal-type human being who is comfortable with being insignificant in the face of enormous social forces but engages with the task of making a difference to a social organism which threatens to fall apart and needs help with growing up. Ultimately, such a stance is of course compatible with both Bion and Foulkes who stressed, in their different way, how the group conductor had to be experienced in a sufficiently holding, containing and mindful way. In the large group setting this means that the conductor becomes visible, graspable and identifiable in the analyst's role. Being a group analyst means maximising the opportunities for 'ego-training in action' through verbal and non-verbal interventions. Modelling the analyst as envi-ronmental mother in this conscious way means that the conductor makes himself known to the group at the start and end of each session. Letting the group guess who the conductor is re-enacts the mother who is more needy than the baby and overburdens the group with the development of a false self which functions to satisfy the conductor and protects him from holding the baby. The large group can be trusted to produce enough destructive and regressive forces without the conductor adding to their development by his actions or inactions.

A Foulkesian large group conductor

At the Group Analytic Society's Symposium on *Destruction and Desire* in Copenhagen (1996) I made the attempt to heed, as the conductor of the daily large group, Foulkes's advice and base the conductor role on its three constituent parts: the analyst, the dynamic administrator and the translator (Foulkes 1986). The group analytic assumption was made that the large group is not just potentially mad but also healthy and that a basic trust in the group by the analyst is needed to facilitate any kind of communication and the construction of a matrix. Furthermore, it was assumed that large group work is essentially a form of social, psychic and cultural working through or *Trauerarbeit* (mourning work) as Mitscherlich has called it (Mitscherlich 1993).

THE ANALYST

The role of the analyst in the large group is rooted not just in Foulkes but also in current analytical thinking in Britain which views the relationship between analyst and analysand as an interactive triangle that always results in the creation of what Ogden called a 'third subject'. Transference events are not a re-enactment of the past but a scenic re-dramatisation of internalised experiences in the here and now of a group context. Although the interaction is characterised by transference and counter-transference relating to the family of origin, it can only be described with reference to the here and now because the pattern of interaction has never been seen like this before and has never been shaped by such a group. It is a unique act of re-creation between those caught up in the current group and its surrounding social matrix. Group analysts can go further than Ogden and say that the interaction between analyst and analysand is always shaped by the context, and the mind and culture of the group are formed by the dyadic and triadic alliances within it and the social foundation matrix surrounding it. The group, the analyst and analysand form an interdependent Gestalt, analytical insights need to be combined with scenic understanding and what modern ethnographers call narrative instead of paradigmatic thinking (Carrithers 1992). Apart from this modern view of analysis, the large group conductor needs to stick to Foulkes's recommendation that group processes cannot just be viewed through the lens of individual analysis. In addition to classical psychoanalytic notions about transference and countertransference, we require specific concepts like mirroring, resonance, location, figuration, matrix and socialisation to help the process of mutual sense-making between the analyst, the individual, the subgroup and the group as a whole.

THE DYNAMIC ADMINISTRATOR

The 'dynamic administrator' role was regarded by Foulkes as highly as that of the analyst. The task is simply that of dealing with the creation and maintenance of a setting for the work in a psychoanalytic as well as administrative way. In the Copenhagen group which I analyse below, this work involved selecting the setting and planning the movement of people to the group room. As a conductor I made sound and sight tests to establish where it would be ideal for me to sit so that I could see and hear and be recognised and understood. This practical work is part of working in a group analytic way with the group, and the time spent with the organising committee of the symposium, its chair and the manager of the sports hall symbolised one of the most important group analytic interventions. This became clear when the workers who built the amphitheatre seating in which the large group met took the structure almost completely down on the morning before the last group session. If it hadn't been for the sports hall manager the group would have turned up for an empty space. It was the manager's understanding of what we were trying to do and his social conscience which made him intervene and insist on having the amphitheatre seating rebuilt in time for the session. Without this intervention all the analytic work by the group and the conductor over the previous days would have lost its meaning.

THE TRANSLATOR

In the 'translator' role the group analyst assumes that the therapeutic process is the same as the process of communication. For Foulkes this meant that people exchange information on four levels, that the problem of disjointed communication, so typical of large groups, is not located in any one person but between people, and that the conductor must translate attempts at communication from the more autistic and unconscious to the more verbal and conscious level. Discharging the translator role means locating symptoms in the matrix and perceiving them as expressions of 'un-relatedness' and 'dis-ease'. It also means that the conductor needs to be humble and realise that no metaphoric expression or scenic dramatisation of a psychic conflict can ever be translated accurately. Like a translator of poetry, the analyst can only convey the approximate meaning of what the speaker meant to communicate. Any ideas that the conductor's interventions as translator are truer or more accurate than anyone else's in the group cannot be sustained but nevertheless, what comes into the conductor's mind is connected with what is happening in the group matrix. The conductor is, like any other speaker or actor in the large group, a location point for transference processes and what someone says is, in essence, a statement on behalf of the group. In other words, a large group conductor can never succeed in occupying the role of the neutral, blank screen observer but must be content with the primary task of the action researcher, which is to be the clinician and the ethnographer and to make sense of the material in the group with the help of its members, not on their behalf (Schein 1990). The conductor needs therefore to try to intervene dialogically, leaving a space for feed-back and giving the group the power to decide whether an interpretation fits or not.

Section III

The conductor as 'participant observer'

Let me now come to my description and analysis of five group sessions at the 1996 Copenhagen symposium of the European Group Analytic Society on *Destruction and Desire* from the conductor's point of view. By definition the reader will be given snapshots of a participant observer who, like a social anthropologist, was following a dual purpose: first, to learn about the mentality of a strange culture in order to record it and make it comprehensible to others; second, to find more of his own true self through familiarisation with the stranger, the other. Detachment in the 'conductor-cum-writer' role is impossible, and what is reported contains unconscious distortions and reflects the fact that this account would have to be of Proustian proportions to portray the true complexity of the events which took place in the group and in the mind and body of the conductor.

   Large group conducting is not really possible without acceptance of the fact that the experience of the group cannot be grasped in words. An experienced large group conductor knows that some non-analytic knowledge of life and social science is needed to discharge the role in such a way that the group's mind and its foundation matrix can be connected. The conductor of a large group is in a comparable relationship to the object of observation with a modern physicist. What we can hope to find are observable 'traces' of enactments; what can 'hold the senses' of a large group conductor together, in the face of a bewildering array of projections and exchanges, is something akin to the philosophy of science developed by Niels Bohr and Werner Heisenberg (Good 1996). These physicists argued that observations and conclusions must be placed in a triangle in order to attain an approximation of the likely truth of an event. They did not believe that the 'objective observer' role is possible, as the researcher is involved in distorting and shaping the event that follows. They believed in the principles of 'indeterminacy' and 'complementarity'. The first idea suggests that we see what we know and that it depends on the specialism of the scientist whether he sees waves or corpuscles; the second principle suggests that it is better to match the eyes of one onlooker with those of another in order to get what van Gennep has described as the 'dense description' that he defined as the task of a social scientist (Geertz 1988).

Applied to the task of large group analysis this means that the conductor needs to weave into his interpretations references to history, culture and philosophy and arrive at a 'metaphoric story line', which is a distortion because it has been artificially structured but is at the same time shareable and thereby open for verification and disagreement. It is perhaps even more true in the large group that group analysis aims at 'ego-training in action' without knowledge of outcomes, and that a neutral and abstinent posture by the analyst resembles the omnipotent fantasies of pre-Einsteinian scientists in search of the detached, objective observer role. It is time to mourn the loss of such illusions of grandeur.

GROUP 1

As the large group was held in a sports hall, at a considerable distance from the university buildings where all other meetings took place, the large-group members embarked daily on a biblical exodus from the cultured and safe environment of the university into the wilderness of an unknown gymnasium. The journey was short in reality and long on anxiety. People entered the hall, sat in their seats and generated a chorus of noise which denied the existence of time and killed off the voice of the conductor. An anonymous group member got the group to fall silent by clapping her hands. The gesture clarified that we were inhabiting a 'paranoid–schizoid' universe. The group was immediately placed in the context of a bloody century and was compared to a melting pot, a marketplace, a dance floor and a battlefield. The fear of disintegration began to face some of the participants, who started to project their anxiety outward and developed the defence of absolute dependency. The square in the middle of the group became the focus of attention and several people found fault with the carpet, as if they wanted a perfect relationship to the group as mother before they could risk speaking.

The search for a safe relationship invoked a fear of the absence of a belonging group. Survival in the here and now required the resurrection of familiar and recognisable themes. The history of the exodus from the university to the group room was reinterpreted, and the long line of people meandering from the Paenum Institute, where the academic part of the symposium took place, to the sports hall with the help of guides was mentally reshaped into a flock of sheep being led to the slaughter. Suddenly the wandering group analysts embodied a line of Jews who were willingly going into the gas chambers at Auschwitz. A helpful gesture was reinterpreted as the persecution of the group by an evil conductor and organising committee. But the blame position could not be held as some speakers got obsessed with their placid compliance and lack of resistance. The victim–perpetrator– bystander theme continued to dominate but could only be tolerated for short periods. At other times members of the group projected whatever thoughts came into their minds. The force by which these atomised thoughts were expelled and crushed without finding a connection confronted the group with the truth of Bion's claim that thoughts are developed as a defence against a fear of disintegration and that connections between thoughts and people can only be made when high levels of frustration can be tolerated.

The large group at the previous symposium of the European Group Analytic Society in Heidelberg in 1993 was remembered and the theme of the Germans and the Jews reintroduced. In this context, someone spoke up and said that I had been a butcher before I became a group analyst. In response, I felt the need to say something and offered the following thoughts: 'Socrates was a philosopher, Socrates was a Greek, all Greeks are philosophers. According to the group I am in charge of a slaughter house, I am a German, all Germans are butchers. How can this ever be a safe group?' The group then wondered whether the story about my previous occupation and my statement were true or metaphorical. Eventually someone said, 'It is better to have been a butcher and become a group analyst than to have been a group analyst, like Karazic, and then turn into a butcher.' The group had wanted to give itself cohesion through the ritual killing of the leader and his exposure as an inadequate mother. The attack symbolised both the Oedipal killing of the father and the baby's attempt to bite the breast in order to find out whether it can be held and contained, whether it can show its bad and good self and still be accepted by the parent and the group. The conductor's survival enabled the group to integrate the inheritance from previous large groups at these conferences and the Germans and Jews were not left alone as the only perpetrators and victims in the here and now. It was pointed out that bystanders like the Swiss had lived in times where they ended up colluding with those that perpetrated the crime in order to stay safe themselves. An Israeli expressed the desire not to be used again for the purpose of hiding other people's guilt and repressed history. This person wanted to know about the Scandinavian skeletons in the cupboard. I then said that the group was trying to separate from the last symposium and come to terms with the fact that giving birth to something new in Copenhagen would involve the destruction of an idealised past.

The group then wanted to know how the Danes had behaved during the war. Very quickly Denmark was upheld as a rare example of how one should behave in extreme situations. While I listened I was thinking of Bettelheim, who argued that it was a person's nature and not his psychoanalytic training which decided whether someone survived or showed himself to be a decent human being in a context of terror (Bettelheim 1986). Unsure of myself, I decided to remain silent. The group ended with a Danish woman insisting that her nation could not simply be idealised, the Danes too had collaborators in their midst. In her the group had found the counter-location point in its search for the ideal leader or perfect environmental group-mother.

GROUP 2

I had been left with a feeling from the last group that its members were resisting the adoption of the patient role. As I was thinking this and trying to empty my mind in order to be fully present in the here and now, the second group began to be preoccupied with the function of the human senses and the difference between the positions of the observer and the object of observation, the analyst and the analysand. The Greek myth of the three women who have to share one eye was told. The myth exploded the idea that a person can rely on being a separate individual in possession of a skin with a clear boundary between inside and outside, between my senses and your senses. Someone picked up the imagery and revealed their distress about not knowing whether they could retain their sense of self, their sense of belonging or their awareness of being in possession of their own senses. In a frightening way the group lived the reality behind the claims of Foulkes and Elias that there is no such thing as a self-contained 'monad' called the individual which stands in 'glorious' opposition to society (Elias 1974). Both argued that we only possess knowledge of who we are by owning the wounding thought that we have a social self that is inextricably made up of 'I', 'you' and 'we' elements. The myth of one eye and three separate women exposed how the tension between this 'I', this 'you' and this 'we' dimension of our mind is at 'dis-ease' with itself and the surrounding cultural container. In short, 'ego-training in action' is not just a matter for a therapeutic group but is integral to everyday life in society.

The myth of one sense organ shared between three individuals also brought into my mind some of Earl Hopper's ideas on primitive forms of social formation in groups. He borrows the concept of 'fractal' from modern physics and information science and claims, in line with Foulkes's idea that each individual is invisibly connected with all others in a group matrix, that parts of the universe display the fundamental structure of the whole system (Hopper 1996). This affirms the old Buddhist belief that the universe can be contemplated in a flower or raindrop and that it is possible to regard each group member, or each subgroup, as a voice for the group. Applied to the three women it meant that each one holding the eye represented a 'fractal' of their common interdependence and ability to see and construct some common sense.

What the group was facing at this point was the task of making connections so that individuals experiencing their loss of identity could feel safe enough to become conscious 'individual members' (Turquet 1975, pp.87–144) and begin to tolerate the 'dis-ease' between individual and group, and make connections between the thoughts that were being projected into the group in response to this apt myth. A small subgroup projectively identified at this point with the need to co-operate and become fully one's self through interdependence. Unconsciously this minority was acknowledging that fate does not let us escape the dilemma created by the pull to be an individual and to be social. At the same time the bulk of the group was defending against the fear of fragmentation and identified with the absence of two eyes and the limits that this imposed on individual freedom. They were expressing their powerlessness and helplessness in the face of the over-whelming force of the group as mother earth or fate, and the conductor as the father in charge of the primal horde. Secretly, the majority of the group focused on the injustice of fate and how it had deprived each woman of her full entitlement to independence and individuality and forced the three of them into a form of sharing which ran individually counter to their narcissistic needs: a figuration just like the one they were experiencing in the here and now of the group, in the face of having to attach to this imperfect object which was, like all groups, somehow less and more than the sum of its individual parts.

As Bion wrote: 'The individual is a group animal at war, not simply with the group, but with himself for being a group animal and with those aspects of his personality that constitute his "groupishness"' (Bion 1961). Bion is apt here because the women in the story were left by the gods to sort out their work group arrangements. This is similar to Bion's attitude that the work group knows what it has to do when it has been told that it isn't working. Conducting a large group is different in the sense that the gods are present in the here and now in the shape of the conductor and the group. The group analytic conductor cannot be content with leaving the two subgroups to simply get on with it and work it out. It is precisely at such a juncture that a comment from the group analytic conductor is needed. The intervention is designed to sustain the working group and build up the matrix and the culture of the group. This is best done by describing what the conductor has noticed about the patterns of exchanges between different parts and the group as a whole so that the group is made real and can begin to function as a container and an imaginary partner to the conductor. When this begins to work the group and the conductor can together form an internal couple which will help increasing numbers of group members to function temporarily in the depressive position.

After this first phase of the second group, the topic of killing, aggression and violence against people, animals and nature returned. The group suddenly shifted from a fear of being attacked by the conductor or outsiders to a sense of not being able to control the violence involved in the process of separating from each other within the now firmer boundary of the group. The paradox of cutting up a patient in order to heal him, of using sadistic rituals to accomplish a mature task, was developed by a person who said how he had supervised a heart surgeon and his team with a death rate of one in three. The psychic pain got too much for the surgeon and he decided to cope by refusing to do the pre- and post-operative interviews with the patient and relatives. He did the cutting, the others did the emotional backing. That was the only way the task could be faced and seen through. The supervision work taught this group member that splitting can have positive as well as negative functions. The large group had brought this experience back to mind as he could only survive in the here and now by projecting a part of himself into the group to be eaten, digested and transformed.

Interwoven in the responses to this story was a strong need within the group for a victim rather than a perpetrator role. The group identified with the person operated on, not the supervisor and surgeon. Through projective identification the speaking part of the group fantasised itself into the position of the dependent and defenceless child. Everyone suddenly wanted to be safe from participation in dialogue, as communication was equated with violence and a potential offence against the other – be it cultural or natural. Unconsciously, the man who brought the story of the surgeon had delegated the role of the violator of innocence to the group conductor because in his role he took care of the malignancy in the whole body of the group. The members cast the group itself at this moment in the role of the mother who could, if required, break the rules of the Oedipal and grown-up game, restore the child within each of them, even in a treatment situation, and offer individualised care for everyone separately. Unlike the surgeon, and unlike the good supervisor, the group wanted to stay in the 'paranoid–schizoid' position. By invoking the innocent victim, a string of speakers located the less than ideal and aggressive parts of the self in the other, the grown-up.

The actual situation was that each group member had to be a surgeon to himself in the face of being with a lot of envious and threatening siblings competing for exclusion and inclusion during the group formation process. Only sufficient selfishness *and* trust in the group would accomplish the task of being in the group with both heart and mind. But the group was made up of group analysts who, in order to be fully working members of the work group, tried to avoid the risk of speaking in a self-serving way. The moral dilemma of choosing between being a survivor and a helper confronted them internally with their very ambivalent feelings towards the tasks of separating from an imagined dyadic relationship with the group and relinquishing in public a self-object based on the analyst as Good Samaritan. The group, its subgroups and individual members were at this moment struggling to accept the formation of an Oedipal triangle. During this painful transition their denial of aggression, in the face of such potentially shaming pressures, covered up the frightening inner recognition that belonging to the large group could offer a sense of identity, in a communal place and a shared time. The desire to belong could only be fulfilled through a confrontation with envy, destructive ideals and the loss of moral and political innocence.

The sense of the unbearableness of being a grown-up and the disillusioning choices involved in mature dialogue and decision-making was picked up by a woman who told of her daughter's plight at the hands of doctors who had to cut up parts of her body in a series of operations in order to save her life as she grew up. The woman went into great detail and the telling of the story took a long time, with her talking and the whole, massive group listening or fidgeting uncomfortably. The reaction to the woman's action and words in the group was strong and quite split and I felt very lost for a time because the whole scene felt like an individual analysis with the woman as the patient, the group as the analyst and me as peeping Tom. Somebody thought that the woman had abused the group in the same way that the doctors had violated her daughter, because she was trying to turn a container for cultural reflection into an individual talking cure; others were moved by the depth of her pain and held her sufficiently to help her mourn enough to recover her wits before the session ended. It was clear that the disturbed state of the group, in the face of the Oedipal conflict, had triggered this woman's need to unburden her guilt and attempt to purge her own mind in such a public way. She hoped to get reconnected with ordinary humanity through acting out a public funeral rite. She had no inner choice, she was driven to dramatise the elements of the Antigone drama and needed to create a public arena which unconsciously turned into a triangular scene – complete with heroine, anti-heroine and silent chorus – to free herself from the role of responsible adult in the face of overwhelming forces of fate. The timing of her outpouring made sense in that the group had unconsciously come to feel like a fateful being and could use her to explore the split between, on the one hand, those that wanted to show their desire to individuate and start the work of mourning and reparation, and on the other, those that wanted to stay merged and attached to the destructive object and persisted with dependency and attack. The woman had used the large group to destroy her shame and recover her desire to belong, the group had contained and used the woman in order to restore its ability to make connections and develop civilising thoughts and rituals. Above all the woman had acted out the central preoccupation of the whole group throughout the session: How can I begin to play an active role in my own salvation? How can I start to relinquish the defence of blaming my parents, external enemies or an unfair world and begin to own my own part in living out my individual and social fate?

GROUP 3

The group first heard from someone whose suitcase had been lost by the airline and who had been helped out by a number of people in the group. A second person objected to the thought that the group was made up of only kind and helpful people. He reported how his umbrella had been stolen during the last congress, and to emphasise the point he wagged his index finger at the group and wanted participants either to be honest enough to return any object which he might lose this time or own up to being delinquent. He gave the group the message that desire cannot be met without loss, that groups cannot exist without antisocial behaviour. This introductory phase ended in the first real and sustained dialogue when someone claimed that the large group had taken her words away and another person answered: 'Perhaps your words weren't usurped; perhaps someone just tried to speak for you.' This signified that the group's mind was no longer treating all words as bizarre objects which had to be kept 'out there' lest they should increase the psychotic insanity 'in here'. A distinction was tolerated between 'me' and 'not-me', between sense and non-sense. The door was now open for the question of meaning in a shared socio-psychic context. This depressive plateau was used by someone to open up the topic of change, collusion, loss, guilt and reparation.

A young Russian woman stood up and accused sections of the congress of being prejudiced about her people. There was a habit of splitting all participants into perpetrators and victims. She had observed that the Germans in the group accepted collective guilt all too easily, as if they had rehearsed it, but she was not going to comply. She was far too young to accept the blame for everything that was done in the name of the Soviet Union. She had come to learn, to be seen, to look and enter a dialogue about the tragedy that had befallen her country. There followed a series of tentative exchanges between this woman and participants from various parts of the ex-union. The whole drama of how difficult it is to make contact with the enemy, with the stranger, with the outsider was acted out. It was a simple thought that broke the spell and made the boundary between insiders and outsiders translucent. A group member from Lithuania said: 'I never thought it would be possible to find a context in which I could ask a Russian what it was like for them, whether they also had to learn to go to a nuclear bunker as schoolchildren and if they also were frightened? Whether they are not just very different, but also like us?' The vulnerability of the question led to a level of openness which was required to reconnect in the here and now and destroy a slavish dependency on the past.

It was interesting to observe that some people, led by a stern and upright man, could not tolerate this moment of oneness with humanity and immediately launched into a proselytising attack on the group by reminding everyone that there was war and mass murder, rather than dialogue, in Rwanda. Fairburn's 'internal saboteur' with a morbid interest in clinging to the bad object and a desire to destroy mature dialogue raised its head (Fairbairn

1953). The puritans were used by the group to stop the dawn of false hope and helped the collective mind remember that destructive and creative forces coexist in a dialectical tension at any moment in the group. The reinvocation of all the sinfulness in the world was experienced by the conductor as an intrusion into a secular group space that had momentarily witnessed the integration of the sacred and the profane. Yet it closed the circle of time for this session, as the invocation of the propensity for what Hopper has called aggregation and massification, amounting to an attack on thinking and linking, is not just always present in the large group but also in society. This counterpoint connected with the end of the first harmonic cycle in the session when the woman's story of having been lent clothes to make up for the loss of her suitcase was seemingly spoilt by the man who reminded us that there were thieves and delinquents amongst us.

The first reaction by the assembled group analysts to the young Russian, who had broken the ground rules by standing up when she spoke and wearing dark shades so that eye contact was not possible, was suspicion and mistrust. I experienced how the spontaneous disapproval of the young Russian was first denied, after the story had been given a good ending, and then transferred unto the spoilers who couldn't leave the woes of the world behind so that the group could dwell on and internalise the experience of reconciliation. What helped me retain the connection, the relationship between both these forces, in this moment of being pulled in two different directions at once, was a sociological thought. Emile Durkheim taught us that a society can only have a strong sense of order and hold onto shared norms and values when the community is reminded of its worth through the actions of deviants. Order and disorder exist in a relationship that helps define the meaning of each in a context (Durkheim 1933). The positive or negative value of an act or a word does not lie in itself but in its use in a particular context.

It was the moment in this group, and the stage in the group's life cycle, that made one subgroup into spoilers and the other into bridge builders. We can all imagine situations in groups or in life where the roles might have been reversed. I was very aware of this split identification and wrestled with making an intervention. In the end, it felt more appropriate to let the group stay with the tension of violation, reconciliation and the burden of unresolved problems. All the more so when I felt that the Russian woman, apart from being very brave and desperate, had created what Hopper has called 'the unconscious repetition of social situations and processes of equivalence' in this third session (Hopper 1999). He argues that people, who for some personal reason have become 'fractals' of the whole social system, re-create situations in a therapy group with other people which have occurred at a social and political level at another time and space. The re-dramatisation takes such a form that it could be regarded as 'equivalent' to the historical and cultural one. For the development of the group it made sense to let reconciliation occur and help it move to a higher level of functioning. I decided to act on this feeling and let the group end in a state of ambivalence about their membership of humanity.

What the spoilers had put me in touch with, when I tried to understand the connection between the woman's struggle to be included in the group and their negative reaction to the way in which she had done it, was the fact that successive Soviet leaders, starting with Stalin, had first violated their dependants in the satellite states and then seduced them into re-joining the 'socialist brotherhood' of mutual love. What the group had witnessed and helped re-create was an attempt by the woman and the ex-members of the former Soviet Union to re-enact a social and cultural trauma and thereby reduce its hold over each of them. It is important at such moments in a large group to let this process of re-dramatisation be acted out rather than talked away because it serves as a substitute for mourning work that cannot yet be accomplished by those involved. Had I offered an interpretation at this point, I would have become embroiled in a defensive stance to avoid taking sides in a split universe that had at that very moment suspended its belief in irreconcilable differences. The spoilers had, in actual fact, been sufficiently socialised by the group during the previous two sessions to mention unresolved conflicts and injustices in Africa, rather than between the split membership of the large group, like the ex-members of the former Eastern Block and those who had by chance been born on the western side of the iron curtain. All this was held in the air and could not possibly have been dealt with if one had tried to widen and deepen the communication beyond the ken of the group.

GROUP 4

The Oedipal scene was dramatised in this group through a preoccupation with reputation. Partly, this group fantasy suggested itself through the setting. We assembled in a sports hall where daylight entered through a glass roof, not through windows in the side walls. In addition, the group space was over-shadowed by a giant scoreboard on which the two scores 68 and 69 were displayed. These external factors were observed and brought into the session. After a playful phase, someone suddenly got serious and posed the question:

what would the press see and write if they looked in on us through the glass roof? Would we be revealed as adults, as children or as mad? The idea that we could be sane and mature because we were meeting in this way was split off and denied. The theme of our own sanity and reputation can, as claimed by de Maré (1991), only be faced in a dialogue through the channel of subgroups.

The large group process seems to show that humanity unites and that culture divides us. We learn to tolerate the frustration caused by the divisive nature of culture by idealising our own sub-culture and by denigrating the neighbouring one. For this mechanism to be successful, cultures have the tendency to define the 'we' as pure and the 'them' as dirty. Contact becomes a matter of taboo and touching the boundary signifies an act of danger and pollution (Douglas 1966). On this basis it makes a lot of sense if subgroups in the large group repeatedly return to the theme of virginity and perversion. They want to avoid a mature stance which implies blood-letting, the loss of innocence, and pollution through contact with the stranger. In the large group the polluting neighbour sits next to you and you get a chance to discover that a translucent boundary between the belonging and the enemy group affirms a common humanity and allows the desire to act out destructive fantasies to be contained by sitting face-to-face.

In this sense the answers to the question about the reputation of the group signified the participants' readiness to engage in a genuine cultural exchange between distinct subgroups whose difference could not be resolved but needed to be accepted and tolerated. One subgroup claimed that if someone were looking at the group they would see how we were avoiding mature inter-course by indulging in psychological masturbation. Another subgroup rallied around the idea that the group was full of old colonists, the first generation of pupils of Foulkes, who had been trying to fertilise virgin territory on the continent and in the east and were now segregating into those who wanted to settle down as farmers by fencing off their own land and those who were addicted to the missionary role. A third subgroup challenged the idea of over-powering fathers and innocent virgins, which had repeatedly cropped up as an image, by pointing out that in the group analytic movement young men like the conductor had been missionised and trained by strong older women. The fourth image dealing with the reputation of the group focused on the idea that we were struggling with making sense of the changes in the psychoana-lytic landscape. Psychoanalysis used to shock because of its emphasis on sexuality, now it is challenging because it demands time and depth in an age of global, Disneylike, fast changes. A person from a continent not involved in the

European east–west split brought the idea into the group that the concern for virginity and a good reputation was linked with the collapse of the old order and the sharing of the Cold War inheritance. 'The west has lost its sense of unity, the east has made the word "comrade" unusable. So how can we find fellowship in the large group if we have no words for talking about it? So, we fall back on sexualising the dialogue when in reality we seek companionship. Perhaps that is the dirty picture we don't want to look at. Companionship might remind us of homosexual bonding and attraction.'

We can see very clearly from this how a large group 're-members' and integrates events from a previous session and picks it up again in the service of strengthening the group matrix. The tolerance of the threatening themes of fundamentally different perceptions and of sexuality also demonstrated that the group had moved beyond dyadic interactions on day four and tolerated work on Oedipal themes for a whole session without significant regression. It was also noticeable that I had to say little in this session and that my memory is more in touch with reflections I had afterwards. The group made me think that the theme of sexuality linked to Oedipal conflicts had been faced very openly. This struck me as unusual, as this tends to occur, in my experience, less frequently in an Anglo-Saxon context. Perhaps this is so because in the United Kingdom and also in the USA we have turned away from Freud and adopted Bion's reinterpretation of the Oedipus complex. Bion thought that Oedipus' blindness was to be related to truth, instead of sexuality. To Bion, Oedipus was arrogant, inquisitive, stupid and destructive – just like the generals Bion experienced in the First World War. As an anti-hero to Oedipus, Bion invented the creative mystic, genius and group therapist who must be able to exist in an state of open ignorance. Ignorance, which Oedipus could not tolerate, was for Bion like a dark tunnel in which the singular and new idea would appear like a bright light.

Neither Bion nor Foulkes was, according to Halton, strong on working with the transference and countertransference in groups. They consequently ended up neglecting conscious work with Oedipal material (Halton 1999, pp.71–91) Bion's theory was rooted in the preoccupation of the object relations theorists with the mother–child containing and holding relationship. Foulkes focused on the group as a good object that could be implicitly trusted to reveal the creative potential within it. I share this belief, but would argue that it is the work with Oedipal material that makes the matrix and the boundary of the group strong enough to tolerate the ignorant position for long enough to let the known, but not yet thought and named material, emerge in the group (Bolas 1995). This fourth group, perhaps not surprisingly as it was full of professional group therapists, seemed indirectly to work through the different positions on the Oedipal situation in the current analytical world. The group split into subgroups which were trying to rearrange the inter-family hierarchy amongst these analysts and reevaluate the teachings and learning of at least three to four generations in relation to the founding father of group analysis. At a socially unconscious level, this involved contemplating the idea that the founding of group analysis by Foulkes implied the perversion of the original teachings of Freud (a kind of homoerotic rape) and that the export of group analysis to the continent of Europe, after World War II, involved the violation of the natively grown psychoanalytic traditions. The group's question: 'What would a journalist see from outside?' was really an exploration of the obstacles to further change within the group and the group analytic movement and its practice and theory. The exploration was also concerned with adapting our current professional identity under changed circumstances in the political and clinical environment, in which we have all become subject to scrutiny and outcome research. The paranoid defence associated with this new health philosophy took the shape of competing group fantasies about violations, misdeeds and deviations incurred by previous generations of analysts and carried and suffered by the current one. In other words, we were collectively exploring how we face up to the reality test in the current situation.

The group seemed to suggest that the pressure of exposure through the media, through an open debate in front of an authority figure, generates a need in us to integrate both positions in the Oedipal debate in order for this knowledge to be helpful beyond the clinical setting in a political and cultural discourse. Freud saw Oedipus as a seeker of truth, endowed with heroic qualities, who faced his fate honestly and acted truly, even though the forces of fate were stacked against him. The group searched for such a posture in the face of external doubts and under the threat of surviving professionally through a stiff examination of the actual performance of the therapist. The group also began to acknowledge that the current competition for a dwindling patient pool feels like the Freudian Oedipal drama involving rivalry, possession, aggression and guilt. Steiner modernised our view of the Oedipal drama by shedding light on the other side of the story (Steiner 1933). He showed that Oedipus wanted to cover up his crimes, that he did not want to face his guilt and struggled to maintain a mental status quo rather than purge himself and clean up his royal house. He recommends that we view the

Oedipal situation in terms of the central conflict between the inner and the outer world and look, with the patient, at how the conflict prevents or facilitates change in both these spheres. This is the current Oedipal paradigm and it came to my mind in this group because people were preoccupied with dirty old men and virgins for a long time and struggled to find a way back to a healthier verbal intercourse and professional potency. I heard this as an unconscious dialogue about the identity and the public perception of our profession. The group expressed a deep need for each 'virgin' group analyst to find the courage to explore how those that had slipped, had incurred guilt and given the group a bad name, could be shamed and thus pave the way to restoring the reputation which the profession deserved in its own eyes. The group was looking for its own Oedipus so that it could find the source of pollution within the community. It wanted to find a scapegoat, rather than living on not knowing the future and suffering a sense of knowing that everyone has colluded in bringing the current state of dis-ease about, if only as naive bystanders.

With so much hard work in the Oedipal situation going on, it was like a reward from the Freudian heaven when the group ended with a dream. A woman reported that she had seen two older men taking children into a classroom. She was one of the children, and when they had all settled down she saw that they and the two teachers were all naked. Before she woke up she realised that one of the men stood facing the class and the other had turned around, bent down and showed his bare bottom to the children. The group felt that one of the older men was her training analyst and that the man facing the children was the conductor. He was feared as having the power to strip everyone naked but sat very exposed before the group. The woman saw her own dream clearly but could not make sense of the taste of disgust with which she woke up. At this point I said: 'It is perhaps a degree of self-disgust which you were tasting for the group. You discovered in the dream that children have the power to destroy their parents' reputations and leave them exposed, defenceless and vulnerable. The dream shattered the fantasy that the group is made up of innocent victims and exposed a lot of anxiety about the relationship between the different group analytic generations and between each practitioner and the outside world.' At this point the group ended. It was the first and last time I was allowed to have a final word.

GROUP 5

In terms of the foundation matrix of post-war Europe it was not unimportant that I as the conductor was a German and that the only contribution during the symposium which had a populist appeal and earned open applause was made by a person with the same national identity who was used by the group to draw up a balance sheet of its achievements. The group member said that the search for innocence seemed to have been a defence against the threat contained in the theme of destruction and desire, and pointed out that 'the virgin is, like all other ideals, an illusion. In the group there has been a search for virgin territory, a passion for missionary activities and a desire for power. These are all male fantasies. But we also had some female fantasies which dealt with having a bad press, being introverted, being shamed. The virgin is not a female preoccupation, it is time to acknowledge the strong women, the powerful older generation and feminine themes in the group analytic movement.'

When several speakers linked these thoughts to the Danish woman in charge of the symposium it became clear that the group wanted to avoid having to deal with their dependency on the conductor and the pain of having to separate from him by relocating the problem of their attachment in a victim–perpetrator split. Instead of facing the pain of ending a good enough symposium, which had succeeded in giving the 'German' within and without a place inside the group analytic movement, the person from the 'fatherland' fell back on a split between good mothers and bad fathers. The second-generation tragedy of having to define the self with reference to a 'higher super-ego ideal' was invoked. The group member implied that one becomes someone special when one stands out from the crowd by virtue of being a strong victim. This represented a fall-back to an identity-seeking device employed by second-generation perpetrator children when they 'compulsively steal themselves' into the victim position to avoid having to identify with their 'murderous fathers' and 'colluding mothers' (Eckstaedt 1992). Thereby those burdened with the collective guilt of the previous generation hope to ensure acceptance in the eyes of those whose rejection they fear most. By obsessively looking for external approval, they develop a self with a harsh internal super-ego and end up hating themselves, just as they restricted themselves to hating their parents and denied their love for them. The secret desire to be free of the collective guilt becomes a self-destructive defence mechanism that ensures that the attachment to the transferred guilt is strengthened, and an unconscious identification with the real parents within re-formed.

The person's critical balance sheet in the large group implied that for the children of the victims and perpetrators the good-enough German is female, the bad-enough German continues to be the father. A German large group conductor doing a good-enough job, worth separating from, must remain unthinkable. Thus the dyadic victim–perpetrator scenario needed to be preserved as a self-object matrix. It was an ironic counterpoint in the last session to the intervention of the Israeli expert on second-generation problems in the very first group, who had shown the group how they often 'used the Germans and the Jews' as an excuse for avoiding a confrontation with their own 'destructive' past. The guilt that had accumulated in these five group sessions was connected with the desire of the younger generation to push the older one from the perceived seat of power. An attempt had been made in session three but the group had pulled back from 'parenticide' when it realised that this would lead to dangerous forms of sibling rivalry. Indirectly, the return to the victim–perpetrator theme was an attempt to mourn the loss of collective and grandiose self-objects which the younger and older generation had projected into the debate about relative positions of power within the group analytic movement.

When faced with ending and separation, the large group descends into a split universe between insiders and outsiders. The reason is perhaps that the large group does not end and mourn, it treats the conductor and the projected group ideal like a transitional object which is relinquished, not lost. The 'dis-ease' with the past and about the end of the group was not worked through and towards the end took on a local flavour. Those who are familiar with Scandinavian history will know that relations between Danes and Norwegians are not easy. Against this background a contribution by two Norwegians made a deeper transgenerational sense. They reported that they had been disturbed by the acting-out of the Danish organising committee at the party, which took place the evening before the last session. The two argued that it was not right that responsible committee members had participated in a public prank and thereby exposed themselves as delinquent. Some of those addressed owned up to having enjoyed participating in this specifically Danish form of acting-out at the party as a way of affirming their separate identity in front of a 'foreign' audience. They admitted gleefully to their historical rivals that it might have been inappropriate to act out in this way but that the event might symbolise something for the whole symposium and the large group. Other group members developed the analysis by saying that desire was not only coupled with destruction but also with self-destruction and, importantly, that personal development was tied up with play and boundary transgressions. The collusion of the committee with a prank was making the self-destructive and playful side of everyone visible. The acting-out of the 'responsible people' had shown that the struggle to hold on to an integrated self is never-ending, that power can mean that those who hold it will discharge their duty honourably, but we also know that power awakens the desire to destroy the boundaries and engage in abusive behaviour. 'The group will end,' someone said, 'but it will also have to live on. We will always be tempted by repetition compulsion as long as we live. In life and in this group we will leave a psychological inheritance, some of our projections will be transferred into the large group at the next symposium and the generation there will have to deal with it.'

It made a kind of sense that someone brought a dream with psychotic elements into the group after these 'persecutory' contributions had berated the whole group and exposed the Danish host subculture as vulnerable. At the point of facing separation from the group an Australian man, who felt the displaced aggression in the group, said that he would go away from the large group feeling that it could never be trusted. The sessions had disturbed him, he had been dreaming violently throughout the week and hadn't dared to reveal these private images before. Now, at the end, he felt safe enough to talk about the dreams as he thought they were the property of the large group and did not belong to his own mind. He dreamt that he was the accomplice of a gang of criminals who were selling corpses. When they had run out of dead heroin addicts to sell they started killing ordinary people to stay in business. Eventually it got more and more difficult to find victims and the gang decided to kill him. Having helped the gang he thought this was very unfair and he asked why they picked on him. The answer was that he had been chosen because he had been a helper. At this point he woke up bathed in cold sweat.

The telling of the dream coincided with a time when I as the conductor had been excluded from the conscious mind of the group and felt killed off inside. I used a short silence in response to the dream to make in my role as analyst a final comment containing material which had been held since the first session: 'When I try to review the group in my mind I am left with an image of adolescent desire. This large group wanted to be hedonistic without becoming responsible, desiring but not destructive. I am left with the image of the doctor–patient relationship. Why, I don't know, but it is as if this group struggled to get in touch with the split-off neediness and aggression in the analyst and wanted unconsciously to avoid the experience of being the helpless patient by "monitoring" and "auditing" the conductor's failings. Perhaps the dream allowed me finally to get aggressive enough to impose an interpretation on you as a group, and the dream allowed the group, as a collective body of analysts, to integrate the sadistic and destructive part of your professional role. Perhaps you can go away and accept that a loss of innocence is an integral part of the therapeutic process. Looking back, it certainly was part of my experience of being the large group conductor here that I had to hold the integration of destruction and desire within, to model a containing and holding posture without.'

Before leaving a large group it is important to reassert the difference between self and other. In Copenhagen this meant reasserting the identity of the belonging group. The difference between 'me' and 'you' was worked out by looking at the divide between 'us' and 'them' – Danes and Norwegians, collaborators and resisters, men and women, old and young. The common ground between the departing German and Norwegian critics during this session was that they dealt with the issue of individuation and separation. Unconsciously, they were asking the group to affirm that they had internalised an experience which could help them face a difficult reality after the symposium. The connected foundation matrix issue which the explorations of identity, separateness and the power of each peer group within the large group signified, was the fact that these exchanges mirrored the post-modern 'sibling society' where fathers no longer play a role in the exchanges between a child and an all-powerful mother, and where the only safe place for the individual is to be found in a sisterhood or brotherhood – preferably with a victim status (Bly 1996).

The Copenhagen large group too consisted of peer groups which preferred to criticise and find fault, who experienced separation and moving on as a betrayal of their own group ideal. In this way categories were kept clean and the 'siblings' could be seen as equal, fair and 'virginal'. Siblings don't need to be rescued by a parental couple, as represented by the committee chair and the conductor. They remain independent and politically correct by opting for the side of the innocent victim and they defend against a feared counterattack by avoiding any offence against people, the environment and animals. The subgroups avoided rivalry and mourning and maintained the fantasy of eternal youth and perfect being. Like true siblings, the Copenhagen subgroups avoided over-intimate contact and remained for long periods in a narcissistic universe which is attuned to how the world should be and not how it is (Lasch 1991). The large group revealed its Janus face at the end: one side faced reality, asserted its autonomy and made some progress in the civilising process of the group analytic movement; the other side fled into a fantasised innocence and eternal youth and refused to engage with the process of disillusionment involved in meeting the demands of the group rather than the individual within it.

Conclusion

The split between Bion and Foulkes is mirrored in the way a large group conductor is conceptualised. The two styles of conducting become graspable through the way a conductor handles beginnings, endings and transitions. The Foulkesian 'pro-group' conductor influences the quality of the experience in the large group by the way he makes himself available during the session and by making it known that he exists at the start. The conductor belonging to the Bionic 'anti-group' tradition gives the large group as much space as possible to regress by refraining from saying anything at the start or the end of the group. These opposing stances are in the end a false choice. The competent conductor of a large group needs to hold both perspectives in mind and use Bion to understand the defences of the group and Foulkes to develop a flexible way of conducting it. If we think of large-group conducting in Hegelian and dialectical terms: Foulkes is the thesis, Bion is the antithesis, and the Copenhagen conducting style the *Aufhebung* (the negation of the thesis and antithesis through a process of transformation in which the essence of both is retained and integrated in a new form) into a 'third position' which is analytical, philosophical and humane. Concretely, this means that the group analyst tries to intervene on all levels of the group, addresses the thinking mind in the group, guards the boundary and lets his actions be guided by a sense of how much regression the most vulnerable member of the group can tolerate. If these ethical and professional standards imply that some participants, who have a preference for the madness of the large group and like to see their conductor push its members to the limits of sanity, get their sadistic lust for blood sports frustrated, then so be it.

It is clear that Foulkes's lessons are mostly heeded in the small-group world and here it has been shown that his ideas have been underutilised for the large group. Foulkes claimed that the group conductor has to develop three roles in the service of the group: he has to be the analyst, the dynamic administrator, and the translator. Through training, supervision and learning from experience the conductor eventually integrates these roles and develops a clearly identifiable group analytic self which the members of any group can use, abuse, cathect and de-cathect as an object. What holds the conductor's personality together is his humanity, and more important than his technical tools are his integrity, honesty, directness and care. The boundary between the analytical role, the responsible citizen and the human being has to be translucent in the large group. In this setting, the conductor needs to avoid getting sucked into simplistic 'either–or' scripts and repeatedly confront these reductionist desires with more 'civilising' and non-splitting 'as-well-as' interventions.

The Copenhagen large group demonstrated over five days how threatening this dialectical way of seeing can be for traditionally minded group analysts. The profession is, in part, subject to helper syndrome, which means that the help-giving group analyst denies his own needs and desires by giving to others through his interpretations, which establish a questionable link between symptom and cause. The theme of the symposium was 'Desire and Destruction'. In the large group, desire turned into destruction through self-sacrifice, and the assembled analysts satisfied their own secret desires through a projective identification with idealised patients who were felt to need rescuing. Group and individual analysts tend to denigrate their own desires as neurotic symptoms of their not-yet-perfect helper nature. The large group at the symposium was over-preoccupied with the theme of the virgin and revealed that group analysts en mass can be addicted to the temptation to perceive the world in victim–perpetrator terms. This powerful archetype functions to protect the professionals from the recognition that an interactive conception of the analyst–analysand relationship against the background of a group means that everyone involved will become guilty through the act of participation. Mistakes are what life is made of, and mistakes, especially those of the conductor, are the source of new knowledge in group analysis and facilitate individual and group development in all settings.

References

Balint, M. (1968) *The Basic Fault: Therapeutic aspects of regression.* London: Tavistock.

Bettelheim, B. (1986) *Surviving the Holocaust.* London: Fontana.

Bion, W. R. (1961) *Experiences in Groups and Other Papers.* London: Tavistock.

Bion, W. R. (1962) *Learning from Experience.* London: Heinemann.

Bion, W. R. (1967) *Second Thoughts.* London: Heinemann.

Bly, R. (1996) *The Sibling Society.* London: Hamish Hamilton.

Bolas, C. (1995) *The Shadow of the Object. Psychoanalysis of the unthought known.* London: Free Association Press.

Brown, D. (1985) in M. Pines (ed) *Bion and Group Psychotherapy.* London: Routledge & Kegan Paul.

Carrithers, M. (1992) *Why Humans have Cultures. Explaining anthropology and social diversity.* Oxford: Oxford University Press.

de Maré, P., Piper, R. and Thompson, S. (1991) *Koinonia: From hate through dialogue to culture in the large group.* London: Karnac Books.

Douglas, M. (1966) *Purity and Danger. An analysis of conceptions of pollution and taboo.* London: Routledge & Kegan Paul.

Durkheim, E. (1933) *The Division of Labour in Society.* London: Macmillan.

Eckstaedt, A. (1992) *Nationalsozialismus in der Zweiten Generation. Psychoanalyse von Hörigkeitsverhältnissen.* Frankfurt: Suhrkamp Wissenschaft.

Elias, N. (1974) *Die Gesellschaft der Individuen.* Frankfurt: Suhrkamp Wissenschaft.

Fairbairn, R. (1953) *Psychoanalytic Studies of Personality. London: Routledge.*

Foulkes, S. H. (1986) *Group Analytic Psychotherapy, Method and Principles.* London: Maresfield Library.

Foulkes, S. H. (1990) *Selected Papers, Psychoanalysis and Group Analysis.* London: Karnac Books.

Freud, S. (1972) *Massenpsychologie und Ich-Analyse.* Frankfurt: Fischer.

Geertz, C. (1988) *Works and Lives: The anthropologist as author.* Stanford: Stanford University Press.

Gennep, A. van (1960) *The Rites of Passage.* London: Routledge.

Good, B. J. (1996) *Medicine, Rationality and Experience. An anthropological perspective.* Cambridge: Cambridge University Press.

Halton, M. (1999) 'Bion, Foulkes and the Oedipal Situation.' In C. Oakley (ed) *What is a Group?* London: Rebus Press.

Hopper, E. 'The social unconscious in clinical work.' In C. Oakley (ed) *What is a Group?* London: Rebus Press.

Hopper, E. (1996) *Das gesellschaftliche Unbewußte in der klinischen Arbeit: Reflexionen über die vollständige Deutung und die Quadratur des Dreiecks. Heidelberg: Gruppenanalyse 6, 1, 67–113.*

Hopper, E. (1997) 'Traumatic experience in the unconscious life of groups: A fourth basic assumption.' In *Group Analysis 30,* 4, 439–470.

Kreeger, L. (ed) (1975) *The Large Group, Dynamics and Therapy.* London: Constable.

Lasch, C. (1991) *The Culture of Narcissism. American life in an age of diminishing expectations.* New York: W. W. Norton.

Lorenzer, A. (1995) *Sprachzerstörung und Rekonstruktion, Vorarbeiten zu einer Metatheorie der Psychoanalyse.* Frankfurt: Suhrkamp Wissenschaft.

Mitscherlich, M. (1993) *Erinnerungsarbeit. Zur Psychoanalyse der Unfähigkeit zu trauern.* Frankfurt: Fischer.

Nitsun, M. (1996) *The Anti-Group. Destructive forces in the group and their creative potential.* London: Routledge.

Pines, M. (1998) 'Bion: A group analytical appreciation.' In *Luzifer-Amor, Zeitschrift zur Geschichte der Psychoanalyse 11. Jhrg. Heft 21.* Edition Diskord, Tübingen 58–70.

Shaked, J. (1993) *Die Gruppe als Spiegelbild der Gesellschaft.* Zürich: SGAZETTE 9/93, 12–17.

Schein, E. H. (1990) 'Organisationsteratung: Wissenschaft, Technologie oder Philosophie?' In G. Fatzer and C. D. Eck (eds) *Supervision und Beratung.* Köln: Edition Humanistische Psychologie.

Skynner, R. (1974) 'The large group in training.' In L. Kreeger (ed) *The Large Group.* London: Constable.

Steiner, J. (1993) 'Turning a blind eye: The cover-up for Oedipus.' *International Review of Psycho-Analysis 12,* 161–172.

Turquet, P. (1975) 'Threats to identity in the large group.' In L. Kreeger *The Large Group, Dynamics and Therapy.* London: Constable.

Vella, N. (1999) 'The Social Unconscious in Clinical Work.' In C. Oakley (ed) *What is a Group?* London: Rebus Press.

Weber, M.(1930) *The Protestant Ethic and the Spirit of Capitalism,* transl. Talcott Parsons. London: Unwin.

Part II

Application
Putting Bion's Ideas to Work

3

From Groups to Group Relations

Bion's Contribution to the Tavistock 'Leicester' Conferences

Mannie Sher

Introduction

Bion's interest in pushing further into the primitive in the individual extended to the group and this aspect of exploring the primitive in groups was taken up and developed by his colleagues in the Tavistock Institute, working in particular on the ever-present challenge to memory and desire, to the very human wish that everything should revert to the *status quo ante*. Overcoming these barriers to learning, Bion believed, offered the chance that new, often surprising insights would be generated.

The purpose of this chapter, therefore, is to rediscover Bion's thinking in the light of his own developments and of current changes in institutions, organisations, societies and the emergence of networks within these. Bion himself appeared to be sceptical of the transfer of his ideas on group processes to other situations where group formation and group behaviour are important. Bion considered that the psychoanalytic approaches to understanding groups should be limited in the main to groups that had the task of self-examination. Although Bion sometimes made analogies with other types of groups, quoting Freud on the army, the church and the aristocracy, the language of Bion, and the group he appeared to have in mind, was the psychotherapy group – the group that by definition Bion believed would recover from clinical illness through a process of self-examination and self-discovery.

Consequently, Bion was surprised at the interest aroused by his articles on groups that led to the publication of *Experiences in Groups* (1961). We have an early indication of Bion's interest in 'sovereignty and power' in small groups via his regret at not having discussed these subjects in the book, but he also reveals his scepticism on the subject by declaring that 'sovereignty and power' do not develop to maturity in small groups. Was he talking about small groups per se? Or was he talking about small groups of psychiatric patients who, as a group, we might expect to have difficulties in the area of self-actualisation and with sovereignty of the self? In the small group rivalries can be understood but in a large group they are difficult to come to terms with. At the turn of the century, Empire was an ideal and in terms of British power, was at its apogee. Bion had fought bravely in the First World War for all the ideals of Empire – and experienced the barbarism and futility of war. In the Second World War he had contributed, particularly through War Office Selection Boards, to challenging the selection system of officers that was a legacy of Empire and the British education system that fed virtually unquestioned idealisations of Empire. Empire was an organising myth for the British at that time, so Bion's initial ideas on sovereignty and power have to be seen in this context. Bion lived through a time when notions of sovereignty and power had moved since the confident assertions of the nineteenth century.

Elsewhere, (1961, p.7) Bion alludes to inter-group relations by stating that the mature form of sovereignty and power is extrinsic and impinges on the group only 'in the form of invasion by another group'. Here Bion seems to be struggling with the mysteries of the relationship between internal and external factors to explain dynamics.

As a practising psychoanalyst, Bion was impressed by the fact that the psychoanalytic approach, whether through the individual or through the group, is dealing with different facets of the same phenomena. Bion's major contribution here was to show that the psychoanalytic approach to the individual and the psychoanalytic approach to the group are two methods that provide the practitioner with a rudimentary binocular vision. When these phenomena are examined using the individual method, they centre on the Oedipal situation related to the pairing group. When the phenomena are examined by the group method, they centre on the Sphinx and they are related to problems of knowledge and scientific method. These views appear to presage later work on groups and organisations which were taken forward by Bion's colleagues like A. K. Rice of the Tavistock Institute. But before we examine later stages on the journey from groups to group relations, we also need to take note of another of Bion's assertions that has bearing on our discussion of what kind of groups Bion really had in mind. Bion had been very much influenced by Rickman (1950, 1951) who had led interest into 2-, 3- and n-person psychology that at the time went against the grain of traditional psychoanalysis. Rickman (1943a, 1945), and Bion were involved with the Northfield experiment (Harrison 2000). The *Experiences in Groups* papers were written before Bion's analysis with Klein, but were not published in book form till after. What was the real significance of the following sentence in Bion's Introduction?

> My present work, which I hope to publish, convinces me of the central importance of the Kleinian theories of projective-identification and the interplay between the paranoid–schizoid and depressive positions. (Bion 1961)

Without the aid of these sets of theories, Bion doubted the possibility of an advance in the study of group phenomena. At once we realise that even though relying on psychoanalytic thinking and utilising terminology usually associated with pathology, Bion was turning his attention to phenomena extant in the broader universe outside the clinical one. It became the task of others to translate and transfer Bion's ideas to other areas of study. This was done in the work of the early pioneers at the Tavistock Institute – 'Tommy' Wilson, Harold Bridger, Eric Trist, Hugh Murray, Kenneth Rice, Elliott Jacques, Isabel Menzies, Girth Higgin, John Hill, Fred Emery, Frank Heller, Henry Dicks, Douglas Woodhouse, Elizabeth Bott Spillius, Eric Miller and Gordon Lawrence, and others from the Tavistock Clinic, notably Jock Sutherland, Pierre Turquet, Robert Gosling, John Bowlby and Mary Barker.

But before we move on to discuss the journey, we need to take a clear look at the influence of Kleinian theories on Bion's work and look there perhaps for the keys to the extrapolations from Bion's work on groups to group relations and the Tavistock Leicester Conferences. As a psychoanalyst and follower of Melanie Klein, Bion's emphasis on the importance of psychic mechanisms at the start of life would not be surprising. In his now famous statement, Bion says that:

> in his contact with the complexities of life in a group, the adult resorts, in what may be a massive regression, to mechanisms described by Melanie Klein (1931, 1946) as typical of the earliest phases of mental life. The adult must establish contact with the emotional life of the group in which he lives; *this task would appear to be as formidable to the adult as the relationship with the*

breast appears to be to the infant, [my italics] and the failure to meet the demands of this task is revealed in his regression. (1961, p.141)

One cannot avoid the impression that the reader is being invited by Bion to re-examine theories and concepts, to make new beginnings without being encumbered by previous theories and to see if the exercise might lead to a point at which views of the group and psychoanalytic views of the individual can be compared, 'and thereby judged to be either complementary or divergent'. The statement reflects the fascinating times he and his colleagues lived in, given they were only just emerging from the devastation of the Second World War. New theories and new methods were needed to replace the disintegration, personal and social, they had recently experienced. Yet Bion seemed to hint that these theories would be complementary and convergent with psychoanalytic training and its emphasis on situations of emotional stress.

Transference

To underscore the role of transference, Bion asserted that there were times when he could discern a group's attitude towards him and that he could state in words what the attitude was; he also said there were times when another individual acted as if he also thought the group had an attitude towards him, and Bion believed he could deduce what his belief was; and there were times when Bion thought that the group had an attitude to an individual, and he could say what it was. These observations, and perceptions and the ability to put them into words provide the raw material on which interpretations are based. This whole business demanded, he said, 'an ability, nurtured by training and vigilance, to stay with ignorance and uncertainty without any irritable reaching after fact and reason' (Bion, quoting Keats, in *Attention and Interpretation*, 1970).

Bion is not satisfied with simply articulating observations. There has to be a purpose to the articulation, and that purpose, according to Bion, is the attempt to translate into precise speech the attitude of the group to the individual and of the individual to the group. Groups, like individuals, pass through a series of complex emotional episodes that permit the deduction of theories of group dynamics that are useful in the illumination of what is taking place and in the exposure of nuclei of further developments.

In the journey from groups to group relations, this point concerning the deduction of attitudes and the articulation of them applies also to the perception of a group observer's attitude to *other* groups, and the group's behaviour based on its thinking of what the other group's attitude towards itself is. This is the case for group thinking shifting to intergroup dynamics, which Bion's colleagues in the Tavistock Institute used to develop theories of group relations. Bion's summation of the theories of group dynamics, i.e. their complex emotional episodes, suggests the presence of the 'other' in group life as much as it is present in the emotional life of the individual. For instance, Bion describes discernible trends of mental activity in the course of the group 'doing' something. In other words, the members of the group assemble in order to co-operate in the achievement of a task. The group therefore is orientated towards an outer reality involving other groups, who may also have an interest in the group's task. Co-operation is necessary and depends on a degree of sophisticated skill in the individual who has developed mentally through experience and learning. This is known as the work group; its activity is geared to a task, it is related to reality; its methods are rational and scientific. Its characteristics are similar to those attributed by Freud (1911) to the ego. The observer of a work group will be able to comment on work-orientated attitudes and activities of the members and of the group as a whole, but any interpretation of these will leave much unsaid. Work group activity will also be obstructed, diverted and on occasion assisted by certain other mental activities that have in common the attribute of powerful emotional drives.

Bion's ideas on group mentality emphasised the individual's contribution and the individual's responsibility to modify and take back his or her contribution to group mentality. Nevertheless, Bion lays responsibility on the group for what happens, not the individual. He is trying to understand the dynamic of the group. He does not tell the patient what to do. He hopes the interpretation will stimulate the patient to do something. Therapy would not necessarily have a positive outcome in terms of people functioning better at war or at work. Therefore, it was left to others to transform Bion's methods and make them more focused on work relationships. Trist focused on social interaction between patients that Bion was not interested in. Nevertheless Bion encouraged Trist even though his own methods did not work. Northfield contained different points of view. Therapy was intended to be found in the therapeutic community and the psychoanalytic study of groups at the Tavistock (Miller 1990).

Bion for me

Soon after returning from my first experience of membership of a 'Leicester' conference in 1974, the supervisor of my group psychotherapy practice at the Tavistock Clinic, Robert Gosling, himself a former colleague of Wilfred Bion, said that he supposed my way of thinking about my group of patients would have been changed forever by my 'Leicester' experience. I remember the relief I felt at Dr Gosling's acknowledgement of my difficulties in reconciling my group relations experiences with my group psychotherapist role.

So began a fruitful quest to find instruments to help me bridge competing models that were predicated on the one hand by individual pathology and the paired relationship, and on the other, individual pathology and group-as-a-whole dynamics that included the psychotherapist.

My gratitude to Dr Gosling in helping me make that transition prompts me now to complete the circle and reflect on my recent and first experience of directing the 'Leicester' Conference. In doing so, my recollections of Dr Gosling nearly 30 years ago are of his encouragement to be as open as possible about the swirling, chaotic dynamics of the group, and to use my feelings stirred up by the chaos to deepen my understanding of the group and to find effective ways of sharing that understanding with it. In that spirit of openness, I decided to include in this paper parts of a daily diary that I kept during the Leicester conference. I hope thereby to place before the reader the unique experiences that form part of the director's role, and to reveal something of the power of projections that the membership and staff are grappling with, and how these get 'sent' upwards in the hope that they will be 'dealt' with or resolved 'up there'.

An account of a personal experience of directing a group relations conference and the link to Bion's theories

In April 2000, I directed my first Tavistock 'Leicester' Conference. I had directed other, shorter group relations conferences, but never one as long as the Leicester Conference – 14 consecutive days with a one-day break in the middle. I was anxious about my first attempt at directing this conference whose participants and staff would be well-versed in group relations work. So high was my anxiety that, of the staff group of ten, I had 'unconsciously' appointed eight who were ex-directors of working conferences. Another measure I took to contain anxiety was keeping a daily diary to record my thoughts, experiences and feelings and to set a reflective distance between myself and the conference experience. This helped me to think about Bion's ideas on groups and to use them to give meaning to the chaotic feelings that seemed to be part of the role. I will refer to them here in order to make the link between theory and practice of group relations more cogent and to define the steps from Bion's groups to the Tavistock group relations.

DAY ONE

Members of staff arrived today and there was a congenial and friendly atmosphere, tinged with mild irritation over the process about to begin. They arrived one-and-a-half hours before lunch, wandered about uncomfortably, not wanting to intrude too much in the preparations that were going on in the office at the time. We were under pressure to complete and print papers in time for the first staff meeting at 2.30pm. Some members were expecting the meeting to commence at 2.00pm so they were relieved to have the extra half-hour. So was I because this meant that I would have sufficient time to get through the agenda. A few thoughts to bear in mind: my role as Director is to help the staff in their roles as facilitators and interpreters of their own and the members' here-and-now emotional experiences of crossing the boundary into the conference.

From the vantage point of the director, one catches glimpses of fascinating projective processes moving about the different parts of the conference. I see this enormous 'tsunami' of institutional anxiety roaring towards me. It can be called 'controlling the director'. The members and staff are evidently anxious about this new director, one who makes mistakes of commission and omission, adding to their fears about the safety of the conference. I also discover that both my words and my silence have power. So there is power from the role and there is anxiety from the role. What models do I have to draw from? They suddenly all depart from me and I am left alone to learn that tolerating anxiety and mistakes maturely is necessary for the job, and to do that without splitting into blame, whether of others or oneself. That is a requirement of the staff too – they may want to have a perfect brochure and timetable, a director's perfect opening address, but they would also walk all over it if they had a chance. We all – staff, Directorate and Director – have the job of balancing knowledge, feelings and thoughts, but in my role I must be alert to the tendency for the different parts of the system – the training group, the large study group and the small study group systems – to get me to favour them, i.e. their wish to split the director; and my tendency to forget about/ignore a part of the total system, like when I omitted the training group from the agenda to report on its day's work!

I am reminded of Bion's (1961, p.161) assertion that the basic assumptions of a group seem each in turn to share out between them the characteristics of one character in the Oedipal situation. However, in the conference these characteristics are interwoven between the members, the staff in their different sub-systems and the director. The membership contains the alternative conference leader, except that he is hidden, at the beginning certainly. The hidden individual is the leader, and although this appears to contradict the constantly reiterated statement that the director is the leader, 'the contribution is resolved through Oedipal fantasies of destroying or replacing the work-group leader, because he arouses a dread with which a questioning attitude is regarded'. The conference being 'the object of enquiry, itself arouses fears of an extremely primitive kind' (Bion 1961, p.162). The attempt to make a rational investigation of the dynamics of the conference is perturbed by fears, and the mechanisms for dealing with them are characterised by splitting and attacks on the father/director.

DAY TWO (START OF THE CONFERENCE)

In the morning, staff of the three sub-systems (large study group, small study group and training group) met in their respective groups. My confusion about my two roles, director and consultant, soon became apparent. I feel bad because it shows my lack of experience and this has consequences for carrying out the task of learning about managing oneself in different roles. This confusion occurred several times and although it can be understood in terms of the conference dynamics, I am concerned that too much emphasis may be given to 'dynamics' and not enough to the realities of my incompetence. To be sure, I had several good moments too where I believed I remained on task and in role and helped to advance the learning. 'Wolfgang' entered the conference lexicon to refer to the dangers of the large study group which lies waiting for the director to trip himself up. A few Germans, led by Wolfgang, are ready to form the opposition. For others, the position is simple: 'If Mannie Sher can direct, why can't I?' In the working conference staff meeting there were rumblings about competitiveness between staff members who unconsciously wish to take my job, but also wish for me to be a clear-thinking and dependable director.

Oedipal dynamics were present, but I wonder: if 'father' is already dead, the unconscious wish must be to promote someone to replace him, leading to sibling rivalry, rather than of Oedipus. But here too I am less certain, thinking rather along the lines of Bion's and Lawrence's (2000) ideas on Sphinx, focusing on organisation, leadership and the personification of the ideal in the person of the leader so that the fantasy can be made manifest – having a good, sound Tavistock Group Relations conference led by a competent, vitalised visionary. The obverse of this is the fear of being in the grip of the dead 'ancients', a dead Tavistock and a moribund methodology. It was the fear of being identified with a dead past that I believe got into me.

In the opening plenary later this afternoon, a member asked whether the staff could say when they were being management, when they were being consultant and when they were being personal, suggesting an attempt to exercise control over chaotic feelings in the first gathering of the members. This must be the challenge of today and of the whole conference – can ambiguity, ambivalence, multiple roles, diverse emotions and thoughts be tolerated and managed successfully by the membership (and the staff) when the director appears unable to do this himself. I have just remembered! I did not make introductions in the first pre-conference staff meeting, nor did I mention in my introductory remarks to the plenary that 'conference time' would be according to the clock in the foyer! First major institutional boundary problem occurs. One of the buildings was locked when the members arrived for their small study groups. One consultant was alone with one female member for ten minutes before the others arrived. The members had a field day attacking the Tavistock and the director: 'Isn't anything reliable any more?' 'Doesn't the director know what is going on?' or 'Is he deliberately misdirecting us?' 'The staff too either have no knowledge or are in chaos.'

DAY THREE

I felt better today after reflecting on the awfulness of yesterday. I slept well but no dreams were remembered.

The day began with the first sessions of the large study group in which a member demanded that I offer a stand-up scripted apology for my mistake of yesterday. There were attempts to play down the error, mostly from men who said they should have been more alert to their own direction-finding abilities. But later comments about impotent/withdrawn male consultants strongly suggest an attack on the traditions, roles, and primacy of the Tavistock Institute and the Leicester Conference. The 'mother of all group relations conferences' had lost its appeal and other organisations around the world were vying for the title and believing it was within their grasp. The men try to show off their potency but the real competition is among the women. The men present intellectual, flashy images of war but are in fact taking flight from their experience of the large group. It appears the large study group do not know what to do with me in consultant role, perhaps fearing that if they annoy me in this role, I may retaliate against them in my director role. The imagery of the large study group has elements of the Divine Comedy replete with Circles of Hell. The group resembles a spaceship under command of ground control who have placed the ship on automatic pilot following a computer crash. The 'cock-up' of the director may have liberated them, but more likely sent them into space.

Bion states that the group, eager to allay the anxiety state of its leader and exhausting itself supporting the leader, is the dual of basic assumption dependency. Coping with its dependency on an anxious leader consumes the energies that might be devoted to the realities of the group task.

Another mistake! In the intergroup plenary meeting, I announced the end of the intergroup event would be on Monday at 3.30pm instead of Sunday at 6.00pm. I am annoyed with myself because of these mistakes. This time it was because I had not cross-referenced the different timetables. It is unbelievable that there are two timetables, each with errors. I should have checked them and double-checked. There are details in the timetable I should have changed, e.g. there is no rationale whatsoever for having two-hour intergroup sessions in the evenings. In fact, every argument points to having the evening intergroup session the same length (one-and-a-half hours) as all the other sessions.

Another problem lies in managing the reporting of the sub-systems – small study group, large study group and institutional event – in the limited time available in the general staff meeting. The programme is too tight and I am concerned that staff will not be able to hold up for two weeks with this kind of pressure. Some are suffering from backache and some from colds.

Today I bumbled less and I think I held to the boundary of reporting, thinking and processing reasonably well, utilising the explicit and implicit communications to extend our understanding of the conference and its sub-systems. But contempt and arrogance, unlikeability and scorn are apparent in most of the group sessions. These seem to be held mostly by the American members and consultants, and the depressed, dispirited feelings held mostly by the European women.

DAY FOUR

I did not run the general staff meeting well because:

1. Too much time was spent on preparing for the hand-over (feedback of information regarding the training group was satisfactory). I should have gone over the hand-over material and made myself more proficient in it. And this is the horrible truth – I did not have the intergroup event in my mind and did not have it on the agenda. Where are your planning, notes, agenda items, purpose and time allocations? Because of the lack of leadership, the meeting drifted until a frantic D had a temper-tantrum. Your staff want you to lead. (See your note on Day 3 on the group exhausting itself supporting their anxious leaders.)

2. Time-keeping. I had changed the time of the staff meeting from 7.30pm–9.30pm to 7.30pm–9.00pm and then at D's request, and with everyone's agreement, we finally agreed the meeting should be from 7.15pm–8.45pm. At 8.45pm K, who had agreed to the change of time, said she thought the meeting was due to continue until 9.15pm! She was following the old timetable, about which I was so resentful. I had inherited it, and did not think to go over it very carefully and examine every event, every session, every detail and make a decision on them on whether they were right for 'my' conference. S asked why the intergroup event at night should extend for two hours when every other event lasts one-and-a-half hours. It only adds to the confusion, he said. I did not know the rationale for it and yet I took it into 'my' conference without question. There were other mistakes in the conference timetable tonight and K. helped me correct them. She suggested that in future at the beginning of the pre-conference staff meeting, I should take the staff through the timetable detail by detail. My anger and despair about the timetable and the mistakes I am making nearly made me want to stop work tonight. It was late. I was tired and depressed, but F persevered and with K to help, we finished the revisions to the timetable successfully.

Discussion about the conference co-sponsorship was good, but also made me aware of how little substance there is in the co-sponsorship. More could be done by our co-sponsors to promote the conference. Few applications came via our co-sponsors. It seems that the Leicester Conference is not in people's minds. The isolation of the conference makes it vulnerable. This point helps me to realise why I was so disengaged from the reporting of the intergroup event. As the director role is on the boundary of the two co-sponsoring organisations, my experience of the intergroup event, I felt, reflected the absence of relatedness between the Tavistock Group Relations Programme and other group relations organisations. There is a kind of virtual relatedness in which working at developing relationships seems optional.

This was strongly reflected today in the small study group sub-system, which seemed divided along the lines of English-speakers and non-English-speakers. The non-English-speakers work harder on seeking and basing their knowledge in their experience of understanding less, and therefore having lower expectations than English-speakers. Bion is clear that the agreeable emotional states in the group that make the individual 'feel better', and the disagreeable emotional states that makes the individual 'feel worse', are kept isolated from each other and from the individual's awareness that these agreeable and disagreeable feelings may have something to do with the individual's membership of the group. Putting it another way, the members of the group privately search for locations of social concern; they find it difficult to ask for help and they cannot comprehend how to manage limited resources.

DAY FIVE

A satisfactory day. Things went well in all sectors: training group, large study group, small study group and intergroup events, but we did not have time to review the intergroup which had two sessions today. At coffee, I heard concerns expressed about a member who seemingly was unable to comprehend the effect of his behaviour on other people. There was some concern about him becoming a casualty, but I looked out for him and saw that he seemed to be getting along satisfactorily. S had him in his inter-group territory and he reported that the member was fine but experiencing high levels of anxiety.

There are Jewish/black/refugee/colonial/slave issues floating around in the conference, but these are not well articulated. Either the Jewish theme has been overworked or the conference has difficulty dealing with the presence of two Jewish members of staff from two major centres of group relations, and who even look alike and are said to resemble Freud. Certain themes of the International Jewish Conspiracy were present, but not easily dealt with. Perhaps this masks feelings about the change of leadership at the Tavistock Institute from a true British tradition to a racially hybrid one from the colonies. The development of group relations institutions in the world and the role of the Institute in providing leadership, raises issues of power and sovereignty in which 'The Tavistock' is held in a semi-permanent iconomatic position, that is to say, 'The Tavistock' group relations model is regarded as necessitating change and is also criticised for changing. In any event, the message from the membership appears to be that they seek safety in the small study groups from their experiences in the large study groups – saying that they do not like what they are learning, especially about the individual's connectedness to the group. One particular non-p.c. piece of learning concerns the attractiveness of aggressive men to women.

I am struck by the relationship, both imprisoning and freeing, with tradition and how bound I have felt by it in taking up the role of director. The 'big one' centres on whether the conference must be held at the University of Leicester in order for it to remain as 'the Leicester conference'. There are other issues which require immediate attention:

- e-mails (provide facilities for them)

- the gates to the garden (unlock them and make the Botanical Gardens accessible as a pathway and a place to relax in).

- the barman (ensure he does not organise the party for members on the last night).

DAY SIX

Today was difficult. It stated with O 'rushing' at me with warnings about casualties unless my staff addressed the negative transference. In spite of having discussed this issue with my staff several times and believing that they were doing so satisfactorily, I still felt burdened by this message. Once more, I felt I was not doing my job properly, but nevertheless I resolved not to burden my large study group colleagues with this message. I recall Bion's reference to the effect of his presence in a group, i.e. even though he desisted from talking about himself, the group seemed excessively curious about him, a curiosity that for the group turned into Bion 'forcing' himself upon it.

> However irrelevant it may appear to be to the purpose of the meeting, the (group's) preoccupation with my personality certainly seemed to obtrude itself, unwelcome though that might be to the group or to myself… We are constantly affected by what we feel to be the attitude of a group to ourselves, and are consciously or unconsciously swayed by our idea of it. (Bion 1961, p.31)

Despite my resolve, five minutes before we went into the large study group, when K asked me why I was looking worried, I told her and the others of my concern about the consequences of not dealing with the negative transference. The effect of this comment was to produce 'memory and desire' in the staff group and to limit their spontaneous participation in the large study group. I too found myself unable to complete my sentences, or to think clearly during the session.

Next, I had to tell the barman that for entertainment on the last night of the conference, I would prefer the membership to approach the conference administrator and not him for assistance.

DAY SEVEN

We are approaching the end of the first week. The changes in the timetable, the end of the first week, the day before the break, all produce tension. There are signs of the membership collectively preparing for the break through various consolidations of their learning. In particular, women appear to be struggling with identity conflicts. One female member was upset at being seen as sexy, because, she claimed, it impedes women's progress in the world of work. The issue for women appeared to be facing the consequence of claiming their sexuality and the breaking up of women's solidarity. Other themes expressed longings to belong to one's own group or culture, and the difficulties faced in achieving this through membership of the large group. The large study group broke out into multicultural themes with tunes and poetry used to express national and cultural feelings. The membership appears to need to re-find traditional and familiar roots as it gets ready for the break.

It seems to me that there is a large number of people who have not yet spoken in the large group. I wonder whether the non-speakers are 'holding' the question of relevance of the conference. There is also a question of whether the conference is a British or international conference and whether ethnic differences and multiple roles can safely be talked about. I have an uneasy thought that if a significant part of the conference cannot raise ethnic, national and cultural differences, might it be a reflection of a director who may not have fully dealt with his own ethnic, racial, religious and national issues.

Today we had the working conference plenary. The lesson, as always, is preparation – knowing what is happening and where everyone is, in what role, every minute of the day. Think ahead and plan, revise and decide.

A key issue is to limit the number of roles one is carrying. Today at the conference institution staff meeting (the total staff group), I attempted to report on the state of the working conference staff (all staff except the training group staff), believing that as director of the working conference I should know what is going on everywhere. But being at that moment the director of the total conference system simply made it impossible, and I ground to a halt. O suggested I should delegate. I asked E to report, which he did willingly and well and things went smoothly. I ask myself why I did not delegate the task in the first instance and I link the large study group's concern about the pernicious consequences of colonialism, the group's fear of its own power, and preserving the male consultants for future roles, to Bion's statement about Saint Augustine and the individual's relationships with the State. Saint Augustine in *The City of God* postulates a heavenly city in which the relationships between individuals become harmonised through each individual's relationship with God (Bion 1961, p.129). But, he continues, this is an example of the work-group changed in order to maintain contact with the basic assumption – in particular with the dependent basic assumption. Saint Augustine was concerned to defend Christianity, but in the process he is alleged to have undermined Rome's capacity to defend itself against a real external enemy. Leadership in relation to the work group must be taken forward confidently. Consensus leadership does not work in all situations. The group got anxious and angry and the work task was defeated tonight. Clear vision, determination and confidence to act are required together without losing the capacity to consult with others.

DAY EIGHT (FREE DAY)

A successful day! Time to gather together and relax. Prepared for meeting with the University's conferences organiser about the gates to the Botanical Gardens. No problem. She came to the meeting with the solution already in hand. The porter would open the gates at 7.45am and lock them at 10.00pm. Problem solved. Question: What prevented the solution being available earlier in the week?

Decided to stay in tonight. Good decision. Went shopping with L, giving us a chance to talk. Returned and talked with K who had suffered a family bereavement. She has decided to stay as consultant and continue working in the conference. I am relieved. I cannot deal with another thing like that right now. The next week is before us and we have an important boundary to manage: the Institutional Event. I wonder what preparations I have omitted.

DAY NINE

I feel fine as all the staff reassemble for the second week of the conference. Everyone is present and they seem to have made good use of the free day – some went home, some stayed in and toured the area or simply relaxed. K has decided to stay on in the conference and I am relieved, although she wondered whether she would be distracted and not available mentally for work. But she is OK for now. I feel admiration for her determination and her sensitivity.

Gender relationships are revealing a pattern – men and women seem to be increasingly relating to each other, but women-to-women relations appear absent. Is open naked ambition between women hidden? Male and female sexuality manifest differently – men in the conference are described as denying their sexuality and relying on polished intellectuality while women avoid open competition, but 'sleep their way to the top'. An obvious, visible male–female pair in the membership has formed. Their behaviour is challenging and disturbing, but I cannot understand it. I wonder whether this pairing expresses hope or is a flight. Feeling surprisingly asexual myself, I am inclined to think that this is flight from a more difficult kind of intercourse, viz. global, political and religious dynamics as they are reflected in the authority roles in the conference.

DAY TEN

We are in the Institutional Event, now working in public, and the drama of my 'mistake' on the first day and subsequent mistakes are still reverberating around the conference. The membership is preoccupied with questions of whether it was a genuine mistake or a ploy by the staff to gauge the membership's response. The confusion resulting from the first mistake has been compounded by a second in the plenary of the Institutional Event when I am reported to have combined the training group and the working conference into a merged 'membership'. I know I referred to both separately in my opening address but it is possible that in reply to a question, I may have inadvertently referred to the availability of consultancy to 'the membership' in general. The sensitivity of the training group members to their new status, and their wish to retain a distinctive identity, need to be recognised. Only the day before they had become transformed into consultants to the review and application groups.

Competition within the staff group is an issue regularly referred to, but not fully discussed, partly I guess because I do not want to have to deal with staff's feelings about my competence. O supports me, but when she spoke to a member about competence, meaning his, I took it to mean mine. I must look up the difference between competence and mistakes.

A point from the large study group: it is a salutary lesson that when one speaks to a feeling or a thought, one discovers its existence in people's minds where it has lain suppressed until a consultant's remark brings it to the surface. My remarks over tea to a member were obviously discussed in her small study group, and in turn were reported in the general staff meeting as the director favouring a member. Today I was freer in my associations and the transference to me as Jewish and South African. Fantasies about pairing with the Jewish male consultant, the 'international Jewish conspiracy' fantasy, more people engaging and 'joining' the large study group – all this is evidence that the group is getting more competent. The large study group consultants are beginning to 'enjoy' the membership.

DAY ELEVEN

There are issues relating to directorship that need considering – experience, seniority and confidence, holding the boundaries and keeping to task. These qualities allow for the proper management of the conference task, which is to allow opportunities for learning from experience to take place. It is a conference of the mind. The realities of the conference: interaction, daily habits, administrative practicalities, are subservient to the primacy of the mind. This is the only conference method available with this kind of emphasis. Thinking thoughts are essential requirements for this type of work. It is an art, a skill and a science. The point I am making is that it cannot be taken lightly, ignored or dealt with inconsistently. Otherwise confusion and madness enter. Responsibility means sticking to one's role under all conditions, i.e. to keep thinking and to offer thoughts even when under pressure, to avoid sarcasm and frivolity, to ponder and deliver carefully and helpfully. Of course, one does not always think or feel that way, as with S's warning that staff are not paranoid enough. Watch out for what is happening, especially the subtleties, and pick them up. Look out for connections, relationships, who is doing what to whom, who represents whom. Watch out for niceness. As for transference feelings, they are the essence of the experience: what exists in members' minds regarding authority figures and each other. Hold several people's interventions in one's mind at the same time. And make it real.

At the Tavistock Institute, group relations continues to be developed and articulated. Theory and practice are closely linked and this linkage forms the basis of the Tavistock approach, insofar as one can be said to exist, i.e. that change takes place principally as a consequence of the mutual engagement of the consultant and group: in other words, extending Bion's assertion that the transference can be used to discuss the group's attitude towards the consultant and the consultant can state in words what the attitude is, the purpose of this articulation being to illuminate what is taking place within the boundaries of the engagement.

DAY TWELVE

Today misgivings about the membership's capacity to learn are heard. I feel a pang of self-criticism, an unwelcome reminder that the director might have done more to ensure an easier path to learning, e.g. created a different conference design, appointed different staff, or selected a different membership. Had the Tavistock Institute miscalculated in the appointment of me as director of the conference? On the basis of my feelings, I am drawn once more to Bion's view that the conference is quite unable to face the emotional tensions within it without believing that some sort of higher authority is fully responsible for all that takes place (Bion 1961, P.38). But as the end of the conference draws near, members become more anxious over unfinished business and they appear to have to identify others who would either appear to have learned less than them, or find a culprit to blame for not better facilitating their own learning.

DAY THIRTEEN

The end of the conference is in sight and today there is a plethora of nautical and religious imagery – the conference feels like a large ship with no one at the helm; a Noah's Ark containing a sinking hope; rudderless ship; the conference arranged around religious festivals: Easter and Passover, suggesting questions about which orthodoxy would prevail.

Once again, anxieties are expressed about the safety of the Tavistock Institute, and there is anger towards the 'ancestors' for not bequeathing a safer structure. I feel somewhat confused over what boundaries I am trying to manage – a Tavistock Institute boundary or a boundary around a group relations community? The issue of succession is inevitably in the air and there are anxieties over whether or not that too will pass safely. It seems to me there is a parallel between the perception of the membership towards the Tavistock

Institute that mirrors a general perception that the nexus of containment has passed from organisations to networks. Today personal relationships more than formal employment contracts sustain work. The death of organisations means the loss of ancestors, and the membership ask themselves: 'Why are we here?'

DAY FOURTEEN

Despite continuing challenges to the authority of the staff and complaints about unfinished business, (e.g. competition between women was not explored) there was evidence of learning having taken place, perhaps especially in the sense that most individuals had felt themselves meeting up with the group collective unconscious, while still maintaining individual differences.

Today there was much poetry and many metaphors and dreams in evidence, as if it was easier to integrate diversity now without exaggerating it.

The staff felt that events were ending well, that important personal growth had taken place. They believed themselves to be holding the right container. I felt I had come through. It had been an absorbing complex conference and important learning had taken place by members and staff alike.

DAY FIFTEEN

A question which I had pondered before the conference, and again within it is: How does the working conference reflect contemporary organisational life? Is there relevance between the conference and the members' back-home situation? Or, is the conference a haven? A spa in the mind? It is everyone's view that the design and the theory encourages a pull to the personal and not to the system. The culture is narcissistic, more focused on the 'me', and when staff taken up issues of authority they are regarded as inhuman and impersonal. Staying in role makes one a bad person, yet paradoxically, learning to stay in role is what people come to the conference for.

The conference is a container and its success can be measured by the extent that diverse role relationships can be explored without losing one's core. Towards the end of the conference, more links were being made to members' organisations. Some groups did try working with leaderless teams, only to discover that leaderless teams kill each other.

The members asked for our honesty and complained that we were covering up. Can one have a public role with integrity? Or, are we ourselves experiencing the collapse of our public roles? Group relations conferences hold values. If we are not honest, members will push us to be integral.

People come to conferences with hopes and dreams; also to deal with the crazy images in society. Group relations is an important network of relationships to help people keep afloat in a schizoid world. It seems, therefore, we must conclude that it is the network, not the organisation that is important. The network, like the family, evokes loyalty and trust. If the conference institution can be trustworthy and loyal to its members, then pairing with the director, not replacing him, becomes a possibility.

Thinking and learning

Bion was concerned to further the application of his theory of functions to the theory of thought processes. He starts from Freud's idea that thought fills the gap between tension and its discharge, i.e. that thought is an experimental version of activity; thought is a way of dealing with the intolerance of frustration. According to Bion, at primitive levels of development, no distinction can be made between the material and the psychological, and the frustration will either be evaded or modified. If evaded, an attempt is made to unburden the psyche, and we have called it projective identification.

Bion published *Experiences in Groups* in 1961. Earlier these papers had been published in the journal *Human Relations*, the journal of the Tavistock Institute of Human Relations. Subsequently in his impressive canon of published work Bion referred to groups in his papers, discussions and seminars. This is often forgotten. As David Armstrong points out:

> I believe it is possible to trace in this later body of work lines of thought which complement, modify and extend the ideas presented in *Experiences in Groups*, and the relative neglect of these lines of thought by practitioners in 'group relations' contributes to the sense of self-inflicted theoretical and methodological atrophy which seems to surround those who work in this field. (Armstrong 1992)

Bion's ideas on groups were incorporated into the thinking that has lain behind the group relations training programme of the Tavistock Institute of Human Relations. The working conferences that were developed to further this method were sponsored initially by the Tavistock Institute and the University of Leicester and latterly by the Tavistock Institute and the

Tavistock Clinic. The leadership of the late A. K. Rice in this development is undisputed. The form, content and method of these original conferences have been replicated in other parts of the world by a number of institutions such as the A. K. Rice Institute in the USA. At present, such conferences are organised in various parts of America, France, Germany, Sweden, Norway, Denmark, India, Australia, South Africa and Israel, for example.

What Bion would have done if he had developed such working conferences is unknown. We do have his observations in a letter to his wife from the time he took part in an American conference in 1969:

> ...Ken Rice, looking white-haired and older, was the same as ever. It soon became evident that R. S. was very nervous, as this was his first experience as Director of the Conference. He was scared stiff of A. K. R. and self, though I did not get wise to this, or its extent quick enough or I would have tried to keep my mouth shut. After the plenary I was so unfortunate as to be talking when the meeting ended and the Staff walked out. I had not realised that according to the real rules of Groups – as laid down by Ken – he insisted on split second termination of each meeting, and by the time I had finished my sentence the Staff had disappeared round the corner and I couldn't find where they had gone... It ended with my being very depressed and inclined to pack my traps and clear out. (Bion 1985)

The working conferences now have a substantial history since their beginnings in 1957. The original formulations of Bion on small groups have been overlaid by the learning from new events to explore the social processes in groups of different sizes. As it is, thinking about Bion's hypotheses is suffused with 'memory and desire', to borrow his own phrase, which have their roots in past experiences of this kind of work and the various psychic and political defences that are inevitable with the process of institutionalisation which has been necessary for development of this kind of educational method.

Traditional group relations training, based on Rice's interpretation of Bion on groups, has the focus of power and authority. But what is left out? Where is binocular vision? If there is too much preoccupation with K, the discovery of 0 is never possible. Knowledge/science is necessarily a public activity and thus involves the group, though it is also the group that resists it. Thoughts require groups. It may be that there is a taboo about K in groups that cannot be broken. The idea that 'thoughts are just there' may be impossible to be recognised. Basic assumptions, therefore, can be thought of as defences against something apprehended. It seems that Bion's personal relationship to groups was that he seemed to want to escape them, but remained fascinated.

Bion thought of group therapy as having two meanings:

- The treatment of a number of individuals assembled for special therapeutic sessions: an exploration of the neurotic trouble of the individual, sometimes turning on the catharsis of public confession.

- A planned endeavour to develop in a group the forces that lead to smoothly running co-operative activity; the acquisition of knowledge and experience of the factors which make for a good group spirit.

This sense of the good group spirit was important in terms of the task he undertook in setting up a training wing in the Northfield military psychiatric hospital. His first task there was to set up a structure to find out how far the pursuit of neurosis being displayed in such a structure was a problem of a group and what would this mean in terms of timetable and organisation. He took the view that men gathered in the psychiatric unit had the benefit of such therapeutic value as lies in military discipline, good food and regular care. He was convinced that what was needed was a kind of discipline achieved in a theatre of war by an experienced officer in command. He thought that psychiatrists in charge of the wing must know what it is to be in a responsible position at a time when responsibility is having to face issues of life and death; and what it is to exercise authority in circumstances that make his fellows unable to accept his authority except insofar as he forcibly has to sustain it. The psychiatrist in authority will realise that his task is to produce self-respecting men socially adjusted to the community and therefore be willing to accept these responsibilities whether in peace or war.

Bion's reference to the need for discipline foreshadows his idea on the need for structures in the mind. The well-functioning group links with his notion of the optimal social environment.

Distinctions between group analysis and group relations

Bion considered that knowledge and experience were required for developing a good 'group spirit'. It resembled the old fashioned idea of morale, or the 'good group'. The idea of the 'group' came to the fore in the Second World War. Bion regarded the group itself as a theatre of war and in turn wars were run by groups.

Bion struggled to differentiate his experience as an officer and his role as doctor. It was a struggle between the focus on individual needs that interfaced with group functioning and the focus on group needs. Was it a false dichotomy? Was it the beginning of Bion's 'binocular vision' theory?

In war, the enemy is the external danger. He wondered what the danger was in the group, and used war as a model for thinking about the group. If the notion of an enemy increases group cohesion, when there is no war situation, does group discipline require a substitute for the 'common enemy'? Bion thought of neurosis as the enemy within the group and his task to create self-respecting, thinking people with the capacity to take up social roles in peace or war.

Working with groups today faces one with dilemmas of 'helping' or encouraging action. Bion was troubled by medicalising 'social distress' versus giving the individually distressed, unemployed, homeless person self-respect so they can protest. The psychiatrist as combatant officer respects the men and that sustains his authority, as opposed to the noncombatant officer who treats men as cannon fodder. If the psychiatrist feels guilty at returning men to the war, he may sabotage the treatment of the neurosis. Returning men to their self-respect produces 'social adjustment' and gives them the power to choose death willingly.

Neurosis is a problem of the group, not only of the individual. Bion works constantly with the paradox of the disturbed group treating itself. The 'transparent wall' enables the group to observe itself by stepping outside the frame. Within the enclosed space, neurotic behaviour can be displayed for the whole group to see – behaviour that is not clouded by the influence of others or by self-deception. Members of the group see themselves through the observer's eyes. This move outside the frame fractures the boundary of the group and enables seeing the inside of one group by being in another group. It is not enough just to be enclosed in a 'one-group-identity'. A transparent space is three-dimensional – time, place and inner-world.

Bion had seen the danger in the training wing coming from defining neurosis as a disability of the community, not only the individual. How does the group help its members to adjust to the distress of society? How could it help people to choose to find something bigger than themselves when they do not appear to have choice? One of the options was to choose the group view and join the war. The thing to treat was the social. Bion's genius lay in risking his authority and status on this innovation, i.e. to help the men to choose to join the war. Contemporary organisations are more complex, leading us to think that what we experience inside is more straightforwardly Oedipal conflict and what we experience outside is concerned with Sphinx.

The value of Bion's experiment lay in the possibility of training the total community in interpersonal relationships. By approximating to this theoretical construct, members of the training wing (seen from outside the framework) could look with detachment and growing understanding upon the problems of its workings.

Bion's skill and those of the men in the training wing was in being available to look at the phenomena in their group in a manner that nobody had used before. By attending to the boundary, and paying attention to see the space, though the space would not change, the perception of it from outside the framework opened possibilities for relearning and undoing the neurosis. The link here to group relations is self-evident.

Bion imposed certain basic regulations upon the men in the military hospital as a prerequisite for developing and studying group forces. In particular, the daily parade which was 'the first step towards the elaboration of therapeutic seminars (Bion 1961, p.16) had both overt and covert intent. The expressed intent was for making announcements, etc., and the veiled intent was to allow the men to step outside as detached observers of the group's behaviour. Bion attempted to invite the men to move from the individual to a communal position.

In 1942 there was considerable uncertainty about the outcome of the war (the Dunkirk debacle occurred in 1940; Singapore fell in 1942) and serious questions were being asked about the quality of leadership in the army. Was Bion therefore reflecting a wider concern in challenging the status quo? The same overt and covert dynamic operated in that he was using a military culture (the parade) for his own ends, which were to do with inviting the men to step outside the (military) frame and comment on what was occurring within the group. They became spectators of their own experience. Bion appears concerned to ensure that the men become responsible for both their own behaviour and for examining it. Bion may have been acting intuitively and seeing this work as the beginning of group relations, i.e. treating the parade as a therapeutic seminar. Or did that all come later? Whatever it is, it is clear that at a practical level the experiment failed, for it was eventually shut down because of the men's behaviour and leaves the impression that Bion may have been construed as subversive.

The army had a hidebound class structure and Bion, challenging his officer colleagues' assumptions about their men as cannon fodder, attempted to find and receive greater respect for them. There is a sense in which Bion was encouraging a form of 'mutiny', but his position was strongly in favour of transition, where men moved from being in a 'patient role' to a 'soldier role'. The use of the term 'subversive' relates to Bion's method or approach rather than action; he is not suggesting radical social transformation, but that men be encouraged to think about the role they take in response to a particular task. Although Bion does not use the term 'role', people can be seen to hold roles in his system. Bion himself was disappointed in institutions. He was deeply affected by the perceived failure of the hospital on the death of his first wife, and his preoccupation with the causes of despair in collections of people may reflect something of his own past. It is possible that flight from institutions was the only way he could gain greater freedom to explore what institutions were really involved in. Bion was interested in helping groups to achieve tasks and not in group relations. Perhaps Bion was more interested in 'thinking flight', and in contrast to Klein, would see the paranoid–schizoid position as potentially representative of creativity. Bion would not have sought the homeostasis implied by Klein's 'depressive pole'.

Bion was puzzled by why men obediently follow orders. He claimed it had to do with their training and discipline, in which the army hierarchy is also construed as the enemy, and the men collude with this process. Yet it was also possible that he felt that First World War thinking folklore was being superimposed on the Second World War in terms of social class and position. Hierarchically ordered sanctions were powerful. Consequently, although those accompanying Bion may have felt that he was giving them power, the question remained as to how they were to use it. Discipline and fear were also controlling factors in the lives of the men. They themselves wished to exercise it when complaining about patients who skived, yet it was also clear that for these particular men, obtaining co-operation by exercising sanctions had failed; the men were no longer frightened by what could be done to them. This may have led Bion to consider that you can only make soldiers by getting men to think voluntarily of being a soldier. It cannot be achieved through fear, discipline, etc.

'What then of love?'

Can men be loved by officers to become soldiers, and is the struggle one between love and hate, expressed as fear/punishment? The struggle is between Bion's love of truth based on the rigour of reflecting and thinking, as opposed to the co-operation achieved by discipline, fear and punishment.

Bion believed that men will co-operate willingly because their officer loves them; the officer can then be free of guilt; otherwise if men act only under coercion, officers may be guilt-laden.

If new forms of leadership were emerging in the army, was there a new model of followership? Certainly there were major changes in society because of the war. Sexual mores were changing and many women now worked at what would have been implicitly construed as 'men's work'. But how much of the respect which Bion indicates an officer should have for his men is synonymous with love? It is perhaps implicit in providing space to look at what is there, that expresses a concern for the well-being of the individual and encourages him to use his freedom to look at reality. Bion was part of a gener-alised set of processes going on in the army about new ways of discovering leadership. There was little on groups before Bion (Freud, Trotter, McDougall, Rickman and the Quaker tradition of leaderless groups in the context of religious practice).

Bion's 'loving concern' may well reflect his experience of human wastage in the First World War, a wastage based on contempt. He is now saying that men have a capacity for making a fuller contribution, indeed, of making the choice about their contribution. The two metaphors of war and religion led to thoughts of a crusade, and Bion's crusade was to see men as capable of reflecting and thinking and making mature judgements and decisions for themselves. His task was to provide those men with the opportunities to do that. It should be noted that Rickman, Bion's first analyst, was a Quaker and psychoanalyst and there may have been a relatedness between the Quaker tradition and group relations. 'Loving concern' may well equate with Bion's 'intuitive sympathetic flair' (Bion 1961, p.22).

Bion saw clearly that psychological means are needed to deal with psy-chological disturbances and his final comments about the experiment at Northfields carries perhaps overtones of his feelings about those who closed down the unit. He clearly believed in the validity of working with groups in this way, and group relations for Bion may have included group interpersonal relationships. Bion seemed preoccupied with what needs of the individual could only be satisfied in a group, suggesting that the choice was between social-ism and narcissism; that it was possible to have thoughts in a group which are not possible alone. For developments to occur, levels of complexity were required, different voices needed to be interrelated, not just integrated into a unity. The group raises hopes that absolute needs will be met absolutely and deficits repaired. But, for Bion, the group never completely satisfies needs. A consultant to a group is not the work-group leader, but one who draws attention to the task: 'You are trying to do "A", but you are doing "B".' Bion considered these questions belonging to large social systems. He saw that Anglo-Indian castes and the English class system were both hierarchies that were the wrong culture and obstructed society's new tasks. Castes were based on division of labour. Class is based on lineage. The result was that the ruling aristocracy could not conduct modern warfare.

The group-as-a-whole – group mentality

Another contribution to group relations was Bion's concern about the question whether the behaviour of one is the behaviour of all. Are all guilty of the cruelty in the group? At Nuremberg only the leaders were punished, but Bion's view was that those who are silent give consent. Negative evidence is that the group supports what it does not repudiate.

Later, Bion took up the theme of the consultant as a probe in the position he occupies in the emotions of the group serving as a measure of 'group mentality'. He provides three postulates of group mentality:

- it is a heuristic hypothesis
- it causes difficulty to individuals in pursuing their aims
- group culture is a compromise formation between group mentality and individual desires.

Bion uses the concept of 'interpretation' here in the sense that his comments are 'interpretations' of unconscious process. His formulation of 'basic assumptions' is a further development on interpretation and they seem to indicate a more inclusive, generalised patterning of phenomena of the 'as if' variety. For Bion himself, the formulation of the basic assumption shifts the tone from 'bewilderment' to something like the possession of compass points adding direction to phenomena.

In any use of basic assumption material, Bion makes two different points:

- the importance of 'giving the evidence' e.g. of how (unconscious) teamwork had been achieved
- implicit indifference to 'outcomes', therapeutic or otherwise.

Working with basic assumption material would seem to have made Bion more 'scientific', more detached and less of the novelist. This emerges as the other side of something quite depressed, his feeling 'left stranded', unable to convince himself, suggesting connections between scientific creativity and the role of depression in this. For Bion, patience was significant, adopting a long timescale, bracketing out action and outcomes; these were ways of managing depression – preparing to receive the 'significant fact', reparation and 'giving things their due', allowing something to emerge and attending to minute particulars. Whether group therapy or group relations, tolerance of frustration was taken to an extreme.

Basic assumptions and interpretation

To Bion, the group was a phenomenon that was greater than the sum of its parts. The totality of events in the group-as-a-whole could be discerned and described, and in particular its unconscious representation of the transcendent which is immanent in the life of the group. Bion's 'interpretation' – his basic assumptions – were intended to make links between the environment containing the group and the group's ability to 'know', both consciously and unconsciously (Lawrence 2000, p.155). He wanted to take the group and the individuals in it beyond immediate phenomena.

Bion may have introduced basic assumption terminology to signify his attachment to a Kleinian framework of paranoid–schizoid and depressive positions, while not wishing to be too rooted in a structure that he believed needed to be more open and fluid. In Bion's groups the concern is about the failure of leaders' and groups' attempts to find a substitute that satisfies. Such a leader will usually be a man or woman with marked paranoid trends; if the presence of an enemy is not immediately obvious to the group, the next best thing is for the group to choose a leader to whom it is. Bion found that in groups where he had been chosen to be the leader, it was he who came to be experienced by the group as the enemy and the group consequently came together in order to put an end to his interventions. Bion focuses repeatedly on the processes of a group coming together as a group. It may resemble parts of human life, such as the family, but it is not the same thing as a family. The leader of a group is not the same thing as a father of a family, although in certain circumstances the leader approximates to a father. But if any member of a group displays parental qualities he soon finds that he has none of the status, obligations or privileges usually associated with a father or mother. As a psychiatrist, Bion was expected to display parental qualities, but his position in the group became anomalous by reason of his exclusion from the group because his behaviour had already made him the enemy of the group. Bion finds that his interpretations do not make a scrap of difference to the behaviour of the group. He draws attention to the similarity with the analytic situation when a patient's lack of response is revealed at a subsequent session to have been very partial. In fact, an interpretation by Bion in one session appeared to be enacted in the next, in one case, his interpretation that the group had met for purposes of pairing off. He provides an example of what happens to individuals as the group passes from one group culture (fight–flight) to another (pairing) and back again. In the fight–flight group it was difficult for individuals to pay much attention to what Bion said or did. In the pairing group it was difficult for any individual to sustain a conversation with Bion. For Bion, the psychiatrist, in the two group cultures (fight–flight, pairing) the job is made difficult by the basic assumption. This makes a group unprepared to receive the contribution that the consultant makes.

The individual in group therapy has to work within the emotional state of the group. He contributes and is also automatically caught up in the group's one, and only one, basic assumption in operation at the time. More than one wouldn't make any sense. Bion assumes that in basic assumption fight–flight or pairing, the individuals function as adults; in basic assumption dependency they do not. In fight–flight basic assumption other elements are extruded. The experience of the group, however is that there is chaos and the basic assumption is a defence against it. Basic assumption fight–flight reduces anxiety regarding chaos. Social factors contain psychosis for issues that cannot be dealt with in the group. It is coincidental that a particular male or female pair get mobilised by the group. The pair is meant to maintain a productive relationship.

The group's hostility is mobilised against a leader: the formation of a pair is to create a new leader. The basic assumption dependency leader gets stuck and anger and jealousy are more easily expressed. Dependency soon reappears. Fight is too frightening and things have to be made comfortable again.

Dependency

For Bion the dependency basic assumption is meant to provide an external object whose function is to provide security for the immature organism. This means that one person is always felt to be in a position to supply the needs of the group, and the rest in a position in which their needs are supplied. The group experiences relief temporarily, but once the culture becomes established, individuals begin to show their discomfort. One phenomenon is the emergence of feelings of guilt about greed. There is a sharp clash between the basic assumption of the group and the needs of the individual as an adult. In the basic assumption fight–flight and pairing, the conflict is between what is required of the individual as an adult, and what the individual as an adult feels prepared to give. In basic assumption dependency the psychiatrist is regarded as a parent and with this come the complications and difficulties of resentment at being in a dependent position. Anger and jealousy are more easily expressed but are not so great as to arouse the fear they do in the fight–flight group. Unlike a dependency group, in the fight–flight group there is no reassurance that the leader will prevent untoward events.

Group therapy and study groups

Inevitably in groups, the members face conflict between individual desires and the culture of the group and this idea took Bion from groups of patients to groups that met for a purpose. Are group relations events concerned with therapy? The Tavistock groups were concerned with questions of morale because of the war and were not therapy. In fact, therapeutic follow-up studies were critical of Bion's methods (Malan *et al.* 1976). Bion's therapeutic groups addressed groups as a whole, not the individuals in them. Patients said they did not find the therapy groups a useful experience. Did basic assumption dependency overwhelm the task of learning?

The aim of therapy groups is for patients to help each other. The therapy group's job is to help with the psychological difficulties of its members and to help change the perspective of the therapeutic process. In the early days the Tavistock had evening social clubs which were a version of psychotherapy. Bion retained the interpretative role as in a self-help group. After the war the healing aspect of therapy, i.e. providing an epistemology of the human mind, shifted, and a new generation of healer arose which offered an outcome that was different from thinking. Healing and intellectual debate got divided between disciplines. In the historical context, healing is temporary; psycho-analysis brings growth and development and the two were split. Bion did not meet up with Foulkes and Anthony because of the Freud/Klein split. The Northfield experiment was regarded by many as a failure, although Bion does not give the impression that it was a failure. Those patients, however, did not choose to come to the groups. In war there was a common context, i.e. patients' symptoms (fear) that prevented them from fighting, had to be treated, an aim that Bion felt uneasy with. Between the war and the book, there is a shift in tone showing Bion's interest in scientific investigation only, not in therapeutic outcome. His aim was to get people to try to think as members of a group and individually. He would interpret the patient's role in his own problems. He disavowed therapy; it was about having an experience. He would be engaging with the imaginary twin of every patient. Bion the observer would be looking at himself too. Twinship is a form of omnipotent control, but the effect of Bion's looking at groups was that they never appeared the same way again.

Bion's work is about the mystery of communications that rely on the mechanisms of projective identification; hypothesising that envy of the group accounts for their silence; that the death instinct exists in groups and is destructive of its task. For example, the patient does not let on that anything has been understood. Envy prevents it being known, but something goes in. The patient, after all, may want to hang on to his insight. Bion was concerned with the language of rebellion – if the individual rebels, would it make any difference? Bion believed that daring to rebel against prevailing numbing norms leads to an alteration of the emotional field of the group. Rebellion in society during times of crisis does not make any difference, but he was interested in what kind of statement enabled the individual to shift the culture of the group.

Self-preservation as the group's aim

Bion carefully drew attention to the differences between the individual's and the group's assumptions of the purpose of coming together, and his observations led him to outline the sequence of basic assumptions; and more importantly, the rationale of these changes.

> …it seems to be a basic assumption, held by the group and the pair concerned , that the relationship is a sexual one. It is as if there could be no possible reason for two people coming together except sex… (Bion 1961, p.62)

Bion emphasised that whilst two people can be meeting for any number of purposes other than those of sex, there must be considerable conflict between the desire of the pair to pursue the aim they have consciously in mind, and the emotions derived from the basic assumption that two people can be met together for only one purpose, and that a sexual one.

The next shift is interesting in that whilst the couple are dealing with their preoccupation (on behalf of the group too), the group has a different preoccupation: the basic assumption of the pair does not conform to the basic assumption of the group.

For Bion, psychoanalysis is a technique of investigation that depends on the presence of two people taking part not only in the investigation of one mind by another, but also as taking part in investigating the mentality of a pair. If his observation of the basic assumption of the group is correct, he says, it is not surprising that such an investigation seems to demonstrate sex as occupying a central position with the emotions as more or less secondary. But he continues with the question, 'If the basic assumption of the pair is that they meet together for purposes of sex, what is the basic assumption in a group about people who meet together in a group?' The basic assumption is that people come together as a group for purposes of preserving the group. For example, the group's preoccupation with absentees suggests that changes in groups are sources of anxiety about the feared disintegration of the group. In a group it takes some time before individuals cease to be dominated by the feeling that adherence to the group is an end in itself.

Bion suggests that the group seems to know only two techniques of self-preservation, fight and flight. 'The frequency with which a group resorts to one or other of these two procedures, and these two procedures only, for dealing with all its problems, made me first suspect the possibility that a basic assumption exists about becoming a group' (Bion 1961, p.63).

Bion posits subsidiary assumptions, viz. the individual feels that in a group, the welfare of the individual is of secondary consideration: the group comes first; in flight the group is abandoned; the paramount need is for the group to survive – not the individual.

Self-preservation and task

The basic assumption of the group conflicts very sharply with the idea of a group met together to do a creative job. The paradox appears to be that basic assumptions are both preserving and disintegrating. There is a paradox that people should want to come together – whence the notion of 'groupiness'. Elements of dependence are hinted at, plus that of adhesion: 'The belief that a group exists, as distinct from an aggregate of individuals, is an essential part of (this) regression, as are also the characteristics with which the supposed group is endowed by the individual' (Bion 1961, p.142).

'What makes a group worth preserving?' In trying to process the experience of the two World Wars, Bion felt that 'surviving at all costs' might represent a heroic national delusion. He felt a better way forward was to ask whether a basic assumption exists about learning in a group?

In another example of Bion moving from group therapy to study groups and group relations, he states:

> The attempt to use the group as a seminar was intended to keep the group anchored to a sophisticated and rational level of behaviour, suitable to the fulfilment of the aims individuals wished to pursue; it was as if without some such attempt this procedure would lead to the obtrusion of a kind of group that was a hindrance of the conscious wishes of the individual. That attempt failing, there began to emerge the group that is dominated by the basic assumption of unity for purposes of fight or flight. If you can only fight or run away, you must find something to fight or run away from. (Bion 1961, p.66)

Given the high level of objection from members at group relations conferences about staff's strict adherence to punctuality, it is well to remember Bion's question (1961, p.86–88). When does the group begin? Does the group begin at the stated time? When it assembles? When the group is in the mind? What is it that begins? What are the group phenomena which Bion sees as 'not beginning', but as continuing and evolving? The dilemmas about being in a group are always present in the mind. Does beginning mean 'beginning to attend' to these ongoing phenomena? Attention is a psychological act that continues indefinitely.

These challenging questions shock many people when they join a group relations conference for the first time – there is no agenda, the group does not appear to 'do' anything. What is group relations about? Bion's contribution to group relations is that it is about what is 'out there' and what is 'in here'. Unconscious fantasies have no beginning. Group phenomena are timeless. The Bionic puzzle forces one to address eternal dilemmas.

Every group is a continuation of previous experience. Every group is a fractal – embodies an image of the whole. An image of all that was and ever will be. The eternal image. Flow is continuous. The individual is universal at the same time. The group is a set of individuals at the same time. The individual is the dual of the group. The group is the dual of the individual. The individual is persecuted by intimations of emotional movements in the group. These internal objects are the group inside us; our ancestors; our primordial 'group objects' – forefathers, parents. The individual ignores the group links and strives to develop as an individual. We are all the same, having the same ancestors, in that sense no different from each other. The twin is both identical and completely different.

Conclusions

Group therapy is a setting for individuals to seek help for their psychological problems. They may expect to receive that help from the group therapist, from other members of the group, and from within themselves. Basic assumptions will be influenced by this fact. Bion took account of the strivings of individuals in groups only insofar as they revealed anything about the transcendence in the group as a whole. In group relations, groups studied the behaviour and mental life of the group as a whole; that included Bion, and this study of the human mind would, he believed, be furthered by group-wide interpretations. Group relations evolved into an enterprise in which individuals learn about the formal and informal roles they take or are given in groups, and was not about the public scrutiny of individual personalities for improvement in social and personal functioning.

Bion depicts the uniqueness of each basic assumption and particularly the emotional state associated with and preceding the assumption. Group members behave as if they were conscious of the assumption as individuals, but unconscious of it as group members (1961, p.94). The interpretation carries conviction because it gives meaning to the group's behaviour. In the herd we are unconscious, but as individuals we can become conscious of what is going on. The sophisticated individual is swept along by the group. Individual = mind; herd = non-mind. Mind can only exist in a group if the herd is ready for it to exist, i.e. if it is ready for the interpretation.

All basic assumptions are driven by fear of annihilation. Every leader is dealing with fear of annihilation preventing him from admitting ignorance. That would be a disaster. Group pressure is for the leader to be omniscient and make the group feel secure.

Individuals defend against unpleasant feelings by splitting and isolating themselves from the group in order to avoid the conjunction of feelings. Group members cannot think and they feel unsafe, longing for an omniscient leader who can think for them and make them feel safe. On the other hand, being with the herd is a survival mechanism. Wandering off is wandering into danger. Bion dislikes the herd. Being in the herd means telling lies about the past and the future. The herd ceases to have a purpose or justification for survival. It seems that Bion became disillusioned with group propaganda, thinking that the survival-value of being in the group was futile and tragic. He states that the narcissistic individual always tries to construct a closed society, because an open one sets free the critical powers of man (Bion 1992, p.122).

Equally, however, the individual can never get it right. Whatever position he is in, there is always another he is attracted to for security or out of fear. Membership of a group means making the best of a bad job. We are part of the herd and it is the herd that counts, whatever we experience individually. The basic assumptions are all delusions of certainty. Bion's text sounds authoritative, but it reveals uncertainty. The basic assumptions are about certainty, security and survival.

If group life is all about illusions, then conflicts are based on alternative illusions. A basic assumption is a temporary delusion. For the delusion to operate there has to be an illusion, e.g. we shall overcome. The delusion is a defence against psychotic anxiety, the fear of annihilation. The illusion is necessary to get away from the psychotic anxiety and the sense of futility. The belief has to be sustained that we are getting somewhere and have meaningful goals. We move in and out of basic assumptions without knowing 'what matters', trying to find a value that we can depend on or adhere to. For Bion it is enough to have survived in the herd. If you move from the herd, you start to think, giving rise to the potential to survive uncertainty and arrive at a new thought.

Can herds be safe? We live in a world where risk is an endemic part of productive forces. The risk is of breaking the existing conceptualisation of the group. Sticking with the herd is sticking with the past. Therefore, leaving the herd threatens both the individual and the group. Basic assumptions offer a paradox: surviving, but without thought or reality testing. By staying with what you have got, you go broke. But a new choice may also fail. Either way it is a gamble. That is the essence of learning from experience in group relations.

Acknowledgements

A number of people have contributed to the thinking out of this paper. In particular I acknowledge the contribution of the Bion Reading Seminar (1994–2000) established by Gordon Lawrence and Jon Stokes, and its members David Armstrong, Peter Goold, William Halton, Paul Hoggett, Colin James and Judith Szeckacs; the members of Anton Obholzer's seminar at the Tavistock Clinic on 'Consulting to Institutions' and to the members of my Sunday morning workshop for consultants (1990–1999).

References

Armstrong, D. (1992) 'Names, thoughts and lies: the relevance of Bion's later writing for understanding experience in groups.' *Free Associations Vol. 3*, Part II, No. 26, pp.261–282.

Bion, W. R. (1961) *Experiences in Groups*. London: Tavistock Publications.

Bion, W. R. (1985) *All My Sins Remembered and the Other Side of Genius*. Abingdon: Fleetwood Press.

Bion, W. R. (1970) *Attention and Interpretation*. London: Tavistock Publications.

Bion, W. R. (1992) *Cogitations*. London: Karnac Books.

Foulkes, S. H. and Anthony, E. J. (1965) *Group Psychotherapy*. London: Pelican.

Freud, S. (1911) 'Formulations on the two principles of mental functioning.' In *The Complete Psychological Works of Sigmund Freud*. Vol. 12. London: Hogarth Press.

Emery, F. (1959) *Characteristics of Socio-Technical Systems*. London: Tavistock Institute.

Harrison, T. (2000) *Bion, Rickman, Foulkes and the Northfield Experiments*. London: Jessica Kingsley Publishers.

Klein, M. (1930) 'The importance of symbol formation in the development of the ego.' In M. Klein (1948) *Contributions to Psychoanalysis*. London: Hogarth Press.

Klein, M. (1946) 'Notes on some schizoid mechanisms.' In M. Klein *et al.* (eds) *Developments in Psychoanalysis*. London: Hogarth Press.

Lawrence, W. G. (2000) *Tongued With Fire: Groups in Experience*. London: Karnac Books.

Malan, D. H., Balfour, F. H. G., Hood, V. G. and Shooter, A. M. N (1976) 'Group psychotherapy: A long-term follow-up study.' *The Archive of General Psychiatry 33*, 1303.

Miller, E. (1990) 'Experiential learning in groups II: Recent developments in dissemination and application.' In E. Trist and H. Murray (1990) *The Social Engagement of Social Science, Vol. 1. The Socio-Psychological Perspective*. London: Free Association Books.

Rickman, J. (1943a) *Paper on Group Therapy*. Draft of W. R. Bion and J. Rickman (1943). Rickman Papers, archive of the British Psycho-Analytic Society.

Rickman, J. (1945) Contribution to the discussion of W. R. Bion's paper on 'Intra-group tensions in therapy: Their study a task of the group' given to the Medical Section of the British Psychological Society, 19 Dec. 1945. Rickman Papers, Archive of the British Psycho-Analytic Society.

Rickman, J. (1950) 'The factor of number in individual and group dynamics.' *Journal of Mental Science, 96*, pp.770–773.

Rickman, J. (1951) 'Number and human sciences, psycho-analysis and culture.' Reprinted in J. Rickman (1957) *Selected Contributions to Psycho-Analysis*. (ed W.C.M. Scott). London: Hogarth Press and The Institute of Psycho-Analysis.

Further Reading

Lawrence, W. G. (1999) 'Centring of the Sphinx for the psychoanalytic study of organisations.' *Socio-Analysis. Journal of the Australian Institute of Socio-Analysis, Volume 1, Number 2*, pp.99–126.

Miller, E. (1990) 'Experiential learning in groups I: The development of the Leicester model.' In E. Trist and H. Murray (1990) *The Social Engagement of Social Science, Vol 1. The Socio-Psychological Perspective*. London: Free Association Books.

4

Alcoholics Anonymous as Medical Treatment for Alcoholism

A Group-analytic Perspective on How it Works

Jeffrey D. Roth

I. Purpose of this paper

Despite the widely acknowledged efficacy of Alcoholics Anonymous (AA), the original and best known of the Twelve Step programs, little systematic attention has been given to its mechanism of action. If we conceptualize AA as a 'pharmacological' intervention in the treatment of alcoholism, we might raise questions about appropriate doses of AA, frequency of administering doses, and different brands of the AA medication. If the alcoholic patient stopped taking the AA medication, the clinician might attempt to understand this noncompliance in terms of side effects that the patient experienced from this treatment.

In terms of dose alone, units of AA may occur in meetings of varying duration, usually sixty to ninety minutes per meeting. The units may be taken at widely varying frequencies, from once per month, once per week, once per day, to multiple units per day. Dosing strategies are available as part of the oral tradition of AA; the most common prescription at the beginning of recovery is to attend ninety meetings in ninety days.

Further complicating this pharmacological picture, AA meetings come in different brands. Some meetings consist of a speaker sharing a personal story of recovery. Other meetings use a format of members sharing comments about a particular topic of discussion. Still other meetings focus on the literature of AA like the Twelve Steps and Twelve Traditions. (*The Twelve Steps and Twelve Traditions* (1952), published by Alcoholics Anonymous World Services, Inc., New York, offers a detailed description and illustrations of how to apply the Twelve Steps and Twelve Traditions.) Each different brand of AA meetings might have a different effect on the disease of alcoholism.

Even this rudimentary examination of AA as a pharmacological intervention maintains a view of AA as a 'black box.' In order to understand the mechanism of action at a 'molecular' level, we need to examine the structure of the AA molecule. Because AA is first and foremost a group, I suggest that a group-analytic perspective is useful if not essential in characterizing the 'pharmacological' basis of AA as a medical treatment for alcoholism. In this paper I hope to establish a foundation for understanding how AA and other Twelve Step programs work.

II. What are AA, the Twelve Steps, the Twelve Traditions, and how did they evolve?

The history of addiction treatment and recovery is well documented elsewhere. (White (1998) provides a systematic and thorough account of the history of addiction treatment and recovery in America.) From the beginning of AA in 1935, the next Twelve Step program, Al-Anon, for the family and friends of alcoholics, was officially started in 1951. With the birth of Al-Anon came the first glimmering of the concept of addiction as a family disease. This transformation of paradigms is essential to a scientific basis for understanding the mechanism of action of Twelve Step programs. If alcoholism were understood to be a disease whose sole site of infection is the individual, then individual treatment would be indicated and expected to be effective. If, on the other hand, alcoholism were a family disease whose site of infection includes the family system, then treatment would include a group-level intervention intended to offer the affected individual a healthy model of group functioning that is absent in the diseased family. Historically, the contagion of potentially healthy group functioning may account for the spouses of alcoholics recovering in AA to have formed Al-Anon. Consistent with this hypothesis, this paper offers as one conclusion that the successful Twelve Step group accomplishes the task of functioning as a healthy work group or family. How these programs manage this feat in the face of the disease of their members may be understood by reference to the Twelve Steps and Twelve Traditions.

III. AA's influence

The Twelve Steps of AA gradually evolved from a group process initiated by the founders of AA. These same Twelve Steps have been adapted and modified by all of the other Twelve Step Programs. These programs include Al-Anon (see above), Overeaters Anonymous (OA), Gamblers Anonymous (GA), Debtors Anonymous (DA), Narcotics Anonymous (NA), and many others. The first and twelfth steps are the only steps that mention the specific substance or process that forms the basis for the addiction. For AA, the First Step is 'We admitted we were powerless over alcohol – that our lives had become unmanageable.' Steps Two through Eleven outline a spiritual process through which the addict may recover from the disease of addiction. For AA, the Twelfth Step is 'Having had a spiritual awakening as the result of these steps, we tried to carry this message to alcoholics, and to practice these principles in all our affairs.'

Consistent with the development of the Twelve Steps as part of a group process, the first and twelfth steps emphasize the group quality of recovery in the use of the plural pronoun 'we.' The profound insights of AA's founders are summarized in these two steps as follows: 1. that the addict cannot recover until admitting powerlessness over the addiction by him or herself; and 2. that only by carrying the message of recovery to other addicts can one remain in recovery from the addiction. The act of sharing, which necessarily involves the presence of an 'other,' and forms the nucleus of a group, becomes the backbone of recovery. This idea is expressed in the AA slogan, 'in order to keep it (sobriety) you have to give it away.'

This idea of carrying a message is frequently confused with evangelical proselytizing, that one somehow wins the right to salvation by converting others. AA is quite clear, however, that the purpose of carrying the message of recovery is to continue the practice of one's own recovery, independent of the impact on the alcoholic who still suffers. Thus carrying the message differs from proselytizing in that carrying the message is a process whose aim is change for the carrier, whereas proselytizing is goal-driven towards changing other people. Using the family disease model, carrying the message is then understood as living in a healthy, adaptive manner that includes openness to sharing with others for one's own benefit, rather than controlling other people.

The Twelve Traditions evolved after the Twelve Steps as guidelines for maintaining the Twelve Step group as a well-functioning, task-oriented system. Like the Twelve Steps, the group of early pioneers who were recovering from alcoholism developed the Twelve Traditions (see Table I). Because the traditions relate specifically to group-level functions, an understanding of the traditions from a group-analytic perspective may illuminate the mechanism of action of the Twelve Step groups. As described in the introduction, Twelve Step meetings may be like a class of therapeutic agents with different specificities, dose-response curves, etc. Some Twelve Step meetings may function less than ideally, and the specific liabilities of these meetings may impact different patients in widely varying ways. This paper examines the ideal Twelve Step group, which operates in accord with the Twelve Traditions, while acknowledging that any meeting inevitably operates imperfectly. Significantly, the traditions are explicitly suggested as guidelines for group functioning with the understanding that they will be followed imperfectly. This imperfection in group function mirrors the expectation that the recovery of any individual AA member will be imperfect.

Table I: AA Traditions[1]

During its first decade, AA as a fellowship accumulated substantial experience, which indicated that certain group attitudes and principles were particularly valuable in assuring survival of the informal structure of the Fellowship. In 1946, in the Fellowship's international journal, the *AA Grapevine*, these principles were formulated in writing by the founders and early members as the 'Twelve Traditions of Alcoholics Anonymous.' They were accepted and endorsed by the membership as a whole at the International Convention of AA at Cleveland, Ohio, in 1950.

1. Our common welfare should come first; personal recovery depends upon AA unity.

2. For our group purpose there is but one ultimate authority – a loving God as He may express Himself in our group conscience. Our leaders are but trusted servants; they do not govern.

3. The only requirement for AA membership is a desire to stop drinking.

4. Each group should be autonomous except in matters affecting other groups or AA as a whole.

5.	Each group has but one primary purpose – to carry its message to the alcoholic who still suffers.
6.	An AA group ought never endorse, finance or lend the AA name to any related facility or outside enterprise, lest problems of money, property and prestige divert us from our primary purpose.
7.	Every AA group ought to be fully self-supporting, declining outside contributions.
8.	Alcoholics Anonymous should remain forever nonprofessional, but our service centers may employ special workers.
9.	AA, as such, ought never be organized; but we may create service boards or committees directly responsible to those they serve.
10.	Alcoholics Anonymous has no opinion on outside issues; hence the AA name ought never be drawn into public controversy.
11.	Our public relations policy is based on attraction rather than promotion; we need always maintain personal anonymity at the level of press, radio and films.
12.	Anonymity is the spiritual foundation of all our traditions, ever reminding us to place principles before personalities.
	While the Twelve Traditions are not specifically binding on any group or groups, an overwhelming majority of members have adopted them as the basis for AA's expanding 'internal' and public relationships.

IV. Bion's Group Psychology

One model of group psychological functioning has been proposed by Wilfred Bion and developed at the Tavistock Clinic in London and the A. K. Rice Institute in the US. Bion described groups functioning at two levels (Bion 1961), explicit and implicit, which correspond roughly to the two levels of individual psychological functioning, conscious and unconscious. Any group has explicit parameters defining task, roles for its members, and boundaries within which to accomplish its work. The clarity of these parameters determines the group's ability to function in an adaptive manner, which Bion defined as a work group. Bion also described three potential disturbances in the group's availability to perform its work, which he called basic assumptions, because the group acts as if its primary task were something other than to perform its work. In basic assumption *dependency*, the group elects a leader to care for the group members, who then experience being helpless and de-skilled. In basic assumption *fight–flight*, the group elects a leader to mobilize the group to attack or retreat from some imagined enemy. In basic assumption *pairing*, the group elects a pair to join with each other with the goal of producing offspring, which represent the group's hope for its future.

Bion's work has frequently been misinterpreted as suggesting that the healthy group operates exclusively in the work-group mode (Lipgar 1993). Bion states explicitly that depending on the task of the work group, the group may need to mobilize different basic assumptions in support of its task. For instance, the church relies on basic assumption dependence, the military on basic assumption fight–flight, and the aristocracy on pairing. Health is defined, therefore, not in the exclusion of basic assumptions, but in the degree of success in making them explicit and harnessing them in the service of the task. Another misinterpretation posits the existence of the basic assumption in pure form. Just as the work group inevitably incorporates elements of the basic assumptions, the basic assumptions themselves represent extreme positions, which do not necessarily appear in pure form in natural settings. Bion describes usual group function in a fluid manner, with groups becoming dys-functional in their stuckness in one basic assumption.

V. Applying Bion's framework to AA

Let us now turn to the examination of group psychological functioning as guided by the traditions of the Twelve Step programs. Just as Bion recognized that the basic assumptions might rarely be found in pure culture, one would expect that the traditions, to the extent that they concern basic assumption functioning, would overlap one, two or all of them. For the sake of simplicity, then, the following discussion divides the Twelve Traditions into three groups to illustrate their major emphasis on each of the three basic assumptions. A vignette illustrating the traditions will follow the description of each tradition. These vignettes have been collected from patients and colleagues. They are presented in first person to protect the anonymity of their origina-tors.

A. Basic assumption dependence

Critics of Twelve Step programs frequently argue that the success of these programs is simply the result of substituting a pathological dependence on the Twelve Step program for the addiction (Ragge 1998). Tradition Two addresses this argument directly: 'For our group purpose, there is but one

Ultimate authority, a loving God as expressed in the group conscience. Our leaders are but trusted servants.' This tradition, therefore, specifically warns against basic assumption dependence, which relies on the group electing a leader who is powerful and omniscient. All members of AA have admitted through the First Step their powerlessness over alcohol. And each member of AA is assumed to have something of value to offer as a 'trusted servant' of the group.

Twelve Step groups may founder or stagnate if they fail to follow this tradition. Meetings do occasionally form under the leadership of a charismatic leader, and these particular groups may, in their allegiance to a person playing Higher Power, become rigid, cult-like and unavailable to support recovery. Thus the deviation from this tradition towards basic assumption dependence is the source of its dysfunction. Well-functioning Twelve Step meetings typically rotate leadership positions on a regular basis, with the explicit understanding that the experience of serving the group in this way is an essential part of recovery.

> At my first Twelve Step meeting, which was in Al-Anon, an older woman approached me and asked who was the alcoholic in my life. When I told her that I did not know if there were alcoholism in my family, and that I was a psychiatrist, she looked at me skeptically and stated that professionals were not ordinarily welcome at this meeting, but I could stay for this meeting if I wanted. I became aware of shame with the accompanying message that I was intruding in a place that I did not belong. Only when I became aware of the traditions did I realize that this woman was not authorized by the group to exclude me. Indeed, I have come to believe that I elected her as my Higher Power at that moment as my defense against becoming dependent on the group. Once I had acknowledged my own ambivalence about joining the fellowship, I was never again challenged by anyone with regard to my right to be a member of the group.

Having suggested that dependence be established on a Higher Power interpreted through the group rather than through the individual, the traditions elaborate three safeguards to ensure that dependence on authority does not result in abuse of the individual member or the group. Tradition Four suggests that each Twelve Step group within the fellowship is autonomous, except in matters affecting the fellowship as a whole. Thus the rights and prerogatives of each individual member within a particular group, and those of each group within the fellowship, are given the widest possible scope of freedom consistent with the safety of others. For instance, critics of AA sometimes assume that in order to attend an AA meeting, the potential member must already have stopped drinking. While a particular AA group may decide not to include intoxicated members, most AA groups welcome the intoxicated member provided that the intoxication is not accompanied by behavior that disrupts the meeting and thereby threatens the utility of the meeting to others. In this way the Higher Power of the group provides a means of becoming dependent that is not jealous, punitive, or critical of other dependencies.

This Higher Power stands in contrast to basic assumption dependence, where individual needs and dependencies become subservient to the group's need to depend on an idealized leader. Thus basic assumption dependence leads to the distortion and obliteration of individual identities and differences between individuals in the group. The Higher Power of the Twelve Step group, on the other hand, values individual differences as necessary to support the healthy collaborative function of the group. This dependence on the Higher Power of the group does not distort, threaten or obliterate identities and differences between individuals and groups.

I had often heard in meetings of Overeaters Anonymous the preference that members avoid mentioning specific foods to minimize the risk of triggering others in the group. I was surprised, therefore, when I started attending noon hour meetings that members of the group ate their lunch at the meeting. As a recovering anorexic, I was particularly attuned to the importance for me to abstain from skipping lunch. I was also in a distinct minority, as most of the other group members were overeaters. I believed that if I brought my lunch to eat at the meeting, I would be discovered to be eating 'bad' food. Only when I shared this belief explicitly at a meeting did I hear from other members that all of them suffered intense shame in relation to eating in front of the group. Indeed, the process of eating at the meeting contained significant benefit for most of them.

Tradition Seven states that each group is self-supporting through its own contributions. This tradition further promotes the autonomy of each group. The group and fellowship as a whole do not accept outside contributions, which might foster dependence on any source other than the Higher Power manifest through the group conscience. The stance of the group is one of mutual inter-dependence rather than helplessness. Contributions are always voluntary and do not affect the member's status within the group.

This tradition also has important implications for the relationship between health care professionals and the addicts whom they treat. If AA is viewed as the medication prescribed for alcoholism, then the task of the treatment provider is to recommend appropriate treatment and work with the alcoholic to understand whatever resistance emerges to engaging in the prescribed course of treatment. Some treatment providers may blur the distinction between the process of prescribing the medication and the medication itself. For instance, institutions frequently host Twelve Step meetings. These meetings may be open to the public or restricted to those in treatment at the institution. The restricted meetings depend for their existence on an outside contribution of membership from the institution. They therefore carry the attendant risk of violating Tradition Seven, which may lead to enacting basic assumption dependence.

I was assigned the role of hero as a child in my dysfunctional family. So early in my recovery I made an effort to contribute something profound and wise at every meeting I attended. As I became aware of this pattern, I understood that I had taken responsibility for supporting the meeting as if I were the Higher Power of the group. I began to appreciate the usefulness of remaining silent at some meetings, allowing myself to be supported by the comments of others without obeying the compulsion to give something back. Only by actively taking the freedom whether to contribute or not could I become truly dependent. At that point my contributions were voluntary and I could begin the process of letting go of my role as group hero.

Status is also not accorded to professionals within the fellowship, who are consequently attending meetings only for their own benefit. Tradition Eight, which defines Twelfth Step work as non-professional, guards both the fellowship and recovering professionals from basic assumption dependence. Recovering professionals (also known as two-hatters) are protected from having their ability to depend upon the group subverted by being cast in the role of all-knowing dispensers of truth. The fellowship is also free to grow along lines determined by the collective experience, strength and hope of its members and is not limited by the ideological or theoretical limitations of leadership that would arise from professional training. This freedom from theory and orthodoxy is strikingly parallel to the ideal espoused by Bion for the group analyst, whose commitment is to remaining attached to the here-and-now experience of the group (Bion 1961).

Conversely, Tradition Eight also offers both the fellowship and recovering professionals the opportunity to benefit from each other. AA maintains as part of its service structure a committee responsible for outreach to treatment providers and institutions. This service structure represents the tangible manifestation of AA's commitment to cooperate with the professional community. Likewise, recovering professionals may receive substantial benefits through their potentially enhanced ability to identify with the struggles of their recovering patients.

> One challenge for me as a two-hatter has been encountering my clients at the Twelve Step meetings I attend. Aside from the technical issues in therapy that are common to any extra-therapeutic contact (remaining alert to the client's thoughts, feelings and fantasies about the encounter), I have needed to remain focused on making sure that I am open to receiving support for my own recovery. Since the number of meetings in my area is limited, I became aware that attempting to avoid my clients would severely compromise receiving support essential to my recovery. I explored this issue with my sponsor and my therapist. I examined whether having clients at my meetings impaired my ability to share honestly. I have come to believe that the critical issue for me is not the presence of clients at a meeting, but the presence of enough group members over whom I have no authority. The diversity of people I hear at meetings protects me from being held hostage by the dogma of my disease.

B. Basic assumption fight–flight

Another source of criticism of Twelve Step programs arises from the mistaken idea that AA, for example, has temperance as its agenda. These criticisms assume that in recovery, the substance of abuse is the enemy. Such a stance would pull the Twelve Step group into basic assumption fight–flight. For fight–flight processes to be successfully incorporated into the task of the Twelve Step group, the traditions provide for a clear statement of the group's membership requirements. Tradition Three states that the only requirement for membership in AA is a desire to stop drinking. In this manner, the group is mobilized to fight and flee from the disease process, not each other, other people, or substances.

The successful harnessing of basic assumption fight–flight toward the disease of alcoholism also provides a model for letting go of power struggles in the process of treatment. The role of treatment is transformed from fighting with the alcoholic to stop drinking to working with the alcoholic to join a process of recovery. This transformation finds expression in the folk wisdom of AA: 'AA may not stop you from drinking, but it may stop you from enjoying it.' To the extent that the alcoholic uses drinking in order to engage in power struggles, Tradition Three provides an alternative means of relating to the group.

When I was drinking, I had a love–hate relationship with alcohol. Sometimes alcohol was my best friend; sometimes it was my worst enemy. I broke up with alcohol and got back together with alcohol more times than I can count. Coming to AA was like getting an amicable divorce. I no longer hate myself for the life I had as a drunk, and I do not resent alcohol. Instead I recognize that if it were not for alcohol, I could not have gotten the benefit of the love and support I receive from the fellowship of AA. Today I recognize that I have a disease, and that this disease can bite my behind whether I pick up that first drink or not. All I need to start my crazy thinking is to forget that I am an alcoholic and to believe that I can handle alcohol by myself.

Tradition Five extends this principle. The primary purpose of the group is defined as carrying the message of recovery to the addict who still suffers. This tradition, therefore, promotes cohesion in the group to engage in a fight against the disease and in attachment to those who suffer from the disease. Importantly, those who still suffer include current members of the meeting as well as prospective newcomers, since all members are considered equally vulnerable to relapsing into the disease behavior.

Newcomers to AA are encouraged to ask someone at a meeting to be their sponsor. The process of sponsorship is a microcosm of the process in any Twelve Step meeting. Meetings are defined as any two people joining together for the purpose of recovering from the disease of addiction. Therefore any meeting between sponsor and sponsee is a Twelve Step meeting. While the sponsee authorizes the sponsor to support the process of recovery, the relationship is not hierarchical in the fight–flight style of the military. The sponsor may be fired at any time, and a member may work with more than one sponsor.

> For my first several years in recovery I wondered why my sponsor would listen to my whining about everything and anything. When would he get sick of me? What kind of crazy person must he be to listen to my drivel? Only when I began to sponsor others did I understand that being a sponsor is entirely selfish. If I opened up to listening to someone else's crazy thinking, and I identified with his insanity rather than judging it, I became more accepting of my disease. I was no longer struggling alone. Being a sponsor offers me the gift of serenity. If I am not getting tangible benefits from sponsoring someone, I talk to my sponsor about the situation. I get the support I need to change my attitude or let go of sponsoring the person I cannot handle.

A further protection from primitive fight–flight dynamics is provided by Tradition Nine. Twelve Step programs are not organized. No hierarchical structure exists. Service boards function as clearing houses for information about meeting times and places. World service organizations function as clearing houses for gathering information on group conscience within the fellowship as a whole. Neither local committees nor world service organizations exercise any executive authority over the individual Twelve Step groups or members. The fight is therefore transacted via service rather than conscription.

Service includes any activity that a recovering member performs that supports the function of the group. Attending meetings, being a sponsor, chairing a meeting, taking the role of treasurer, setting up chairs, making coffee and ordering literature are all considered service to the group. All of these activities are understood as enhancing the recovery of the individual. Indeed, the primary motivation for service is to support the individual's recovery. The energy of each individual fighting the disease through service to the group is thus harnessed and usable to support the work of the group. No one is coerced to serve the group because service is a valued, selfish activity. This dynamic of voluntary participation has been called 'obedience to the unenforceable' in the Twelve Step programs. Obedience of this kind stands in stark contrast to the experience of enslavement to the disease of addiction.

> My whole concept of leadership has changed as a result of my recovery. I used to think that being a leader was an opportunity to control other people or take on overwhelming responsibility. As I watched other people chair different Twelve Step meetings, I saw how some leaders regularly sought group feedback in order to make decisions. Frequently these leaders would be gently supported to make a decision on the group's behalf. Other leaders would charge ahead heedless of feelings among group members. These leaders would inevitably be challenged on their dictatorial styles. When I developed the courage to chair meetings, I found that my own leadership style began to change effortlessly. The service that I gave the group by leading was repaid abundantly in my growing capacity to exercise leadership sanely.

Fighting among group members who might compete for leadership is protected against by Tradition Twelve. Anonymity is sometimes only understood as a means of protecting the recovering addict from gossip or shaming. The more useful role of anonymity, that of preserving healthy individual and group function, may then be overlooked. Anonymity, operationally defined in the group as placing principles before personalities, offers each group member an opportunity to experience humility. This emphasis on service rather than competition supports the adaptive use of fight–flight basic assumption impulses.

Anonymity is often confused with secrecy. To the extent that the Twelve Step group respects the anonymity of its members, the need for secrecy within the meeting may relax enough for members to share painful and shame-filled experiences. Honesty, openness, and willingness to share become the hallmarks of recovery, and these traits are utilizable in the service of fighting the disease. Conflict avoidance through intoxication gives way to conflict resolution through commitment to open sharing of feelings.

> While meetings have usually provided quiet opportunities to get support, I
> have occasionally become frightened by the open outbreak of hostility in
> the group. Someone may feel hurt about being interrupted by the chair of
> the meeting or angry during a heated discussion of group business. At
> these times I am vulnerable to judging whomever I deem to be the
> disruptive member of the group, which leads me to becoming distant and
> unavailable to receive help. What helps me stay connected is remembering
> to place principles before personalities. Then I find a way to identify with
> the person who feels hurt or angry and examine what we are doing as a
> group to support each other. I am able to let go of protecting myself with
> isolation from my fear in order to join with the group.

C. Basic assumption pairing

One of the hallmarks of unmanageability for the practicing addict is the
inability to sustain meaningful committed relationships at work or in the
family. The role of basic assumption pairing for the practicing alcoholic is to
pair with alcohol. Part of the oral tradition of Twelve Step programs has
defined 'thirteenth-stepping' as the pairing of two addicts for the purposes of
a sexual relationship that may ultimately lead to one or both of the pair losing
their recovery. The ability of the group member to attach to the group may be
understood as requiring the group to harness the energy of basic assumption
pairing in a manner that pairs each member to the group rather than to a single
substance or person.

The First Tradition suggests that the common welfare of the group should
come first; personal progress depends on unity within the fellowship. This
tradition recommends that each group member surrender to a pairing with
the fellowship of recovery. Meetings themselves are the primary locus of this
pairing; many meetings have informal social gatherings before and after to
facilitate this attachment. Beginners in recovery may also be encouraged to
ask a more experienced member to be a sponsor. Oral tradition suggests that
the sponsor is not the sole source of recovery. The sponsor–sponsee relationship may be terminated at any time without justification. The group member
may have more than one sponsor. Of central importance is that the sponsor
takes the role to support the sponsor's own recovery. The pairing, therefore, is
explicitly selfish and does not generate some specific product for the group as
a whole. Historically, beginners are also encouraged to seek sponsors of the

same gender to avoid sexual pairings that would lead to 'thirteenth-stepping' (see above).

> As my son entered early adolescence, I watched him struggle with compulsive behavior that was familiar to me from my own addiction. I invited him to come to my Twelve Step meeting with me. He ambivalently agreed. After he attended several meetings, I happened to go to that meeting alone. A member of the group raised the issue of young teenagers attending the meeting. I felt hurt and afraid that my son's opportunity to receive this help was threatened. Several group members spoke about how they were uncomfortable with choosing what they would discuss in the presence of a young teenager. They were also very clear in owning their discomfort; they explicitly recognized that the parent was responsible for a teenager's attendance at the meeting. Poignantly, one member spoke passionately about the wish that his parent had been in recovery and introduced him to Twelve Step meetings earlier in his life. The group ultimately decided to include teenagers as members of the group.

The remaining traditions provide protection for the fellowships from the consequences of pairings outside of the fellowship. Tradition Six states that the fellowship and its groups do not endorse, finance, or lend their name to any outside enterprise. Since the only product, or offspring, desired by a Twelve Step group is its own recovery, the act of connecting via basic assumption pairing would covertly draw the group into products such as profit, prestige, or power.

Twelve Step programs have avoided pairing with each other. Since many addicts in recovery suffer from more than one addiction, increasing numbers of addicts attend more than one kind of Twelve Step meeting. For instance, an alcoholic who eats compulsively may attend both AA and OA. Since both AA and OA use the same basic steps and tradition, some addicts attempt to recover from any and all compulsive behaviors in one fellowship. This tendency may be resisted by some meetings that work to concentrate their discussion on the disease that unites their specific meeting. Maintaining a clear focus is supported by Tradition Six.

The clear boundaries of my Twelve Step meetings support me as a recovering therapist. Sometimes I need to speak at meetings about conflicts and problems that I encounter as a therapist in recovery. If a group member approaches me as a therapist, I am aware that my clinical practice is an outside enterprise. Being in recovery has affected my clinical practice, both in how I conduct treatment and in my reputation as an addiction treatment provider. When I am at a meeting, I am simply another member of the fellowship who happens to be a therapist. I am not attending the meeting to solicit referrals; therefore I do not have to appear to be healthier or more polished than I am.

Twelve Step groups are also discouraged in Tradition Ten from taking positions on outside issues. The danger of ideological pairing, producing theoretical offspring unrelated to recovery, is therefore avoided. Relevant to this paper, the ideological pairing produced by incorporating an understanding of group dynamics into the Twelve Traditions is not a Twelve Step activity. Note in this regard the attribution/disclaimer in Endnote 1. Alcoholics Anonymous World Service, Inc., received a request to reprint its Twelve Traditions as part of this paper. They granted permission with the condition that this attribution/disclaimer be included. This boundary, which is an immediate consequence of Tradition Ten, preserves the integrity of AA and also facilitates sharing of experience with outside enterprises.

Like many Jews who attend Twelve Step meetings, I was initially alienated by the meeting's use of Christian-sounding prayers and the meeting location in a church. During a meeting in late December several group members talked about feelings that arose in relation to memories of intoxication around Christmas and New Year's celebrations. When my turn came to share, I started talking about my associations to Hanukah. Another group member interrupted me, reminding the group about the importance of not bringing in religion as an outside issue. I was enraged and I self-righteously accused the entire group in my head of the most heinous antisemitism. Fortunately for me, my Christian sponsor freely and non-defensively acknowledged the likelihood of some anti-Semitism in the meeting, and he gently supported me in examining what this experience meant to me. He also confronted me about personalizing the interruption, thereby setting myself up to discount the support of the interrupter in reminding everyone that our group is not a religious program.

In addition to being problematic from the standpoint of pathological dependency, charismatic leadership also threatens the nature of the members' attachment, or pairing, to the group. Tradition Eleven therefore provides a safeguard concerning the entry boundary to the Twelve Step group. The public relations policy of Twelve Step programs operates through attraction rather than promotion, assuring that pairing occurs on the basis of principles rather than personalities (see Tradition Twelve above).

This tradition is also consistent with the customary prohibition against advertising in the medical profession. Ideally treatment involves a pairing of patient and treatment provider for the purposes of getting help for the patient and providing professional gratification for the treatment provider. Ethics violations typically involve the treatment provider promoting some interest external to the tasks of the treatment relationship.

One consequence of longevity in recovery is that I have witnessed several Twelve Step meetings in the process of birth and death. Meetings are born when two or more people commit to sharing a process of recovery. If the meeting grows and thrives, the original members may leave without harming the vitality of the group. My recovery is supported by my attachment to the group, but my recovery does not depend on the vitality of any one group. As I have grown in recovery, my needs have changed and I have sought different meetings to satisfy these changing needs. I am free to discover what meetings I am attracted to. I have also watched meetings die. My acceptance of the death of these beloved meetings has helped me to trust that nothing is removed from my life without something better becoming available. This trust is an extension of the surrender that enabled me to let go of my addiction, believing that something better in the form of recovery would take its place.

VI. AA as a work group

The success of a Twelve Step group as a work group is highly correlated with its adherence to the Twelve Traditions. Ideally, the traditions allow the group to utilize the power of the basic assumptions, fighting against addiction, depending upon each other, the group, and the fellowship, and pairing with the goal of recovery from addiction. The task of this work group, as clearly defined by Tradition Five (see above), is to support its members in achieving recovery by working the Twelve Steps. As a work group, each well-functioning Twelve Step group has a mechanism for monitoring its use of basic assumption group functioning.

A naïve explanation for the efficacy of Twelve Step programs might invoke the cathartic value of talking about one's difficult experiences with addiction. The simple recounting of past episodes of addictive behavior has been called a 'drunkalogue' in AA. While drunkalogues are not forbidden in Twelve Step programs, group members are encouraged to share not only how it was, but also what a life in recovery is like for them, and how they got to whatever phase of recovery they are now in. Therefore Bion's insight and framework of group psychological functioning, which includes an understanding of work as a process, supports the view of Twelve Step programs as sophisticated work groups. The Twelve Traditions protect the Twelve Step group as an effective work group whose members can attach and connect to the task of recovery. Thus, in addition to providing an opportunity for individual members to share their stories of personal recovery, Twelve Step meetings also typically dedicate some time for discussion of questions that are relevant for the group functioning as a work group. These discussions are called taking a 'group conscience' and are explicitly understood as a means of authorizing the entire group to participate in making decisions that affect the group as a whole.

In conclusion, Twelve Step programs like Alcoholics Anonymous may be therapeutic agents with 'pharmacologic' activity far more extensive than commonly appreciated. One limitation in our ability to understand their mechanism of action may have been the absence of a group-analytic perspective like that pioneered by Wilfred Bion. This discussion of the Twelve Traditions in terms of basic assumption group functioning provides an introduction to such a perspective. A more substantial appreciation might be obtained by active participation in one or more Twelve Step meetings, preferably in several different Twelve Step programs. The appreciation of the underlying dynamics might also be enhanced by participation in group relations conferences conducted in the Tavistock model. Garrett O'Connor directed several such group relations conferences in the 1980s with a focus on the dynamics of addiction and recovery. A more comprehensive examination of the dynamics of Twelve Step groups in a Tavistock conference design remains to be accomplished.

Some implications of this group-analytic perspective on the Traditions of the Twelve Step programs for the treatment of recovering addicts have been examined in this paper. Conceptualizing addiction as a 'group' or 'family' disease establishes a basis for using a group treatment that prescribes the group medication of a Twelve Step program. The Twelve Traditions of these programs describe both the therapeutic mechanism of action and some guidelines for their optimal usage. These considerations affect the manner in which health care professionals approach the recovering addict, engage with the community of Twelve Step programs, and potentially participate in their own personal process of recovery.

References

Alcoholics Anonymous (1952) *The Twelve Steps and Twelve Traditions.* New York: Alcoholics Anonymous World Service Inc.

Bion, W. R. (1961) *Experiences in Groups.* New York: Basic Books.

Lipgar, R. M. (1993) 'Bion's work with groups: Construed and misconstrued.' In S. Cytrynbaum and S. A. Lee (eds) *Transformations in Global and Organisational Systems.* Jupiter, FL: A. K. Rice Institute.

Ragge, K. (1998) *The Real AA: Behind the Myth of the Twelve-Step Recovery.* Tucson, AZ: Sharp Press.

White, W. L. (1998) *Slaying the Dragon: The History of Addiction Treatment and Recovery in America.* Bloomington: Chestnut Health Systems.

Endnote

1. The Twelve Traditions are reprinted with permission of Alcoholics Anonymous World Services, Inc. (AAWS). Permission to reprint the Twelve Traditions does not mean that AAWS has reviewed or approved the contents of this publication, or that AA necessarily agrees with the views expressed herein. AA is a program of re-covery from alcoholism *only* – use of the Twelve Traditions in connection with programs and activities which are patterned after AA, but which address other problems, or in any other non-AA context, does not imply otherwise.

5

'Attacks on Linking' and 'Alpha Function' as Two Opposite Elements in the Dynamics of Organizations

Hanna Biran

I. Implementing Bion's theoretical concepts

My intention in this article is to elaborate on two central concepts of Bion's clinical thinking. The two concepts – the one of destructive nature (attacks on linking), the other of constructive nature (alpha function) – were coined by Bion for the analysis of object–subject relations, (mother–infant), as well as for the relationship between the psychoanalyst and the patient.

While working with these concepts I discovered, to my surprise, that they are preconceptions by nature, i.e. that they are of an unsaturated essence. This unique quality enables endless playing, elaboration, implementation and development of these concepts into other worlds and dimensions.

Using this application, I wish to emphasize that when shifting from the individual's world to that of the organization, we must think in terms of social entity. A common error is to view the organization from its members' perspective, rather than looking at the members from the organization's perspective. When borrowing Bion's terms for the analysis of organizations, we must keep in mind that we are moving into a trans-subjective world. The processes in the organization do not stem from the people living in it, but are a result of the nature of their lives as members in the organization. My working hypothesis is that people living in an organization are subject to the control of the organizational entity, for better or for worse. The organizational entity may make them flourish or wither, it may encourage their development or hinder it. The organizational entity is stronger than the individuals populating it.

Alpha function

Bion (1963) describes this function as the mother's function. The infant projects into his mother all the beta type elements, which are thoughts that are not thinkable, such as the fear of dying. These are thoughts that are too frightening for thinking. The mother's function is to contain and decipher these elements. She transfers them into alpha type elements. Through this function the mother soothes the infant, rescuing him from a psychotic experience. Once the infant has grown up, he executes this function for himself.

Let's leave the mother and infant behind and refer only to the process. Then, we discover that Bion has identified a process that is the core of the function of thinking. We do not refer here to logical thinking, but to an epistemological one, which binds thinking with experience and concepts with intuition. I opine that this is by nature the kind of thinking responsible for growth in organizations. An organization cannot grow without space for thinking and a process of thinking.

The organization needs such an alpha function, which is responsible for the containment of new and unformulated ideas. This function is a tolerant one, allowing time for ideas to grow. It gives an opportunity for new ideas to be synthesized, allowing space for ideas to be expressed and to find words. This process creates a new idea which Bion calls 'selected fact'. That is to say, this function contains, deciphers, as well as creates, new concepts.

Selected fact, according to Bion (1962), 'is the name of that element in the realization that appears to link together elements not hitherto seen to be connected. The selected fact is the name of an emotional experience. The emotional experience of a sense of discovery of coherence.'

The organization needs the alpha function especially at times of growth and change, and even more at times of crisis. Alpha function is responsible for the organizational thinking that views the many and varied – seemly unconnected – elements inside the organization, and deciphers the connections among them.

Alpha function belongs to the non-psychotic space of the organization, and therefore it is the one preventing the organization from being entrapped by memory, nostalgia or megalomaniac fantasies. With the absence of containment and deciphering functions, such elements might destroy the organization.

Attacks on linking

Bion (1967) mentions this function as belonging to the psychotic aspects of the personality. The basic idea is that of an attack on anything that is felt as connecting between two different objects. The source for this phenomenon goes back to the infant's fantasy of sadistic attacks on the mother's breast, either out of envy or of frustration. These attacks are the prototype of all attacks on objects used as links. For example, the attack on the connection between the parents, at the stage when the infant is not yet ready to accept the loss of his mother as not being entirely his own, acknowledging that there is another person in her world apart from himself. In the domain of psycho-analytic psychotherapy, the attack is on the verbal thinking of the analyst, and especially on any link that the analyst finds. The possibility for a new meaning to grow is thus severed. The patient attacks the links, paralyzing the analyst's thinking.

Leaving behind dyadic situations and moving to the organizational space, we will find out that this process of cutting the links is typical of organizations. This process belongs to the organization's psychotic and destructive part. We may say that through it the organization prevents itself from thinking on the metaphorical level or the all-encompassing level, dealing with different events concretely and through split vision, denying contacts and contexts that would have allowed decipherment and insight.

The attack on the links may apply to links between ideas and feelings, links between words and meanings, between the concrete and the metaphorical, between the organization's past and future, between the organization's internal and external relations, and so on. The connecting links are all activities related to experiences that have an emotional quality. A living organization is one full of emotions. Bion speaks of three main links: L (love), H (hate) and K (knowledge). Each of the three can be under + sign, or under − sign. That is to say that the links occupy a central place in the process of growing, and have the same ability to build as to destroy.

The connecting link is a vital activity, responsible for the emotional experience of learning. The hate of learning emerges from the psychotic part of the organization, and it may lead to an attack on linking, which may cause the organization a block in thinking and growing. Thus, instead of developing meaning, the learning process will draw to a halt, losing any possibility for gaining insight.

The connecting links create the emotional experience of learning. Out of this experience grows the thinking process. Once the links are under attack, the thinking process is disturbed.

Working hypothesis

The said two elements exist in organizations simultaneously. There is no organization which is totally healthy, and in which the processes of thinking and learning undergo constant growth. It seems that the proportions and energies of these two kinds of process may determine the fate of the organization, setting its course towards either growth or decay.

Alpha function sustains blows in organizations, especially in extreme situations of over-success or of crisis. In case of over-success, thinking is prevented and blocked due to megalomania, narcissism and grandiose notions. In case of crisis, thinking is prevented due to paranoid and melancholic elements. It seems that whenever it is possible to analyze the thinking, creative and constructive elements on the one hand, and the attacking elements on the other, it may also be possible to understand the unconscious dynamic of the organization, and perhaps enable the organization, through a consultancy process, to opt for growth by overcoming the destructive and psychotic elements.

In this article I shall analyze organizations of different character, attempting to demonstrate how organizational events could be conceptualized through the said two concepts. I will also demonstrate how this conceptualization could shed light on organizational dynamics, thus facilitating the consultancy process. For each organization I shall try to show how these elements are expressed differently, but if the hidden structure of the destructive side of the organization is understood correctly, it is possible to release the other elements and lead to their growth. This hidden structure is common to different organizations, and it seems that it could be detected in any organization.

II. An organization dealing with land development and the environment: The Jewish National Fund (JNF)

The organization was established in the early twentieth century. When established its primary task was to buy lands in Palestine from Arabs, transferring them into Jewish ownership. This activity was known by the mythical-sounding phrase 'redeeming of the land'. As a child who was born together with the state, I have strong recollections of the solemn moments every Friday, when the schoolteacher would pass carrying the 'Blue Box', and every child would contribute a penny in order to take part in the 'redeeming of the land'. In the collective memory of the Jewish people, the JNF is a mythological organization.

The primary task for which the organization was established was accomplished to a substantial extent. Further, politically and socially, this task now sounds archaic, unsuitable for the current period when attempts are taking place to live peacefully with the Palestinian Arabs, allowing them to live on their own lands, so that the interrelations between the two peoples will be more just and better balanced. These days, when Israeli Arabs are using violence in their struggle for equal rights, this original task has become irrelevant and even immoral.

The organization is independent, but is supervised by the government. It has a general managing director, as well as two chairmen representing the government. The general managing director works with the directorate that includes the board, in which the different organizational functions are represented. The two chairmen head the directorate.

The organization is rich, thanks both to contributions that have been made by world Jews through many years, and to the lands that have been purchased. Due to its wealth and anachronism, voices were raised at the Parliament in recent years demanding the dismantling of the organization and the distribution of its property among the government ministries. Their argument is that the organization has concluded its task.

Because of the external threat, the chairmen decided to reorganize. They became deeply involved in the organization, creating for it a new vision, a new destination and new primary tasks. They also created a more flat organization, in which the management was transferred from the center to three geographic districts: north, center and south. Their aim was to allow growth in each district, and prevent the centralization and bureaucratization that had so far characterized the organization.

The newly defined objectives of the organization were: forestation and the protection of green areas, assistance to developing townships, assistance to poverty-stricken neighborhoods by erecting facilities for the community's use, developing parks for the benefit of underprivileged populations, and so on.

This new initiative seemed positive and constructive. The problem was that all these changes were difficult to implement and met with resistance, mainly hidden, from veteran employees. The change caused strong tension within the organization, while the top management was finding it difficult to understand why the change was not going through, and why processes were still moving slowly, some becoming even more cumbersome than before. Although the organization was reduced from 3,000 to 2,500 employees by encouraging retirement, managers were reporting both superfluous manpower and difficulty in implementing tasks and realizing targets.

I entered the organization as the head of a team of five consultants. The first stage was a workshop for 35 directors, managers and heads of departments, the purpose of which was to allow an open dialogue as well as analyzing the organization and attempting to uncover the hidden emotional processes taking place in it. I will not go here into all the findings or the entire consultancy project, but focus only on the main findings which shed light on the hidden dynamics taking place between constructive and destructive aspects in the organization's life.

As for the hidden processes, the main – and for us, the most fascinating – discovery was that the organization wished to undergo a change in order to grow and make itself compatible with the new age, but simultaneously, and as a reaction to any breakthrough or innovation, the same organization reacted with a halt and with falling back on conservative, traditional patterns, relying on the past. There was no function in the organization that could observe it globally as a whole; no one could observe the synchronization between the two processes. The organization's leaders were too blind to see it, and all managerial levels fell victim to some crippling processes.

It is important to indicate that we are observing two kinds of organizational behavior, which we will term 'organizational behavior A' and 'organizational behavior B'. In this context, when we exposed this internal map to the management, we discovered together with them that these two types of behavior are trans-subjective, i.e. they cross the boundaries of the personal. That is to say, the same manager indicates that he can discern within himself behavior of both types according to the subject at hand, the nature of the specific meeting he was invited to attend, the atmosphere at the meeting, as well as the dominant voices of the speakers preceding himself. It means that the wish to bring about a change and, simultaneously, the blocking of that change, do not occur according to the preferences of individuals, but according to conscious and unconscious processes taking place in different forums. Managers started to detect their own conflicting behaviors. Before the analysis they were incapable of such insight, and could not see the internal contradictions into which the organization was pushing them. They suddenly realized that this situation perpetuates a Sisyphean oscillation between a breakthrough and a halt, forestalling the organization's transformation into a new phase.

In order to illustrate the theoretical concepts developed in this article, I shall describe these two types of organizational behavior as representing the two concepts to which I refer. This division is not very accurate, but it allows viewing the organization as a whole, and for me it is a kind of 'selected fact' that sheds light on the organization's incoherence, indicating the place where the organization is trapped.

ORGANIZATIONAL BEHAVIOR A (Alpha function)	ORGANIZATIONAL BEHAVIOR B (Attacks on linking)
• Looking to the future	• Looking at the past; memory-filled concepts
• Looking at the needs of future generations	• Relying on myths of the founders' generation
• Openness	• Dogmatism
• Bypasses and 'acrobatics'	• Halting and stopping progress
• Concern with external threats	• False optimism and denial of existential threat
• A culture of freedom of thought	• A culture of survival and fear of change

It is important to view this table as existing in constant motion, realizing that the organization is simultaneously constructing and deconstructing itself. Paradoxically, when type A behavior is strengthened, type B behavior is strengthened as well. They don't exclude each other, but rather feed and reinforce each other. In this kind of unconscious relationship there is hidden the fear of catastrophic change (Bion 1970). There is a lack of tolerant alpha function that would contain, soothe and prevent the oscillation. It turned out that type A behavior did not constitute an alternative, but rather a threat.

In this table we may discern in organizational behavior A a phase of organizational thinking and of organizational learning. The terms are not saturated, and are open for change. They have the quality of preconceptions, and therefore dynamically they can continue growing in a type of a spiral process. It is painful to discover that part of the creativity of this behavior has to do with investing in how to bypass and overcome organizational behavior B. Organizational behavior B was experienced as an unavoidable fact.

In organizational behavior B we can see that the attacks on linking operate according to L-H-K, and it is therefore impossible to undertake thinking in that space. This behavior has the characteristic of organizational psychoses. For example: L = love and worship of the myths connected with the early days of the organization. H = hate for anything new undermining the tradition. K = the use of knowledge-saturated terms relying on examples from the past and on ritual words. A dogmatic culture creates impenetrability and lack of tolerance for being in the condition of not knowing.

I shall demonstrate through a vignette from my work in this organization. In a role-analysis group with the participation of six managers, the ability to explore and to discover new things was obstructed on three consecutive sessions. In retrospect it seems to me that there were processes that prevented learning. I was absorbed into an empty dialogue and left the group that day feeling depressed and worthless. The most senior manager of the six produced a painting in which he had painted himself, his function and the organization. It was a painting of nature. His managerial functions were depicted as the energies of the sun and the rain, falling from above regardless of what is happening on the ground. The managerial function seemed to be hanging in the air, bestowing its energy without any coordination with the needs of the employees under him. When I indicated this point, his immediate response was: 'So what, I am optimistic. They will learn how to take from me.' I suddenly saw the vision of a king who is not connected with his kingdom and ignores his subjects' needs.

In the next sessions it was the turn of the managers working under him, who did not react to my earlier dialogue with him. Two of them painted the organization as a prison, and two others as a partially constructed house surrounded with walls. When I attempted to enter the unconscious processes unveiled in the paintings, the senior manager obstructed the exploration by expressing his admiration for all his managers, praising each and every one of them for being so great and wonderful. All the five have been patted by him as he was telling me chapters of their biographies, according to which all had enjoyed great glory in the past, even before joining the organization. The one was a great scholar, the other had a PhD in history, the third was decorated during his military service, and so on. This glorifying, saturated with a kind of phallic mystification, created an atmosphere in which nothing was left to explore. In the fifth and last painting a giant tree was depicted, which looked to me like a phallus turned into a totem, and the group seemed to me to be in a religious state of mind, worshiping the glorious past. Altogether they looked like a lost tribe, holding on to abilities which are irrelevant to the organization as it is today. In the meetings of this group we were in a phase constructed on a high level of anxiety, owing to the changes that had taken place in the organization. The group as a group seemed to me like a blocking wall, similar to the prison in their paintings; a wall blocking the developing of any real dialogue within the group.

I give this example in order to demonstrate a dialogue in which the alpha function did not work on the organizational level, making real organizational thinking impossible. However, it should be indicated that in a dialogue taking place on a later occasion and on a larger forum, the senior manager said that he had felt that many of the functions he had fulfilled in the past seemed to him to be irrelevant, and that he didn't know how to handle the changes and the new power centers in the organization, which weakened him, and in fact pushed him to dig his heels deeper into the patterns of the past. This insight, on a later occasion, seemed like an opening for a different kind of exploration, originating in some question marks and lack of knowledge. It was an alternative to the use of total and obstructing knowledge that had been demonstrated at the role-analysis group. This example illustrates how the same person could demonstrate organizational behavior B in one situation, while showing signs of organizational behavior A in another.

III. Mental health public clinic, the Ministry of Health

I was invited, as the head of a team of three consultants, to a mental health clinic employing some 26 persons in all mental health professions, as well as 10 students who are being trained there. We were invited by the head of the clinic, who complained of bad relations in the team, bad enough to cause a lack of cooperation among the staff members. This was harming the training of the students and even the welfare of the patients.

In the first stage we held a two-day workshop that included role analysis, an institution event, social dreaming and plenary sessions. It is important to indicate that the organizational structure and culture exposed there were typical of governmental institutes of mental health.

These were the main phenomena:

1. All the key positions of management, professional responsibility, team heads, and so on, are held by veteran psychologists and social workers of middle age or above.

2. Of the employees, 80% are women.

3. There is a high degree of conservatism in the therapy given to patients: fixed patterns for intake, diagnosis and therapy based on strictly traditional methods.

4. We were working with underprivileged populations and low socioeconomic levels, mainly with people who could not afford private therapy.

5. An excruciating internship process was imposed on the young psychologists, who are considered 'slaves' and work for meager wages. They must pass a difficult internship test, for which they are trained by the veteran clinic employees. In the test they must cite well-known clinical material, and in order to pass it they must avoid any original, creative or individualistic thinking. They must conform to the establishment.

These rigid elements, which are massively entwined into the organizational culture, obstruct the development of alpha function, creating patterns of thinking according to preconceived schemes. There is a clear hierarchy of knowledge based on age and period of service. The older generation is considered to have the total possession of knowledge. The concepts are saturated with ready-made knowledge written in professional jargon. This knowledge blocks the growth of unsaturated preconceptions. Initiative and innovation by the middle and younger generations are met with suspicion, and considered to undermine the infrastructure of the clinic's work.

Working with this specific clinic, we discovered additional aspects that block the growing of alpha function.

This clinic had always been headed by senior women psychologists, who left their authoritative and mythological mark. The current head of the clinic had assumed her position ten years previously. She was then over 40, coming from the periphery and not a part of the generation growing in the clinic. Her arrival was traumatic, and she suffered much abuse by the clinic's senior employees, who admitted that they enjoyed making her suffer. Our working hypothesis: none of the senior clinic members had dared occupy the mythological chair of the former head of clinic, who died of cancer. When the alien, relatively young head of clinic dared fill the large void, she absorbed anger and hostility, which amounted to an attempt to destroy her completely. The atmosphere was filled with the question which was never asked openly: 'Who is she, daring to step into the shoes of the great, dead mother?'

Since her first year there, the head of clinic has defended herself through keeping her distance and fulfilling her role rigidly in order to survive as a figure of authority, and salvage the managerial function. This rigidity, as in a vicious circle, increased the level of hatred and anger. This difficult starting point cast its shadow over her first years at the clinic. These episodes remained mute, undigested, without being transformed into dialogue, like hard objects filling the space. No explanation was given as to the head of clinic's rigid behavior. These hard objects were hitting the coming generations and the young persons joining the clinic, with no working-through of the history or deciphering of these processes and their meaning. The newcomers met with a rigid, remote head of clinic, who was hiding her personality, acting mechanically and emphasizing discipline. They met with a senior team holding ritualistic professional discussions with no personal contact or human warmth, in a heavy post-traumatic atmosphere. It was a team of senior people who avoided any help and support to the head of clinic.

The next generations joining the clinic manifested the syndrome of 'the Holocaust second generation'. They became cautious, tried not to ask questions, not to cause pain, not to harm, not to open wounds. Avoidance became the central pattern.

In the first plenary session which we held during the workshop, in which we introduced ourselves and the workshop's events and objectives, nobody spoke except for the head of clinic. A freezing silence prevailed. Nobody asked questions. We experienced such high levels of anxiety that it caused paralysis of thinking. No dialogue with us was attempted.

While exploring the history of the clinic we found that soon after assuming her position, perhaps in order to reduce the attacks on her, the head of clinic divided the employees into three interdisciplinary and intergenerational teams. She appointed senior women employees as the heads of each team. She thus isolated herself even further, being the only one not belonging to any team. This way she was left only with super-ego roles. Everyone else, including the senior team, would not accept responsibility, and she alone was left in the role of the one reprimanding employees for being late, checking the number of patients per employee, supervising the keeping of records and so on. She was thus stigmatized as the 'bad mother', while feeling isolated and entrapped, unable to share her feelings with anyone at the clinic.

While the head of clinic was entrapped in her super-ego roles, the three heads of teams became the 'good mothers', the alternatives to rigid management. Each team united around its 'good mother', as in a warm nest. The team became the safe haven, the sanctuary, the relief. Here intimacy was experienced, here the interesting professional discussions were taking place. In the team they were getting emotional support. The team turned into the 'warm house' for which it was worthwhile to come to work.

As we continued on the exploration process, we discovered that those three 'warm nests' in fact stifled the space for thinking, creating a tangle of 'family relations' preventing any individualistic or innovative thinking. While working on role-analysis it was found out that people were entrapped in the teams in a stifling chain of loyalties, with a severe deficiency in the sphere of potential space, required for creativity and self-discovery. Loyalty to the team turned out to be the supreme value. All employees, without exception, said that they felt they belonged to the team, and had no feeling of belonging to the clinic. Each head of team demonstrated an excessive motherly interest and over-protectiveness of her team members, while demonstrating total indifference to what was going on at the clinic as such. In this atmosphere of three 'families', all conflicts within each team were avoided, while the space between the teams was filled with the hostility of each team towards the other two. All the conflicts, tensions, envy, competition and aggression were tunneled into that space. We found a clinic working under the pattern of 'us' and 'them', with the students and patients paying the price. These two groups, who were receiving the clinic's services, became the vessel into which all the unsolved reckoning between the teams was tunneled.

For example, a student who was being supervised by a supervisor from team A, and was giving family therapy together with a therapist from team B, found himself torn in a constant conflict between the two. In one case of family treatment, the mother was treated by a therapist from team A, while the daughter was treated by a therapist from team B, and the family found itself locked in a conflict and professional disagreement between the two therapists.

Under these conditions the most difficult place to belong to was the clinic's large team meeting taking place once a week. This meeting was experienced as an alienated, ritualistic place, a place where no dialogue might evolve. This atmosphere was extremely contrary to the 'total togetherness' atmosphere in the teams.

Already during the workshop we started to break through the tightly guarded borders by designating team-crossing groups for role analysis. In the organizational and social dreaming events the employees had to meet in the large group. On the first day the role-analysis groups were very difficult. The employees were not accustomed to speak outside their 'warm house'. The turning-point occurred at the role-analysis group in which the head of clinic participated, when for the first time there was speaking about the history, and this was carried on into the plenary session, bringing relief, especially for the younger generations. Another breakthrough occurred when the younger generations started to speak up. So far they had been neutralized by being dispersed among the teams and absorbed into the Oedipal-motherly aspect.

A painting by a woman psychologist of the middle generation reflected in a fine metaphorical way the distress of the generations which were blocked and absorbed. This psychologist painted identical figures standing in a uniform, straight line, all on tiptoe like ballet dancers. She also painted heavy bricks and working tools, with a pyramid in the background. The figures seemed very colorful. The associations were: walking carefully, waiting in line, imposed equality, erasing of individuality, turning the individual into a mold. The bricks and the pyramid were immediately associated with slavery. In the Jewish culture, the slavery of the Israelites under Pharaoh is the most prominent symbol of slavery.

The conjecture I made based on this painting was that the clinic was experienced as an organization in which it was dangerous to stick out, in which there was a hidden injunction to toe the line and conform with everyone else. Because of the colorful figures the conjecture also came up that there was some gratifying and convenient side to the life of slavery, along the line of 'I loved my master'.

In the group discussion the participants identified with the painting to a great extent. A dialogue ensued in which it was stated that it was dangerous to step out of line because of the aggression and envy it might raise. A heavy feeling was expressed, according to which any duty in the clinic was randomly distributed, not according to ability and talent. On top of this the fact stood out that central positions were distributed only according to age and years of service. The conclusion was that the elders were harboring an unconscious, mute and acute envy of the young. We also found that there was a high degree of replacement in the middle generation; whoever could open a private clinic would leave the moment they could.

This conclusion found further corroboration during the social dreaming event. A great difficulty in narrating dreams was experienced. The dreams which did come up reflected difficulty in entrusting to the clinic the aspect of the young, playful, creative child. A striking dream relating to the intergenerational relations was narrated by a male psychologist: 'I am dreaming that I am walking along with my father. I am smiling. The atmosphere is pastoral and pleasant. Suddenly he kicks me hard, and I realize he is crazy.' This dream made it possible to view the pseudo-pastoral atmosphere filled with hidden violence which erupts in the dream. The dream also contains a hint at psychosis in the system. An organization which kicks the next generation is operating under some kind of madness.

Describing the dynamics in the clinic I tried to illustrate the absence of creative elements wishing to grow, blocked by the psychotic aspects which do not allow the links to exist. If the important links are discovered, it is possible to turn from an incoherent to a coherent state allowing growth.

I shall attempt once more to demonstrate the two types of thinking, the function that thinks as opposed by the function that cuts and blocks. Here too it is possible to discover the hidden structure, reflecting two different ways of organizational thinking. Through the consultancy process it is possible to strengthen the alpha function, which exists mainly in a hidden, fractured and damaged way. If the alpha function is strengthened in a containing and non-menacing way, there is a chance that the psychotic elements will undergo a transformation from a destructive to a constructive mode.

Alpha function	*Attacks on linking*
• opening the space to many languages	• use of fixed, old-fashioned and closed clinical jargon
• opening a potential space for subjective knowledge	• rigid knowledge hierarchy according to seniority, age and position
• the opportunity to retell the subjective and different narratives of the organization	• single, undigested narrative, which casts its shadow over the organization
• an open and flowing connection between role and person	• depersonalization in running the clinic – the role takes over the person (head of clinic), vs. over-personalization – the person takes over the role (heads of teams acting like 'good mothers') – (Larry Hirschhorn's terms 1997)
• viewing the organization through the sphinx. Exploring the infinite possibilities to be found in roles. (Gordon Lawrence's term 1999)	• Oedipal relations between the generations to the extent of creating a perverse working place, turning it into a kind of enslaving, sick family. These relations are experienced as given and final
• opening a dialogue among the generations for the sake of mutual fertilization and joint construction	• undigested envy of the young by the elders, unconscious, murderous thoughts in the different generations one towards the other
• developing the ability to dream as a kind of epistemological thinking	• focusing on the daily routine; reducing the ability to dream; adhering to the concrete
• connecting concept and intuition in order to allow preconceptions	• use of concepts saturated with clinical knowledge; blocking of emotional knowledge

IV. Current reflection of alpha/beta elements in Israeli-Palestinian relations

In an article concerned with the peace process published in 1997, I described alpha function as responsible for the holding of dialogue between Arabs and Jews, as against beta-type elements, which do not undergo transformation and recur as violence and terror acts without any change. I argued that these elements are bursting out of the psychotic aspects of society. Since 1997 this argument has received ample corroboration through what has been happening in the relations between the two peoples.

Following the analysis of the first organization presented in the current article, which demonstrates that organizational behavior B is strengthened in response to the strengthening of organizational behavior A, it occurred to me that also in relations between the two peoples the two kinds of behavior are not disconnected, but rather, an alarming reciprocity can be detected between them. It became clear that as the peace process makes progress, and as the road for a sane dialogue, for compromise, for territorial division, is being paved, just to the same extent, on an escalating curve, and in response to the peace process, more and more violent and savage forces are gaining strength (as in the lynching of two Israeli soldiers by a crowd of several hundred Palestinians, and in unnecessarily violent acts of Israeli soldiers towards young Palestinians).

The dialogue, which is based on alpha function, and which has room for question and doubt, is being blocked and attacked by extremist forces who ask no questions. These forces are getting more and more loaded with a kind of apocalyptic religious energy, which is not connected with thinking processes. Against the attempted dialogue, a rioting crowd is getting stronger on both sides, united around mutual slogans of total destruction. This is an incited crowd, speaking the language of graves and holy sites. Lately alpha function has become thin and fragile, facing the impulsive frenzy, which has a psychotic hue, and which is willing to lead to total destruction.

Referring to the unconscious social processes taking place on the level of relations between the two peoples, it is possible to unveil a strong connection between the hand extended for peace and willing to make a generous compromise, and the escalation of violence. It is difficult – and may prove impossible – to compensate the Palestinians for 33 years of occupation. The moment when the option of peace appears, the repressed rage breaks out. This rage is inflamed by religious-extremist Moslem leaders, who encourage terror attacks by suicide bombers. Facing this tide, the Jewish population finds itself frightened and almost helpless.

Rage which is colored by mystification and holiness is not translated into thinking, and therefore cannot make dialogue possible either. Alpha function cannot translate a rioting crowd into a dialogue. This may constitute one of humankind's greatest tragedies. This tragedy exists beyond time and place, and it does not exclusively belong to the Middle East. It belongs to all social situations in which dark instincts overcome the ability to think.

To sum up: an organization requires a constant reservoir of preconceptions so that transformations allowing new thinking can take place. These transformations are created by alpha function, which is an infinitely creative function. Alpha function is of spiral nature. It has the elements both of containment and of innovation. This function is in charge of the world of dreams, images, metaphors and vision. Against it Bion presents the concept of 'attacks on linking'. The meaning of this concept is that a link constructively connecting two components is destroyed by an attack which is unconscious and psychotic in essence.

When we regard an organization from a psychoanalytical point of view, while emphasizing Bion's contribution, we may discover damaged links, links under assault or already destroyed. These same links are supposed to connect between parts of the organization, between organizational behaviors, organizational cultures past and present, a person and his role. When these links are under attack, organizational creativity is harmed.

Bion mentions unconscious envy as the source for these attacks. It seems that in contemporary organizations there are other variables which harm the links. These variables are connected with the quick pace of changes, which are not always digestible, and which create a high level of uncertainty and instability. In a world filled with existential fears, which reinforce the need to survive, thinking might stop in favor of conservatism and dogmatism.

According to Bion, all the attacks on the links are such as to block the potential for growth. These attacks make it impossible for unsaturated preconceptions to grow, while protecting saturated, stationary and even dead concepts.

When a preconception is created but is not allowed to grow, being saturated by memory or desire, it loses its ability to serve as a link and fertilize the organization. Sometimes groups representing the organization's veteran members saturate the preconception with memory. Sometimes groups representing a new wave saturate the preconception with desire. This idea allows us a fresh encounter with the famous dictum: 'Without memories and desires'.

References

Bion, W. R. (1962) *Learning From Experience*. London: Maresfield Reprints.

Bion, W. R. (1963) *Elements of Psycho-Analysis*. London: Maresfield Reprints.

Bion, W. R. (1967) *Second Thoughts*. London: Maresfield Reprints.

Bion, W. R. (1970) *Attention and Interpretation*. London: Maresfield Reprints.

Biran, H. (1998) 'An attempt to apply Bion's alpha and beta elements to processes in society at large' in Bion Talamo and Borgagno (eds.) *Bion's Legacy to Groups*. London, Karnac Books.

Hirschhorn, L. (1997) *Reworking Authority*. MIT Press.

Lawrence, W. G. (1999) 'Centering of the sphinx for the psychoanalytic study of organisations.' *Journal of the Australian Institute of Socio-Analysis 1*, 2, 99–126.

Reed, B. (1976) 'Organisational role analysis.' In Cooper, C. L. (ed.) *Developing Social Skills in Managers*. London: Macmillan.

6

Learning at the Edges between Knowing and Not-knowing

'Translating' Bion

Robert French and Peter Simpson

To come to what you know not,
you must go by a way where you know not.

St John of the Cross (The Ascent of Mount Carmel, I, 13: 11)

And this gray spirit yearning in desire
To follow knowledge like a sinking star,
Beyond the utmost bound of human thought.

Alfred, Lord Tennyson (Ulysses)

...better discuss no further, since we are in the dark.

Job (37:19)

Learning arises from working at the edges between knowing and not-knowing. This idea is a direct 'translation' from Wilfred Bion's thinking about psychoanalytic method into the context of our own work as teachers, consultants, researchers and writers. In their book on Bion's clinical thinking, Symington and Symington (1996, p.3) summarise the point very succinctly. They write that the '*only* assumption' underlying Bion's thinking was that 'the mind grows through exposure to truth' (their italics). By growth of mind, he meant the ability to act more consistently and rigorously in relation to truth.

While 'learning' equates well to Bion's 'growth of mind', our translation of 'exposure to truth' as 'working at the edges between knowing and not-knowing' requires more careful explanation.

Bion used the symbol 'K' to represent 'knowing' and the symbol 'O' to represent his notion of 'truth' which, in direct contrast to K, he defined as both unknown and unknowable. O is often rather grandiosely described – following Bion himself, it must be said – as ultimate reality, ultimate truth, the godhead or, in Bion's borrowing from Milton, as the 'formless infinite' (Bion 1984a, p.31). As Eigen writes: 'O can be the ultimate reality of a session, emotional truth of a session, growth of the experience of an analysis, the ultimate reality of the personality. It can be creatively explosive, traumatically wounding, crushingly uplifting' (Eigen 1998, p.78).

Bion's notion of O becomes more accessible, however – and more usable – when another aspect is brought into play: that the truth of O is also 'immanent' (Bion 1984b, p.147); that is, O is truth or reality *in the present*. O is the reality of the here and now, what we refer to as 'truth-in-the-moment'. Hence his description of the encounter between analyst and patient as 'the intersection of an evolving O with another evolving O' (Bion 1984a, p.118).

By definition, it is not possible intellectually to know the full reality of each passing instant: 'O does not fall in the domain of knowledge or learning save incidentally; it can be "become", but it cannot be "known"' (Bion 1984a, p.26). However, it is Bion's assumption that exposure to truth-in-the-moment can lead to growth of mind. Such truth is, therefore, worth pursuing because it has an impact upon us and can inspire learning, even though it remains unknowable and unknown.

Our assumption is that working at the edges between knowing and not-knowing offers the possibility for exposure to truth-in-the-moment, hence opening up the potential for learning. The edge is important because whilst the truth-of-the-moment never enters the domain of knowing, it is through encounters at the edge that we may be subject to its influence.

It could be argued, for example, that such things as the gardener's 'green fingers', the painter's brush stroke, the actor's gesture, the confident tennis stroke, the consultant's intervention, or indeed the scientist's insight, depend on being in touch with truth-in-the-moment. In none of these situations can the moment of insight be either controlled or predicted. The knowledge gained is a 'gift', rather in the way a forgotten name is often remembered or the solution to a mathematical problem is 'discovered', only when one stops thinking about it.

Traditional approaches to accessing truth-in-the-moment

Our understanding of the nature of not-knowing and of its positive value for our work has been formed in exploring the interaction between ancient tradition and Bion's thinking. This exploration has been enhanced by the fact that Bion himself explicitly worked with some of these same traditions, as represented by Meister Eckhart, St John of the Cross, the Bhagavad Gita, poetry, philosophy and the Bible.

Bion's use of 'O' to denote present but unknowable truth, for example, echoes the use of the circle in the Zen discipline of painting, in which O is regarded as 'an expression of enlightenment – an experience of completeness – at each moment' (Tanahashi 1994, p.ix; also Schneider 1994, p.xviii.)[1]

The truth-in-the-moment of the Zen master's brushstroke (Herrigel 1988) is also the 'nothing' of Meister Eckhart (Smith 1987, pp.68–9) and the *nada* (nothing) of St. John of the Cross which is the beginning and end of knowledge. In Bion's view the very capacity to think develops from the infant's experience of absence, of 'no-thing' which, well enough contained, can become a thought (Bion 1962, pp.31–7; Symington and Symington 1996, pp.102–3).

The centrality to human development of the unknowable truth of O is well illustrated in the icon paintings of the Eastern Orthodox tradition (Ouspensky and Lossky 1982; Temple 1990). Icon images are quite familiar outside the East, from book cover illustrations or from Christmas cards. What is probably less familiar, however, is that these images can be read as an early example of 'organizational role analysis' (Armstrong 1997; Reed 1976). In the case of the icon, the organization is the cosmos, and the role being depicted is the cosmic role of the human agent: that is, our role in relation to O, to the unknowable and unknown.

The modern eye tends to focus on story or on the historical accuracy of events, also on colour as decoration and on the authenticity of the emotional impact. In a sense, however, none of these matters in icons – even the story, at least as history: 'The icon never strives to stir the emotions of the faithful. Its task is not to provoke in them one or another natural human emotion, but to guide every emotion as well as the reason and all the other faculties of human nature on the way towards transformation' (Ouspensky 1982, p.39). Everything has its impact and gains its meaning from the symbolic sense: 'In the art of icons, it is content that is the criterion of form' (Burckhardt 1982, p.7).

What is represented in Figure 6.1, for example, symbolically represents a ladder similar to the ladder of Jacob's dream. Like the ladder in Jacob's dream, this is a ladder between heaven and earth, stretching from the hand of God in the top corner to the rocky earth at the bottom, and right down to the cave in the corner, representing the lowest place of existence, 'the dark place in ourselves where God has not yet entered' (Temple 1990, p.132).

A double movement is portrayed, therefore: starting with God we can see his power, in the form of the Divine Ray, being transmitted through the human to the earth. Here, by submitting himself to God's power, the saint is able to master the power and strength represented in different forms both by the white horse and by the dragon. The dragon is not killed but mastered – and in many such icons seems almost to look lovingly at the saint as though gladly acknowledging his superiority.

Figure 6.1 St George Killing The Dragon, Crete c. 1500 (in Weitzmann et al. 1982, p.328)[2]

This movement on the 'ladder' can, however, also be reversed: humans are born in the darkness of the cave, Bion's Ur-catastrophe, perhaps (Eigen 1993). Icons of the nativity generally portray Christ's birthplace as a cave, caves also being seen as 'focal points for the exchange of cosmic energies' (Pherykedes in Temple 1990, p.21.) We then have work to do, work of understanding, development and self-control, in order to master or come to terms with the powerful forces represented by the horse and the dragon (the *id*, perhaps). Only then can we begin the transitional or transformational work, which is required at the edge between the known earthly realm and the unknown spiritual realm.

So the icon's function is to draw our attention to the edge at which we may have some contact with the Divine and to our unique role in working at that edge. The image and the movement depicted are equally 'true' in terms of the individual psyche or the relationship between the individual and the human community, or humanity and the rest of the natural world. The very formalised style of icons, which can seem so static and foreign to the modern eye, should not blind us to the fact that the experience or reality they depict is far from static. The edge is not reached once and for all, but must instead be the object of constant attention in each and every present moment.

In a way that is very similar to psychoanalysis, the practice of the mystical traditions to which icon painting belongs depends on a training which involves particular forms of 'spiritual exercise' (Hadot 1995). The purpose of these exercises, whether for the contemplative or, in Bion's view at least, for the psychoanalyst, is to develop a level of awareness and attention that can make possible moments of insight into or from the unknowable unknown. Access to truth-in-the-moment depends on the development of this state of awareness and attention.

Parallels to Bion

The hand of God, which appears in the centre of one of the top quadrants of many icons, is accompanied by a segment of a circle, rather like a section from a halo. In diagrammatic form, the energy of development in the icon of St George (Figure 6.1) moves from the hand of God through the saintly figure – represented in Figure 6.2 below by the saint's halo – to the earth.

If one were to finish this diagrammatic representation of the icon image, therefore, by filling out the circle – always left incomplete by the painter – the symbolic truth would be made explicit (see Figure 6.3).

Figure 6.2 Dragon's cave, saint's halo, God's aura

Figure 6.3 The completed 'O' representing God

The movement of the 'Divine Ray' is from the 'completeness-at-each-moment' of O, the divine realm, the unknowable unknown, to the misshapen 'O' of the primal cave. To work at this movement leads to growth of mind through exposure to truth, and each movement of development inevitably exposes another edge, where the encounter with our not-knowing or ignorance and limitation may block us or free us to further growth.

The very incompleteness of the circle at the top of the icon is clearly significant: it indicates the impossibility of finding any adequate way of representing 'heaven', the divine realm, the 'formless infinite' of Bion's O. The darkness of the cave, on the other hand, suggests the incomprehensibility of infantile emotional experience, that is, Bion's 'beta elements': 'initial catastrophic globs of experience', 'raw material, primal thoughts, nonthoughts, mindless hallucinatory globs' (Eigen 1993, pp.216 and 217).

There is another striking, if somewhat fanciful, pictorial parallel in Bion's work. His 'Grid' – 'a method I have found useful in thinking about problems that arise in the course of psycho-analytic practice' (Bion 1963, p.6) – could be thought of as a visual representation of the movement from the 'cave' of blind ignorance to 'O', the unknowable truth.

It is interesting to 'read' the Grid (Figure 6.4) rather as we have suggested icons should be read; that is, to take the *form* as the key to the whole. If one tries merely to understand whether a particular event or interaction belongs in B3 or C4, then the focus is on the content of each individual 'box'. If, however, the Grid is turned on its side – and overlaid with the earlier diagrammatic icon image – (see Figure 6.5), it too could be seen as representing a kind of ladder linking 'earth' and 'heaven'; in this case, stretching from the earth or cave of Bion's beta elements up the ladder of successively higher-level abstract conceptualisations – in the direction of an always unattainable truth. If there is also a reverse movement, it is stimulated by the impact of any encounter with the truth: the truth is always available, and the mind inevitably grows when exposed to it.

This reading of Bion's Grid highlights the importance of 'edges' and of movement; for example the movement across the edge between 'conception' and 'concept', or between 'inquiry' and 'action'. As development always involves movement up the 'ladder', the boxes themselves can become a distraction or a seduction, if we become preoccupied with how things *are* to the exclusion of what they *are becoming.*

The focus of our work has to be on the intersection of evolving Os, that is, on the edges where known meets unknown in our shared experience. As in

	Defini-tory hypo-theses 1	ψ 2	Nota-tion 3	Atten-tion 4	Inquiry 5	Action 6	...n.
A β-elements	A1	A2				A6	
B α-elements	B1	B2	B3	B4	B5	B6	...Bn
C Dream thoughts, dreams, myths	C1	C2	C3	C4	C5	C6	...Cn
D Pre-conception	D1	D2	D3	D4	D5	D6	...Dn
E Conception	E1	E2	E3	E4	E5	E6	...En
F Concept	F1	F2	F3	F4	F5	F6	...Fn
G Scientific deductive system		G2					
H Algebraic calculus							

Figure 6.4 Bion's Grid
Note: © 1970 by W.R. Bion, reproduced by permission of Paterson Marsh Ltd on behalf of Francesca Bion.

Goethe's *Faust*[3], what matters is growth of mind rather than attainment, that is, the ability to strive constantly to find a new edge without 'someone who KNOWS filling the empty space' (Bion 1991, p.578).

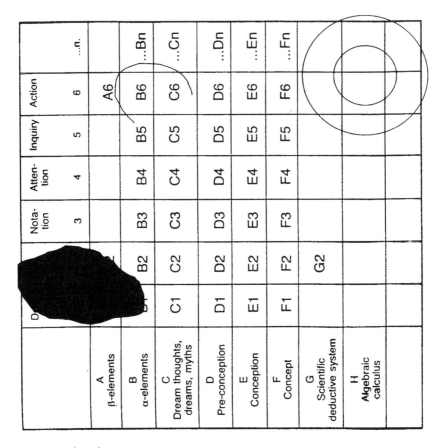

Figure 6.5 Bion's Grid as icon

The emotional experience of the edge

It is important to emphasise that the experience of reaching the edge of our knowing can be unsettling as well as stimulating and fruitful. It can, as a result, set in motion well-worn defensive routines. The edge is not a comfortable place to be.

The image from Paul Klee's etching entitled: 'Two men meet, each supposing the other to be of a higher rank' shows vividly the tensions and defenses that the experience if the edge of not-knowing can evoke (see Jaffé 1972, p.13). Clearly the two men have a real problem. All the usual marks of recognition that would help them to know – to know who the other is and therefore how to behave – all these signals have been removed with the removal of their clothes: 'It is an interesting question how far men would retain their relative rank if they were divested of their clothes. Could you, in such a case, tell surely of any company of civilised men, which belonged to the most respected class?' (Thoreau 1910, p.18)

In the visual language of icons – and Klee's entirely non-specific, rocky background is very reminiscent of an icon – clothing is used to depict the inner state of a person. The removal of clothes or outer garments can therefore signify a psychological change of state, a transition from what is outer and seen to what is covered and within. The problem for Klee's two men, however, is that they cannot give up their hold on knowing. Their transition to what is within simply uncovers their state of inner dependency on knowing. Completely thrown, therefore, by not knowing and by the resulting anxiety, each tries to outdo the other in the depth of their bowing.

The emphasis in Klee's title on 'higher rank' clearly directs us to the picture's social critique. However, this should not obscure the fact that at every level we clothe ourselves with our knowing. So although we may feel somewhat superior to these ridiculous-looking elderly men, their anxiety and deep bowing is precisely what can happen to us every time we bump unexpectedly against the edge of our ignorance. Not to know even the littlest thing can make one question one's competence – and even identity. Just at the moment when working at the edges between knowing and not-knowing can allow space for a new thought, it can also let in the anxiety of one's nakedness.

Ordinary work at the edge

In our experience, the remarkable thing about working at the edges between knowing and not-knowing is that whilst at times it can appear esoteric or mystical – that is, extra-ordinary – it is also, at times, very ordinary and practical. For example, during a recent role-analysis consultation, my [RF's] client said: 'I want to ask you a question. Do you think I'm naive?' Two people had told him that he was naive and he had clearly experienced this as an accusation. He was now seeking some kind of reassurance. I was hesitant but said a few things, feeling as I did so that I was just stalling till I could find something useful to say. For the first time, however – and as a direct result of being engaged in thinking and writing about the ideas in this chapter – I became consciously aware both that I did not know what was going on and that I could actually choose to work as though my ignorance might be the indicator of a potentially creative edge. So I assumed for a moment not that I knew – knew the client, his presenting problem (that is, naivety) or the solution (reassurance) – but, instead, that I did not know and nor did he.

This is clearly a very limited context and a really very everyday encounter. We were not dealing with 'ultimate reality'. However, the imminent truth of that moment was indeed that neither of us knew what we were talking about – and acknowledging that brought about an immediate change. The recognition of not-knowing enabled us to explore what 'naive' might actually mean to each of us – and to the two others, his wife and an aggressively competitive male colleague. For example, why did he assume that to be called naive was derogatory rather than, say, a high compliment? The shift away from our naive assumption that we knew what we meant opened up the possibility for learning in several areas: his own personal and professional history, his expectations of me, of his father, and of his own manager and colleagues, and, as a result, in relation to the leadership and management dimensions of his own role.

Naive versus political: Working with parallel truths

The attempt to work at the edge of uncertainty demands what might be called a 'sophisticated naivety'. This state of mind is reminiscent of the comment attributed to Picasso to the effect that he had learned by the age of 16 to paint as well as an old master, but it took him another 30 years to learn to paint like a child.

The naivety our work demands is the ability to be alive to the impact of each new moment, as though 'born again' in each instant: 'naive' being derived from the Latin verb 'to be born'. Bion's view of analytic work with patients was that 'The only point of importance in any session is the unknown' (Bion 1967, p.272). This is a radical expression of sophisticated naivety.

If 'naivety' involves openness to truth-in-the-moment, the 'sophistication' required is the ability at the same time to remain in touch with *context* and, as a result, to maintain the ability to differentiate between 'truths'. Even in individual work, 'an analyst can not cover all possible meanings of any moment, (Eigen 1998, p.66). Working with groups and organizations, or even with an individual in an organizational role, involves many additional layers of complexity. 'Sophisticated' naivety therefore requires us to recognise that there are indeed many truths in every moment: 'To a certain extent, one can select what O to focus on when' (*ibid.* p.78).

A great part of the skill of the teacher, for example, is to recognise and respond to the truth at any particular moment that will most effectively further the aim operating at that moment. The extreme complexity this involves arises from the fact that the truth of any moment can involve many potentially conflicting emotional, intellectual and/or political needs: of an individual or individuals, of a subgroup within a class or of the whole class, of a colleague or group of colleagues, or of the wider system of department, school or university, or of the local or national community. The excitement and inspiration of the teachers portrayed in the films *Dead Poets' Society* and *The Prime of Miss Jean Brodie* come from a naivety which is radical but not sophisticated: their single-minded belief leads them to pursue only *one* truth. In both films, the ultimate death of a pupil symbolises most graphically the dangers inherent in the exclusion of other 'truths'.

Our suggestion that naivety may be *opposed* to politics is an attempt to capture the complexity of all group and organisational work that incorporates a psychoanalytic understanding of human relations. The ability to select among available truths-in-the-moment depends on the ability to work at the edges between knowing and not-knowing; that is, to recognise a variety of edges, one's own and the client's, and to recognise limitations as well as possibilities. For example, an edge we see as important may be a step too far for the client. Resistance from a client may be a defensive attempt to avoid facing up to a difficult truth, but it may also indicate that we have reached an edge of insight into a previously unknown area which interests us while the client is, as it were, heading a different way and has a different agenda. Entry to the unknown or not-yet-known may, on the one hand, release an individual or group into new areas of creativity or, on the other, make any further working relationship with the client impossible.

A recent case example may illustrate some of these layers of tension between the naivety which can open up a fuller view of the broad emotional, practical, intellectual and political truth-of-the-moment, and the parallel, contingent political truth which may exclude further exploration.

Recently I [PS] was approached by a manager who knew he had a problem – a team which was not functioning properly – and was motivated by a desire to remove the problem by getting the team to work the way he wanted. However, he did not know how to achieve his aim: he had come to the edge of his knowing. He therefore did what many will do in such a situation: he looked for someone, an expert, who would know how to get what he wanted. Some members of his team had worked previously with Bristol Business School and so he approached me for some team-building consultancy. The problem was that I did not know how his aim might be achieved either, nor whether his analysis of the situation was accurate – whether what he *wanted* would be what he *needed*.

As is typical of such instances, it turned out that the situation was indeed much more complex than the manager himself realised. I first conducted a series of diagnostic interviews to try to assess the state of this malfunctioning team – and then spent the subsequent weekend in a state of high anxiety, having been brought very clearly to the outer edge of my knowing and, as a result, also feeling at the edge of my competence. However, I could not give up the desire to know. I could not get the project out of my mind, and tried to find a 'constructive' way to approach it. I saw constantly in front of my eyes a single sentence, spoken by Phil, the manager, which I had written at the top of one page: 'Martin is a problem.' It was so clearly right, partly because of Martin's stance and personality, but partly also because he was being scapegoated. That much was obvious, and it seemed to me important that Martin was offered some individual consultancy – role analysis, perhaps – as a way of helping him to understand and to come to terms with the situation. However, I also could not shake the dark mood that had settled upon me, nor could I get away from the feeling that I was missing the point.

When I met with RF on the Monday afternoon following my troubled weekend, I talked him through the project. The more we talked the greater was our sense of confusion and despair at ever finding an effective way of intervening. The sense of incompetence and mild panic that arises when we don't know was palpable. After about an hour and a half, apparently out of nowhere, RF started to say again what could be done, but this time in terms of what he would like to be able to do, if only it were possible. I felt my dark mood shift. By the time he had finished, we had both realised that we had become completely caught up in the process of the group, the splitting into positive and negative, the scapegoating of Martin, and the despair about ever changing him. What I knew was the historical fact that 'Martin is a problem'. This knowledge stopped me from making the necessary transformation of the truth-in-the-moment that was presenting itself to me: that the dominating pattern within this team was of splitting and projection.

What helped us most was that we managed to continue working explicitly with the awareness that we did not know what to do – even to the point that not only did we not know what to do, we had even lost our sense of how to deal with not-knowing. This double pit, as it were, actually forced us to wait for something to happen.

My subsequent work with this team focused largely on encouraging them to let go of the scapegoating and to explore other possible causes for the blockages in their work together – for example, an overdependence upon the manager, a lack of ability within the team to self-direct, and a huge reluctance to allow each other to make mistakes in leadership. However, I realised at the end of this piece of work that I had based my approach on a false assumption: I had assumed we all shared a desire to find and work at unknown and perhaps uncomfortable truths. This simply was not the case. My own interest in engaging with the truth, whatever it might be, allowed me a degree of naivety that helped me to recognise some interesting and potentially important issues and dynamics. On the other hand, my lack of sophistication blinded me to the *political* truth-in-the-moment, that the manager and I had different commitments. His interest in developing a self-managing team seemed to end at the point where the team might want to do something of which he disapproved. Put bluntly, he wanted them – collaboratively and independently – to reach the decisions he favoured. If they did not, he would almost certainly resort to telling them what to do.

Staying at the edge: A necessary disposition

We have come to realise that in the all too rare moments when we are able not only to recognise that we have come to an edge but also to stay with the experience of not-knowing, we really do not know whether we are doing something or whether something is being done to us. Do we reach for the truth-in-the-moment, or does the truth reach for us? In the same way that Bion wrote of '"thoughts" in search of a thinker' (Bion 1984c, final words), might we think in terms of '"truth" in search of a seeker'?

Reaching the edge of not-knowing and recognising it as such is one thing; staying there is quite another. If knowing does not keep us there, what does? Although the word may not be the best one, we think of this element, to use an ancient term, as a 'disposition' – that is, a state of mind, a way of being, a way of attending to experience. It is this disposition that allows one to bear the experience of encountering an edge.

In writing about his own personal and intellectual development, for example, Paul Tillich chose the image of the 'boundary' to symbolise this experience of living at the edge between knowing and not-knowing:

> The boundary is the best place for acquiring knowledge... Since thinking
> presupposes receptiveness to new possibilities, this position [between alter-
> native possibilities for existence] is fruitful for thought; but it is difficult and
> dangerous in life, which again and again demands decisions and thus the
> exclusion of alternatives. This disposition and its tension have determined
> both my destiny and my work. (Tillich 1967, p.13)

Some people may be more naturally disposed to living on the edge than
others, rather in the way the 'capacity for tolerating frustration' – to which this
disposition may be related – varies from one person to another (see for
example Bion 1962). In addition, many other factors influence the development of the disposition to stay at an edge and the value attributed to doing so
– from the individual's experience as an infant through to the broad culture of
a society, community or organisation. Because the experience of the edge
tends to provoke anxiety, for example, a group or organisation can develop
ways of being, relating and acting, which are designed unconsciously to
protect them against the recognition of the limits to their knowledge.
Defensive habits can then become built into patterns of organising, both into
organisational roles and structures and into ways of relating. This is one way
of understanding the development of 'social defences against anxiety' (Jaques
1955; Menzies 1960) or, from the perspective of systems theory, of systems
archetypes (Senge 1990).

One of the difficulties of even talking about the disposition required to
stay at the edge of one's knowledge – and it is a difficulty we have faced
throughout the process of writing this chapter – is that it is so easy to slip into
making the experience of being at the edge sound acceptable. The uncertainties aroused by the encounter with not-knowing can indeed be exciting and
can provoke significant learning. However, as Paul Klee's image illustrated,
they are often unsettling and anxiety-provoking, confusing and even
terrifying. They can inspire a sense of incompetence and loss of control, and
can obliterate all sense of role and identity and of the task in hand.

The practical, political and emotional pressures on us to *know* are constant
and almost irresistible. It is hard to be called 'ignorant' and to take it as a
compliment, despite the fact that there is a long tradition which asserts the
opposite: 'How can he remember well his ignorance – which his growth
requires – who has so often to use his knowledge?' (Thoreau 1910, p.4) The
disposition which equates growth of mind with ignorance has taken many
forms, from Freud's 'evenly suspended attention' and Keats' 'Negative Capa-

bility' to the 'yoga of knowledge' in the *Bhagavad Gita*. All of these appear in Bion's work.

It is not by chance that one metaphor to describe the emotional experience of not-knowing is of a cloud – not as viewed from a comfortable distance, but with the disorientation and panic one can experience when lost in the fog – the 'cloud of unknowing' (Walsh 1981). Another image is of a dark night – the 'dark night of the soul'[4] (Bion 1984b, pp.158–159). This is not, however, a night as we know the night in our electrified and urbanised experience. It is a truly bewildering and terrifying night, where nothing can be seen, where there are no clear roads as we know them, and where there are, by contrast, real dangers to safety and even to life. This is the basis for Bion's comment that 'In every consulting room there ought to be two rather frightened people: the patient and the psychoanalyst. If they are not one wonders why they are bothering to find out what everyone knows' (Bion 1990, p.5).

The challenge is to stay with the moment rather than to retreat into what Needleman, in an idea reminiscent of Bion's notion of basic assumptions, has called 'dispersal' (Needleman 1990, p.167). Dispersal manifests as a flight from the anxiety of the meeting with the unknown into explanation, emotion or physical action. The method of working at the edges of our not-knowing therefore depends on developing an awareness of one's own particular valency for dispersal, as well as of the strategies of others. Such work requires a training and awareness equivalent to, though not the same as, that of the analyst.

To put it most simply, the disposition required to stay at the edge of uncertainty is one of waiting: 'such "waiting," however, is not dead or inert but intensely alive and accurate in its shifting sense of where the patient [client, student] is moving' (Eigen 1993, p.12). It is 'an attitude of pure receptiveness…an alert readiness, an alive waiting' (*ibid.* p.219). It is a state of openness almost identical to 'the prayer of faith', St John of the Cross's first step in contemplation: 'my counsel is – learn to abide with attention in loving waiting upon God in the state of quiet' (*The Ascent of Mount Carmel*, II, Chapter 12: 11; see also Butler 1926, p.14).

Traditions of this state of mind

Bion and Winnicott both learned to wait: 'to wait and wait for the natural evolution of the transference arising out of the patient's growing trust in the psychoanalytic technique and setting' (Winnicott 1980, p.101). As the

Symingtons put it: 'To the question "How is the analyst to penetrate through the sensuous to the psychic reality?", Bion's answer is that he waits until a pattern begins to emerge and then he *intuits* the psychic reality' (Symington and Symington 1996, p.178; italics in original). To describe this 'alive waiting', Bion used the everyday term 'patience', intending it to 'retain its association with suffering and tolerance of frustration'. With it he described the ability of the analyst 'to be aware of the aspects of the material that, however familiar they may seem to be, relate to what is unknown both to him and to the analysand… Any attempt to cling to what he knows must be resisted…' (Bion 1984a, p.124).

To wait can, however, be the hardest thing to do. Consultant, manager, teacher – and even, ironically, researcher – are all roles where one is inevitably perceived as 'the subject who is supposed to know' (Lacan 1979, p.232). The fear induced by the sense of not-knowing what one is doing really is of catastrophe – possibly as a nameless disaster, but probably as a very obvious one: of one's incompetence revealed, accompanied by a loss of self-esteem, the potential loss of the client – and hence a loss of income.

Underlying the capacity for patience, for alive waiting, is the capacity for faith, which Eigen (1993, pp.211–225) has argued most convincingly is the only effective counter to the fear of catastrophe: 'Faith is openness to truth, to reality, whatever it may turn out to be' (Watts 1983, p.40; see also Simpson 1997).

Bion's own description of the disposition necessary for staying at the edge between knowing and not-knowing is well known: 'Discard your memory; discard the future tense of your desire; forget them both, both what you knew and what you want, to leave space for a new idea' (1980 p.11). In his view, exposure to the unknown truth-in-the-moment demands that the analyst bracket out not only memory and desire, but also understanding and sense perception (1984a, p.43) – even the desire for understanding or the desire for 'cure' (1967, p.273).

This is why Bion was attracted to Keats' notion of 'negative capability' (for example, Bion 1978, p.8; 1984a, p.125). Keats was describing the poet's capacity to wait – and to tolerate the emotional experience of waiting in a state of not-knowing. To have this capacity, he wrote, is to be 'capable of being in uncertainties, mysteries, doubts, without any irritable reaching after fact & reason' (Keats 1970, p.43; see also Simpson, French and Harvey 2002).

Faith in the pursuit of truth – openness to the rich seam of learning that can be mined from the pit of ignorance – can help to get one to the edge, or to recognise those moments when one has, unexpectedly or more or less deliberately, reached the edge of one's knowing. In its turn, the disposition of 'alive waiting' means being able at that edge to attend to the experience of that unique moment, and to survive the encounter with the limits of one's knowledge, in order to let something new emerge, a new thought perhaps, but without any sense of certainty that it will.

All the traditions of this disposition describe facets of 'alive waiting' and an orientation towards the edge of ignorance: 'the slenderest knowledge that may be obtained of the highest things is more desirable than the most certain knowledge obtained of lesser things' (St Thomas Aquinas, *Summa Theologica*, I, 1, 5 ad 1, quoted in Schumacher 1978, p.11). They are also linked by the notion of the discipline, or *askesis*, of learning. Access to truth-in-the-moment may be uncertain, unpredictable and difficult to interpret. However, the disposition on which such insight depends is not random but disciplined: 'The wise student, therefore, gladly hears all, reads all, and looks down upon no writing, no person, no teaching. From all indifferently he seeks what he lacks, and he considers not how much he knows, but of how much he is ignorant' (Hugh of St Victor in Illich 1993, p.16).

In this sense, as we have suggested above, psychoanalysis can be seen as a modern form of the tradition of training which existed in ancient Greece and Rome, and has re-emerged in every age in response to the needs and philosophies of the day: the tradition of 'philosophy as a way of life' (Hadot 1995), learned through the discipline of 'spiritual exercises'.

Ending

In her book *Drawing on the Right Side of the Brain*, Betty Edwards, captures the artist's problem very precisely in terms of the dilemma of knowing and not-knowing. She writes: 'The problem with drawing chairs and tables, as with many other things we might want to draw, is that *we know too much about them*, (Edwards 1982, p.106; italics in original).

Her words are strongly reminiscent of Bion's comment about the way in which, from the very first contact with a patient, the interaction between knowing and not-knowing is of central importance. In one of his lectures he said: 'An individual comes to see me; he thinks I am a psycho-analyst; I think he is a patient. In fact I don't know' (Bion 1978, p.14).

In this chapter, we have struggled with two questions. First, how can we use psychoanalytic theories to bring us to the edge of a new thought? But also, second, how can we let go of all of our theories, psychoanalytic or other, when an experience of truth-in-the-moment makes us face up to our ignorance?

References

Arden, M. (1985) 'Psychoanalysis and survival.' In M. Arden (1998) *Midwifery of the Soul: A Holistic Perspective on Psychoanalysis.* London: Free Association Books, 26–43.

Arden, M. (1997) 'Dreams, imagination and the self.' In M. Arden (1998) *Midwifery of the Soul: A Holistic Perspective on Psychoanalysis.* London: Free Association Books, 102–113.

Armstrong, D. G. (1997) 'The "institution-in-the-mind": Reflections on the relevance of psycho-analysis to work with institutions.' *Free Associations 7*, 1 (No. 41), 1–14.

Bakan, D. (1990) *Sigmund Freud and the Jewish Mystical Tradition.* London: Free Association Books.

Bettelheim, B. (1983) *Freud and Man's Soul.* New York: Alfred A. Knopf.

Bion, W. R. (1962) *Learning from Experience.* London: Heinemann.

Bion, W. R. (1963) 'The Grid.' In W. R. Bion (1997) *Taming Wild Thoughts.* London: Karnac Books.

Bion, W. R. (1967) 'Notes on memory and desire.' *Psychoanalytic Forum 2*, 271–80.

Bion, W. R. (1978) *Four Discussions with W. R. Bion.* Strath Tay, Perthshire: Clunie Press.

Bion, W. R. (1980) *Bion in New York and São Paulo.* Strath Tay, Perthshire: Clunie Press.

Bion, W. R. (1984a) *Attention and Interpretation.* London: Karnac Books. (1970, Tavistock Publications.)

Bion, W. R. (1984b) *Transformations.* London: Karnac Books. (1965, William Heinemann Medical Books.)

Bion, W. R. (1984c) *Second Thoughts.* London: Karnac Books. (1967, William Heinemann Medical Books.)

Bion, W. R. (1990) *Brazilian Lectures: 1973 São Paulo; 1974 Rio de Janeiro/São Paulo.* London: Karnac Books.

Bion, W. R. (1991) *A Memoir of the Future.* London: Karnac Books.

Burckhardt, T. (1982) 'Foreword.' In L. Ouspensky and V. Lossky (1982) *The Meaning of Icons.* Second Edition. New York: St Vladimir's Seminary Press. (pp.7–8).

Burckhardt, T. (1995) *Chartres and the Birth of the Cathedral.* Ipswich, England: Golgonooza Press.

Butler, Dom C. (1926) *Western Mysticism: The Teaching of SS. Augustine, Gregory and Bernard on Contemplation and the Contemplative Life.* Second Edition with Afterthoughts. London: Arrow Books.

Campbell, J. (1988) *The Power of Myth.* (With Bill Moyars.) New York: Doubleday.

Coltart, N. (1985) 'The practice of psychoanalysis and Buddhism.' In N. Coltart (1992) *Slouching Towards Bethlehem…and Further Psychoanalytic Explorations.* London: Free Association Books.

Edwards, D. (1982) *Drawing on the Right Side of the Brain.* Glasgow: Fontana/Collins.

Eigen, M. (1993) *The Electrified Tightrope.* Northvale, New Jersey: Jason Aronson.

Eigen, M. (1998) *The Psychoanalytic Mystic.* London: Free Association Books.

Hadot, P.(1995) *Philosophy as a Way of Life*. Edited by A. I. Davidson. Oxford: Blackwell.

Herrigel, E. (1988) *The Method of Zen*. London: Arkana.

Illich, I. (1993) *In the Vineyard of the Text: A Commentary to Hugh's 'Didascalicon'*. Chicago: Chicago University Press.

Jaffé, A. (1964) 'Symbolism in the visual arts.' In C. G. Jung, M.L. von Franz, J. Henderson, J. Jacobi and A. Jaffé *Man and His Symbols*. London: Aldus Books.

Jaffé, H. L. (1972) *Klee*. London: Hamlyn.

Jaques, E. (1955) 'Social systems as a defence against persecutory and depressive anxiety.' In M. Klein, P. Heimann and R. E. Money-Kyrle (eds) *New Directions in Psychoanalysis*. London: Tavistock Publications.

Keats, J. (1970) *The Letters of John Keats: A Selection*. Edited by R. Gittings. Oxford: Oxford University Press.

Lacan, J. (1979) *The Four Fundamentals of Psycho-Analysis*. Harmondsworth: Penguin.

Louth, A. (1992) 'Denys the Areopagite.' In C. Jones, G. Wainwright and E. Yarnold (eds) *The Study of Spirituality*. 2nd impression (with correction). London: SPCK.

Matthew, I. (1995) *The Impact of God: Soundings from St John of the Cross*. London: Hodder and Stoughton.

McGinn, B. (1992) *The Foundations of Mysticism: Origins to the Fifth Century. Vol I of: The Presence of God: A History of Western Christian Mysticism*. London: SCM Press.

Menzies, I.E.P. (1960) 'A case study in the functioning of social systems as a defense against anxiety.' *Human Relations 13*, 95–121. Reprinted in I. Menzies Lyth (1988) The Dynamics of the Social: Selected Essays, Volume 2. London: Free Association Books.

Milner, M. (1973) 'Some notes on psychoanalytic ideas about mysticism.' In M. Milner (1988) *The Suppressed Madness of Sane Men: Forty-four Years of Exploring Psychoanalysis*. London: Routledge.

Moore, T. (1982) *The Planets Within: Marsilio Ficino's Astrological Psychology*. East Brunswick, N. J: Associated Universities Press.

Needleman, J. (1990) *Lost Christianity: A Journey of Rediscovery to the Centre of Christian Experience*. Shaftesbury, Dorset: Element Books.

Ouspensky, L. (1982) 'The meaning and language of icons.' In L. Ouspensky and V. Lossky, *The Meaning of Icons*. Second Edition. New York: St Vladimir's Seminary Press.

Ouspensky, L. and Lossky, V. (1982) *The Meaning of Icons*. Second Edition. New York: St Vladimir's Seminary Press.

Prokhoris, S. (1995) *The Witch's Kitchen: Freud, Faust, and the Transference*, tr. G. M. Goshgarian. Ithaca, N.Y: Cornell University Press.

Reed, B.D. (1976) 'Organisational role analysis.' In C. L. Cooper (ed), *Developing Social Skills in Managers*. London: Macmillan.

Schneider, T. D. (1994) 'Graffiti on perfectly good paper.' In K. Tanahashi and T. D. Schneider (eds) *Essential Zen*. San Francisco: HarperCollins.

Schumacher, E. F. (1978) *A Guide for the Perplexed*. London: ABACUS.

Senge, P.M. (1990) *The Fifth Discipline: The Art and Practice of the Learning Organization*. London: Century Business.

Simpson, P.(1997) 'The place of faith in management learning.' *Management Learning 28*, 4, 409–22.

Simpson, P., French, R. and Harvey, C.E. (2002) 'Leadership and negative capacity.' *Human Relations 55*, 10, 1209–1226.

Smith, C. (1987) *The Way of Paradox: Spiritual Life as Taught by Meister Eckhart.* London: Darton, Longman and Todd.

Stephenson, R. H. (1995) *Goethe's Conception of Knowledge and Science.* Edinburgh: Edinburgh University Press.

Symington, J. and Symington, N. (1996) *The Clinical Thinking of Wilfred Bion.* London: Routledge.

Tanahashi, K. (1994) 'Preface: On positive emptiness.' In K. Tanahashi and T. D. Schneider (eds) *Essential Zen.* San Francisco: HarperCollins.

Temple, R. (1990) *Icons and the Mystical Origins of Christianity.* Shaftesbury, Dorset: Element Books.

Tennyson, Lord A. (1842) *Ulysses.* In N. Alberry (1994) *Poem for the Day.* London: Sinclair-Stevenson.

Thoreau, H.D. (1910) *Walden.* London: J. M. Dent; Everyman's Library, No. 281.

Tillich, P. (1967) *On the Boundary: an Autobiographical Sketch.* London: Collins.

Walsh, J. (ed) (1981) *The Cloud of Unknowing.* New York: Paulist Press.

Watts, A. (1983) *The Way of Liberation: Essays and Lectures on the Transformation of the Self.* New York: Weatherhill.

Weitzmann, K., Alibegašvili, G., Volskaja, A., Chatzidakis, M., Babić, G., Alpatov, M. and Voinescu, T. (1982) *The Icon.* London: Bracken Books.

Winnicott, D.W. (1980) *Playing and Reality.* Harmondsworth: Penguin.

Endnotes

1. The circle has held some very similar meanings in Western art and architecture. See, for example, Burckhardt 1995, pp.102–4; Campbell 1988, pp.214–8; Jaffé 1964; Moore 1982, p.128.

2. The authors would like to express their gratitude to the Hellenic Institute of Byzantine and Post-Byzantine Studies, Venice, for permission to reproduce 'St George Killing The Dragon'.

3. In Goethe's version of *Faust*, the pact with Mephistopheles is very Bion-like. Goethe's Faust does not 'sell his soul to the devil' unconditionally, in exchange for being provided with everything he might desire. Instead, Faust's soul will only be relinquished if Mephistopheles can offer Faust an experience which satisfies him:

   If I be quieted with a bed of ease,
   Then let that moment be the end of me!
   …

   If to the fleeting hour I say
   'Remain, so fair thou art, remain!'
   Then bind me with that fatal chain,
   For I will perish in that day.
   Faust I, Faust's Study (iii)

Werd' ich beruhigt je mich auf ein Faulbett legen,
So sei es gleich um mich getan!

…

Werd' ich zum Augenblicke sagen:
Verweile doch! Du bist so schön!
Dann magst du mich in fesseln schlagen
Dann will ich gern zugrunde gehn!

(lines 1699-1702)

4. Bion argued that what he called faith (F) is a state of mind that allows the analyst to use 'the piercing shaft of darkness' to shed light on the 'dark features of the analytic situation' (1984a, p.57). Although at this point he derives from Freud the idea of 'rendering oneself "artificially blind"', he is clearly also indebted to the apophatic tradition, as expressed in St John of the Cross's 'dark nights' of the soul and spirit, themselves a reworking of the 'dazzling darkness' of Dionysius the Areopagite (Louth 1992, p.189; Matthew 1995; McGinn 1992, p.175-6). With the need to establish itself as a respectably scientific pursuit in an exoteric age, this dimension of psychoanalysis has remained perhaps necessarily under-explored, although more recently there does appear to be, alongside Bion, a revival of interest. (See, for example, Arden 1985; Bettelheim 1983; Coltart 1985, pp.164–175; Eigen 1993, 1998; Milner 1973). It has been argued by Bakan (1990) that Freud himself was directly influenced by the Jewish mystical tradition. He may also have been indirectly influenced through the impact of his great master, Goethe, who was similarly inspired by these traditions and whose view of science was in radical contrast to Newtonian, reductionist approaches. (See, for example, Arden 1997; Prokhoris 1995; Stephenson 1995.)

7

Narcissism v. Social-ism Governing Thinking in Social Systems

W. Gordon Lawrence

The ego-centric, the socio-centric, thinking and futility

When Wilfred Bion first advocated the use of the 'leaderless group' for officer selection during the 1939–45 war, he was urging that candidates be selected for their ability to cooperate with others. This has to be related to what Bion said on the subject of narcissism and social-ism. In *Cogitations*, which was post-humously published in 1992, where he was working out his ideas before he published them, he wrote in 1960 of narcissism and social-ism as individual-istic impulses:

> These two terms might be employed to describe tendencies, one ego-centric, the other socio-centric, which may at any moment be seen to inform groups of impulsive drives in the personality. They are equal in amount and opposite in sign. Thus, if the love impulses are narcissistic at any time, then the hate impulses are social-istic, i.e. directed towards the group, and vice versa, if the hate is directed against an individual as a part of narcis-sistic tendency, then the group will be loved social-istically... I maintain that in a narcissistic statement, there is always implied a social-istic statement. The two must go together: if one is operating, so is the other. (Bion 1992, p.122)

Even if often unacknowledged, love and hate are basic emotions that are always operating in social systems. In postulating the tension/conflict between narcissism and social-ism, Bion is also indicating the parallel tension, and its underlying reasons, between what he termed Oedipus and Sphinx issues in the group and organisation, and how they interpenetrate each other.

Bion identified the focus of enquiry for system analysis by differentiating the two perspectives that can be taken on groups and organisations. He wrote, in his introduction to *Experiences in Groups* (1961):

> I am impressed as a practising psycho-analyst, by the fact that the psycho-analytic approach, through the individual, and the approach these papers describe, through the group, are dealing with different facets of the same phenomena. The two methods provide the practitioner with a rudimentary binocular vision. The observations tend to fall into two categories, whose affinity is shown by phenomena which, when examined by one method, centre on the Oedipal situation, related to the pairing group, and, when examined by the other, centre on the sphinx, related to problems of knowledge and scientific method. (Bion, 1961, p.8)

It is the problem of thinking, coming to know consciously, knowledge and scientific method, together with the constraints on thinking in organisations and groups that is the concern of this chapter. To state the issue starkly, in organisational consultancy the focus is on Sphinx; Oedipus is left to the therapist in his/her consulting room, or is left as a private matter for the individual. Although narcissism can be interpreted using Oedipal insights, the challenge that Bion sets before us, as I understand it, is to make working hypotheses about narcissism from a Sphinx perspective. It is the thinking that informs the narcissistic state that is to be addressed to satisfy man's curiosity about himself.

The context of this exploration is group relations education as a means of learning of the dynamics of groups, organisations, and social systems in general. Narcissism and social-ism can be seen in all these contexts as they govern the thinking processes of individuals. At worst, group relations education can be seen as a variation on the rescue phantasy that occurs in therapy. This would be to enhance the narcissistic thinking of the participants. At best, group relations education can be seen as providing participants with opportunities to mobilise their social-istic tendencies, by exploring their thinking in relation to the group processes, the politics of the group, the tension between consciousness and the unconscious, between the finite and the infinite, the exploration of *caritas*. And, possibly, the spiritual dimensions of social systems. What is learned in group relations education can be extrapolated to organisations and all social systems. Furthermore, group relations can be an arena in which participants learn the rudiments of 'creative apperception', i.e. learning to rid themselves of compliant patterns of behaviour (Winnicott 1971, pp.65–6).

The *primary task* defines the nature of the work the group, or organisation, has to complete in order to continue to survive. Narcissism and social-ism have to be seen in this context. The primary task will be publicly stated in terms of purpose or mission (the normative task). There are, at the same time, hidden conceptions or understandings of the primary task. These can be at the level of 'what we say we do' (the existential task) and at the level of 'what message our behaviour is saying that we do' (the phenomenal task) (Lawrence 1985, p.236). These three versions of task will always be present. These versions can be used to distinguish the thinking that is taking place in an organisation.

Primary task is a product of thought, either by an individual or a collective. The organisation is brought into being, and continues to survive, through the thinking processes of the people involved. The thinking processes are anterior to the recruitment of people to carry out the work and all the necessary buildings and plant. Subtract this thinking and the organisation would simply be a collection of buildings and machines, existing for no purpose.

Pursuing the notion of thinking, the following hypothesis follows. *The differences in understanding primary task, stated as normative, existential or phenomenal, give an indication of whether the role holders in the organisation are pursuing narcissistic or social-istic goals.*

Narcissism

It is straightforward to identify the immature narcissist and the immature social-ist. They sit at two ends of a continuum. In between there is the mature narcissist and the mature social-ist with the mature, self-managing personality in the centre. Each of these mental positions, or postures, will change according to the context of the environment.

What characteristic marks off the mature from the immature narcissist? The answer is the degree of schizoid characteristics. Ronald Fairbairn discovered the schizoid. Fairbairn was a Scottish psychoanalyst who was a contemporary and was working out his ideas independently of Melanie Klein. Fairbairn gave the concept of schizoid personality flesh. Of the schizoid, Sutherland, who worked closely with and was influenced by Fairbairn in Edinburgh, succinctly summarises:

Adults with marked schizoid features have amongst others three prominent characteristics, even though these may not be overt. They are (a) an attitude of omnipotence; (b) an attitude of isolation and detachment; and (c) a preoccupation with inner reality. As he subsequently points out, it is the last that is the basic feature since the others are derivatives of a situation in which relationships with the outer world have been accorded less emotional significance than those in the inner world. It has to be emphasized, I believe, that these characteristics have one common feature, namely they are attitudes of a whole person; since they have such very early roots, they point to the functioning of the ego as a whole from the beginning. (Sutherland 1989, pp. 97–98)

Notwithstanding Sutherland's belief that the ego functions as a whole in effect, which is a learned response, we are all as human beings subject to the splitting of the ego when we are infants. Few of us can say that we have a totally integrated ego. In actuality, everyone, without exceptions, is schizoid at the deepest level, which can be seen through our dreams where figures in them represent the split-off parts of the personality. As Winnicott said (1971, p.66) 'It is important for us that we find clinically *no sharp line* between health and the schizoid state or even between health and full blown schizophrenia' (italics in original). Whether this clinical observation of Winnicott is true or not is a matter of clinical judgement. The author accepts it from his non-clinical standpoint.

Note on futility

Underlying the schizoid personality is a profound sense of futility. He or she feels that life has no meaning. The idea of futility also means feeling useless, pointless and ineffective. It can also mean focusing on trivial matters, putting aside tragic issues as being too difficult to entertain.

That futility is a condition of being human was well described somewhere by John of Salisbury (c.1115–80):

The brevity of our life, the dullness of our senses, the torpor of our indifference, the futility of our occupation, suffer us to know but little: and that little is soon shaken and then torn from the mind by that traitor to learning, that hostile and faithless stepmother to memory, oblivion.

In a sense, futility is the condition that comes about when we recognise that all will end in death. And no matter what we achieve in terms of learning and understanding, in the end it seems to be for nought. We spend our time acquiring degrees, and the like, to give us a sense of worth but this sense of self pride is also a defence against the horrors of futility. So, what's the point?

As Philip Larkin pointed out somewhere, it is an achievement each day for people to get up and go about their business without being crippled by the thought of encroaching death. If we regard ourselves as being the be-all and end-all, creatures of Oedipus, and do not see, or construe, ourselves as having a place in the struggle for consciousness – in that great multi-millennial long human drama of bringing thinking into being – we can only take up the position of futility.

The schizoid person is such that he/she withdraws emotionally from relationship with their interlocutors with the consequence that they feel ignored. This, as Fairbairn pointed out, means that the schizoid is in an affective state that is similar to what Jung called introversion. The tendency to live the self-enclosed life is always a temptation, not recognising that to join with others is to enter into the thinking processes that are the product of being a human being. In many ways we all evince schizoid behaviour, even temporarily, for all of us feel at various times a sense of hopelessness and futility. The thinking of the narcissist is self-enclosed in the inner world, whereas that of the social-ist is open-ended and engaged with the reality of the environment.

We were born with an intact ego. It was the experiences in the first months and years that caused this intact ego to become split. The mother becoming a rejecting object causes this splitting. The split-off internal object together with the part of the ego that has offered love thus becomes split-off from the ego. It is this sense of frustration when oft repeated that results in a sense of hopelessness and futility. None of us has a perfect childhood. In acute examples, this would result in a pathological state. However, for many of us this does not mean that we are pathological cases, but it does mean that we will always be defending against the basic futility that sits at the core of the schizoid personality.

There is, I believe, once we have first experienced, understood and negotiated repeatedly the oscillation between the paranoid–schizoid and paranoid–depressive positions a second psychic achievement: the tragic position, the recognition that life is tragic and not to be gainsaid. This we may do in psychoanalysis. In this way, a very real possibility of putting this sense of futility into perspective is achieved. The acceptance that life is tragic is the key to this understanding. It is tragic that we shall die. To arrive at the point of understanding that it is the meaning, and the quality of that meaning, that we make for our lives that makes death worthwhile, is a seeming paradox.

We can work creatively with the sense of hopelessness and futility that we all, on occasion, experience. In our worst experiences we wonder if we are a formless blob, worth nothing, a fated person without any hope of rescuing a sense of destiny. At the most profound levels of mood we capture the schizoid sense of futility. If we wallow in it, we become schizoid personalities clinically, bordering on being immature narcissists. If we attempt to work with it – to recognise the meaning of futility (the meaning of meaninglessness) – we can be freed to transcend it by living in a life-giving manner through making meaning to life despite this bedrock of futility and hopelessness.

Fairbairn saw the schizoid state as a diagnostic category. I think that when the schizoid can be seen as a being in a pathological state, we can see the narcissist at work. The mature schizoid, by contrast, with trace elements of the narcissist, has the qualities that make for creativity. This is arrived at when the ego learns to make use of its internal objects (split as they may be) for conscious creativity. It is a working partnership between the inner world of objects and the outer one of objects. It is the result of a triumph of the will of the ego. To be sure, the subtlety of the creative process, and the wish to be original, is to make reparation for destructive impulses; to rework in a life-giving way the deathliness of life. This means taking account of the group and organisational processes and social dynamics that bring about the murder of the human spirit, and that continually impinge on human beings.

The normative primary task can give role-holders in organisations a sense of communal or social-istic purpose that obliterates the sense of individual futility. However, the existential and phenomenal primary tasks can indicate how the sense of futility is being grappled with. The more that these are governed by narcissistic thinking, the more they are expressions of futility.

While the person with schizoid tendencies is never completely mature with a normal personality (who of us ever attains this state of grace?), we do know that provided the regression has not gone too far such people are amenable to analysis, for they show a great deal of insight.

Schizoid phenomena tend to be universal, but as Christopher Bollas describes it, the narcissistic personality, who sits at the extreme of the spectrum, loves him/herself only (Bollas, 1987, p.90), and seeks relationship with no objects in the environment for such objects are construed as being part of their own self-system. The narcissist wants to seduce the other in passive ways as he/she gives the other the image of him/herself. They are always in control. There will be no relationship unless this wish is satisfied. Narcissists wish to exercise power and authority over their object relations.

'By inviting the other to fall in love with his image of himself, the narcissist aims to control the other's eventual effect upon him' (Bollas 1987, p.93). How this comes about is that the narcissist takes over the mother functioning and 'mothers himself in an intense and rigid manner' (p.93) because he has decided who will decide what is the fate of the child as a self. This is because mother has failed to enable the child to establish his/her version of self. This was problematic for him/her as early conflicts with mother were experienced. The result is that the narcissist takes the position of the mother. There had been 'considerable frustration and rage with his mother, so in assuming his own care of himself, the narcissist feels a sense of triumph at gaining control and power over the sources of self-esteem' (Bollas 1987, p.93). Consequently, the narcissist controls the image of self as a way of exercising power over the objects he wishes to influence in the environment.

It is, then, the schizoid, with marked narcissistic tendencies, that is the object of my enquiry, i.e. the immature or primitive narcissist. He/she is someone who pursues his/her own course of action, based entirely on the perceptions of his/her inner world. They are ruthless in pursuing their own ends for they can only listen to the dictates of their inner world. By the socio-centric impulse I take it that Bion means entering into the life of the group and the spirit of the other, through being connected by his/her transference–countertransference feelings.

George Soros calls this 'reflexivity' (Soros 1998, p.47). It is the recognition that we are all connected through our feelings. It is in this context that Soros writes of bias in the value judgements that are always part of economics. Bias is an active ingredient and is difficult to work with because it cannot be measured. The point he is making is that the actual course of events contains the effects of the participants' bias. Although he limits his discussion to economic matters, he is making the essential point that feelings (bias) are present and operating all the time, not least in human relations.

The immature narcissist constrains his/her perceptions of the world to the domain of his/her inner world. They have a solipsistic view of the world, construing it only in terms of their own reality. What Soros calls 'bias', we would term transference–countertransference. The narcissist will demand of the other, 'Take back your projections!' for they always wish to limit the strength of what they are introjecting. They rely on a simple economic model, based on control, of how people relate. They want to feel that they are in charge of themselves and their environment. The socio-centric members of a group, on the other hand, will be interested in these as they determine what is the psychic reality of the group, seeing them as part of the thinking of the group. They will be evincing empathy with, and care for, others.

Social-ism

The socio-centric impulses will come out as a version of social-ism. Here, I do not think Bion was concerned with socialism as a political movement but was addressing more common concerns of being human. Here, we can note that there is an immature form of socialism, a literal denotation, which we have witnessed, and are witnessing, in every totalitarian regime. The group or enterprise then becomes a persecuting, tyrannous being. Here, we see the joining of the immature narcissist and the immature socialistic impulses (cf. President Milosevic and the people of Kosovo and the Serbs).

I understand, for example, when I listen to those who subscribe to Trotskyism, Stalinism and the like that they have desperately to believe in their ideology, which they do as a way of defending against the anxiety of the feeling of utter futility. They have found a ready-made solution to the problems of living, which has the self-important advantage of being a political movement, which takes people out of themselves and allows them to sublimate their ego. To be sure, the same can be said of any other ideology, political, religious, etc. I think that when it is clear that the ideology has to be defended against all enemies – revisionists, and the like – then the funda-mental ideology has to be addressed in terms of being a defence. What to replace the ideology with becomes a pressing, existential question that the individual may not be able to answer for they know that it will drive them mad. In such a mental space the individual becomes an immature social-ist.

When the members of the group are able to mobilise their socio-centric impulses in a mature fashion, we see that there is a possibility of thinking together to create a group, which would be truly more than the sum of its parts. I think that this quality of group life is possible when the participants are in a state of ruth, when they are concerned about the other. This, the opposite of ruthless, is a concern for the human condition.

To quote Bion, 'The group is essential to the fulfilment of man's mental life' (Bion 1961, p. 53). The notion of thinking is of critical importance. Here, I mean the Sphinx that Bion identified, i.e. knowledge and scientific method. The epistemology of group life becomes apparent as 'figure', when the Oedipal phenomena of the participants in the group are made into 'ground'. Bion identifies the thinking that brings about the basic assumptions in which both leader and led can be caught. In this the spirit of inquiry – symbolised by Sphinx – into the human predicament is made manifest.

Scientific method is used to arrive at the truth, which, on occasion, will free us from the futility of facts. Thinking can be seen as a continuous process in which the inhabitants of the universe engage. John Wheeler in an article entitled 'Information, physics, quantum: the search for links' suggested that we construe the physical Universe 'as being a gigantic information-processing system in which the output was as yet undetermined' (Davies and Gribbin 1991, p.301). He coined the slogan 'it from bit' by which he meant that 'every *it* – every particle, field of force, even space–time itself – is ultimately manifested to us through *bits* of information'. I will argue that the key element of this process of generating knowledge is thinking. So everything that exists has been brought into existence through thinking. We deal, although it feels to be non-scientific, with *bits* of thinking that are translated into thoughts, i.e. *its*.

It is essential that we see something of the complexity of thinking in this discussion. Thinking, present tense, is putting into words, though not necessarily, our feelings in the context of an experience. Thinking is the outcome of participating in the nature of reality. For that we not only participate in but also partake of reality, or its phenomena. Once the thinking has occurred it becomes thought. Thought is enshrined in our culture. It is that which has been thought and is memory, which results in the past carried forward into the present.

Bion said that there were thoughts in search of a thinker. This view that thoughts are 'out there' waiting to be thought in order to become 'in here' is daunting, at first. This is because we tend to believe that thinking comes from the individual as an entity, or a self, and that all thinking originates from there. In actuality, it makes more sense to say that thinking and thought are, together, a collective phenomenon. To be sure, individuals connect themselves with this when they think, but they are not originators in any real sense.

Bion developed a far-reaching theory of thinking, based on the work of Freud and on Klein's formulation of the epistemophilic instinct in babies. He writes of mental space, which is represented by the phenomenon of verbal thinking and thought. There are three elements to Bion's thinking. They are 'alpha function', 'alpha-type' elements and 'beta-type' elements. I understand the way he uses the terms as follows. *Alpha function*, which surrounds us, operates on the sense impressions and the emotions. When the *alpha function* is successful, *alpha-type* elements are generated, which then can be stored and used by the individual. When they are not successful because the sense impressions and emotions remain unchanged they remain as *beta elements. Beta elements* are not felt as phenomena but are experienced as things in themselves. They are, therefore, undigested facts and are not available for thought (Bion 1962). Whether alpha functions and the like exist is unknown, but I think that Bion has given us a way of thinking how we take and reject aspects of thought.

In so far as this discussion goes, and simplifying it, it is the quality that the individual brings to bear on thoughts that is important. Thoughts which remain unregistered in the emotions stand still as beta elements. If they are internalised and digested then, since they have now become alpha elements, they are available for further thinking and dream work, which is the basis of thinking.

So we have the idea that thought is memory, which is present around us, but that we can each think in relation to what has been thought if we can register thoughts emotionally and internalise them. When alpha function is successful, thoughts become alpha-type elements.

Memory is a collective phenomenon, which, once we entertain it, takes us into the phenomenon of the flow of meaning between people. This is to acknowledge culture in its widest sense. This flow of meaning is more fundamental than any particular thoughts through the actual thinking of an individual. Here the emphasis is on the group, collective effort with individuals seen as a private, idiosyncratic mixture of the collective whole of values, meanings and intentions. The flux that is the interaction between these is the source of new thinking.

Furthermore, thought is a product of the context of the body, the emotions, the intellect, the reflexes and cultural artifacts, which exists in an unbroken field of mutually informing thought. All these components interpenetrate each other. They do so to such an extent that we are compelled to see 'thought as a system'. Included in this system is thinking as a wave function, which occurs all the time either in the buzzing confusion that is our minds or in dreaming, but occasionally it will objectify as a particle.

This holistic perspective on thought and thinking apparently goes against the cultural experience of being in society. In society, we see thinking and thought as being fragmented. We carve thinking and thought up to determine causal relationships, for instance. This is despite the evidence that thinking about the world in this specific, obsessive way goes against the evidence that thinking is the outcome of synchronicity. We live in a world in which factors and events are related in random, surprising ways, i.e. in a non-specific world – 'the chaosmos of Alle', as James Joyce put it in *Finnegans Wake*.

Thinking (Sphinx) in social systems

The immature narcissists' deeply schizoid characteristics preclude their thinking, except in terms of themselves in their self-contained inner world. In particular, narcissists preclude themselves from what we would term the essentially unconscious aspects of thinking, as they occur in social systems. They cut themselves off from thinking of the 'unthought known' (Bollas 1987), and from thinking as dreaming.

There are, I am postulating, four types of thinking: first, thinking as *being*, which is really culture and how we think of ourselves in relation to groups and social systems. Second, thinking as *becoming* which is the process we undergo as we think what we, or the social system, could become. Third, thinking as the *unthought known* and, fourth, thinking as *dreaming* (Lawrence 1999, p.303). The first two types are what we do every day, the latter two in the shadow. They are, respectively, of the 'here and now' and the 'there and then': the present and the future.

Thinking as the unthought known

This refers to the innate thinking that we were born with. It could be said to be part of our imprinted inheritance. It is the thinking that we are part of because we are human. To be sure, it will depend on fate how much of this thinking can be mobilised in life. Fateful circumstances will elicit this unthought known and leave large areas of it to be unused. Similarly I submit that circumstances of destiny will call out of us feelings and thoughts that we never knew we had. I think of people who are called to fill a role and surprise everyone by their capacity to do it. I have always believed that we should always be offering roles to others, which, on the face of it, are beyond their competence. They continually surprise us by being able to take and make the role in an extraordinary way, although there will be disappointments.

We have to consider the 'shadow of the object', which is the shadow the objects of the environment left on the ego in early nurturing. The shadow is carried as a trace throughout life. The child cannot necessarily process this through mental representation but the object (mother, in the first instance) always affects us even though we have not thought of it. Hence, it is an *unthought known,* which is a permanent presence in our lives, though it seems as if it is absent because it is out of consciousness.

In groups and social systems at large, there are as many unthought knowns as there are people. How do we access them? We do so through the use of our countertransference feelings. In groups we tend to limit this to the feelings about authority and those who would exercise leadership over us. But these feelings are not readily identified. 'The most ordinary counter-transference state is a not-knowing-yet-experiencing one' (Bollas 1987, p.203). The not-knowing state is important in the role of taking a group. It is from the consultant who is in a state of un-knowing that one learns the most in a group relations conference. Essential, in my view, is the readiness of the taker to experience countertransference feelings by creating an inner space in which he/she can be available for them, as a route into discerning the transference feelings.

In reliving the group's transference it means that the individual participants of the group's representations of the disturbed bits of the infant self will be experienced in the transference image of the taker. So the room, so to speak, will be full of unarticulated bits of the participants' egos.

We know, then, of the unthought known when we recognise the transference and countertransference feelings that are evoked in social systems as we interact with others. And I believe that these sets of feelings have mostly been denied in many group relations conferences in the last few years. Clearly, this sweeping generalisation has to be modified. The more the staff of a group relations conference feel under the compulsion to provide unequivocal certainty, avoiding all not-knowing, the more they mobilise the narcissistic aspects of themselves. Consequently, they are not available for the ambivalent transference and countertransference feelings of the participants. In effect, the totalitarian state of mind takes over with the disappearance of social-istic, or socio-centric, concerns.

It seems to me that the taker's task is to make available material of which the taker may not yet know the unconscious meaning. This is possible depending on the taker's relation to feelings and thoughts. So to try to grapple with the unthought known the taker will ask him/herself, 'How is the group using me?' After thinking the taker will employ terms such as, 'What occurs to me,' or 'I am thinking that,' or 'My hunch is,' or 'My working hypothesis is,' as a way of generating, or resuscitating, feelings of what is, as yet, known but not thought.

The taker, if you will, is providing a facilitating environment for the group. The key to this is how the taker regards his/her own thoughts. One's own thoughts as a taker are subjective states but they can be put to the group as objects in the space between the taker and the group, in the 'third space'. As such they are transitional objects to be played with, to be scrutinised, rejected, accepted and made into something which symbolises or, better still, gives thinking substance, in some measure, to the feelings of the participants in the group for the taker.

The object is to facilitate the exploration of thinking, particularly in the area of authority and leadership, which has hitherto been inarticulate or inchoate, by making it available for verbal representation. The thinking is about authority, etc. If we can get the phantasy to be made available for inspection we can make the unthought known that much more available for examination. The articulation of the unthought known will make a difference to the life, and the quality of its truth-searching aim or mission, of the group or social system. Otherwise it becomes futile. Here, I think, it is essential that the reality be different from the phantasy because it can then be explored with the taker knowing that he/she is exploring from a state of truth.

The unthought known, and people acting on the basis of it, we can see in Bion's basic assumptions (Bion 1961). The wish to be dependent, as in a baDependency group, is the wish, based on the shadow of the object, to be in a state where all one's needs are catered for. The unthought known is acted out through the baD group.

Similarly one can discern the unthought known(s) in all the other ba groups, which are expressions of the inarticulate elements of the psychic life of the participants. At the same time, we have to recognise that basic assumptions are a primitive form of social-ism, because they are where the participants act out their common concerns. The exception is basic assumption Me-ness (baM) (Lawrence, Bain and Gould 1996, pp.28–55), which is fuelled by ego-centric, narcissistic preoccupations.

Dreaming

When a participant offers a dream in a group, the dream almost always illuminates the truth of the situation in which the group is. This has been found repeatedly. The group, in a sense, becomes a dream screen. A dream, in my view, is always a synthesis of the reality. To be sure, it will be coded. It is, however, as Fairbairn showed, a symbolic narrative of the state of affairs that exists in the inner world as the subject interacts with his/her environment.

Recently on a consultation project which used only social dreaming, I found that the dreams illustrated exactly the situation the clients were in. One participant dreamt of finding the lineaments of a garden hidden by weeds. This expressed the desire of the group to find their roots and to clear away all the detritus of their history in order to find something that they could collaborate around.

The truly creative person is able to make use of his/her dreams constructively in thinking out some new puzzle that is exercising them. Writers, such as R. L. Stevenson and Graham Green, consistently made use of their dreams in their fictions. The chemist Kekule dreamt of a snake that illumined the structure of the benzene-ring and there are many more examples. The truly creative person is able to accept the phantasy of the inner world and put it to use in the external one.

My point is that dreams have to be taken very seriously in group relations conferences. There are differences between the analyst and analysand dream exchange when it occurs socially. First, we have to rid ourselves of the idea that a dream is personal possession. Second, a group provides a container which is different from the classic dyad, and consequently the content of the dream changes to fit the environment for receiving it. (For a discussion of the potential of social dreaming, see Lawrence, 1998.)

The dream also allows us to access the unthought known. In a social system this will often be the secret that everyone knows but no one will talk about. It is held subliminally, below the threshold of consciousness. Once voiced it makes a difference to the system. This is because once the significance of its meaning is made explicit the import and repercussions of it will be acknowledged. If it is brought to the surface of discussion through association and amplification a consensual, agreed meaning will be created.

I would argue that social dreaming be part of the configuration of events of a group relations conference because it is a method of getting to grips with the unthought known(s) of the conference and, incidentally, shows participants the use of dreams, as a form of thinking. Social dreaming has been democratising the use of dreams for about twenty years.

There are other factors to be taken into account. Dreaming is the missing link in evolution. I think that the simplest of cells undergoes a form of dreaming, proto-dreaming, in which the cell is thinking out its relationships with objects in its environment. It is reworking and rehearsing how it will relate to its environment for sustenance and make relationships that will enable it to survive.

Dreaming is always in the form of images in which the subject is also an object. We see the dream from a different, almost omnipotent standpoint, while we are engaged in it. As such, dreaming is always a form of thinking. Remember that all dreamers are thinkers, to echo Bion.

Implications for social systems

To summarise points made so far: the narcissist, who is an extreme form of the schizoid, preoccupied as he/she is with self, precludes him/herself from thinking of the unthought known, and thinking as dreaming. This has far-reaching consequences. I believe we have moved into a social world where narcissism is rewarded publicly: so much so, I believe, that we operate in a society, and its institutions, in which one basic assumption that people work on is that of basic assumption Me-ness, which hinges around survival of the individual. In short, this is the schizoid character that always wants to retain the good, and export the bad from his/her inner world, who works on the simple equation that: good = inner; bad = outer, to state the matter starkly (Lawrence, Bain and Gould 1996).

I see this in group relations conferences where the members will at times become so caught up in their own egocentric worlds that larger social-istic concerns are not part of their agenda. They have come to a conference to learn about groups and their functioning, but they don't want to learn. If you will, they don't want to be sullied by the experience of being in the messy world of basic assumptions. They *know about* basic assumptions. Not for them the infantile feelings experienced in ba Dependency; nor the pain of a failed ba Pairing relationship; and certainly not the mixed emotions of being in a ba Fight/Flight grouping. But as they pursue this existential primary task of 'learning by acquaintance', as A. K. Rice phrased it, they become caught in this other basic assumption group, which I call Me-ness. Then, they feel they will be safe from the horrors of experiential learning, which would result in their *knowing of* basic assumptions and the work group, at first hand.

Once individuals can recuperate their ego functions, they move into the world/group/organisation, which is being driven by the impulses in the indi- viduals of social-ism. Their preoccupation becomes socio-centric and they are able to mobilise their mature narcissistic qualities. They quit the Oedipal world and enter that of Sphinx.

This immature narcissism is rewarded in British industry and commerce, and has been since the Thatcher era. Think of the leaders in British business. Like all narcissists they are consumed by the need for success. They wish to be number one, to be *primus*. They are selected to cope with the anxieties and fears of the employees. The anxiety is about being in a global economy where events and happenings are increasingly non-specific, by which I mean that we are living in a time of synchronicity, to echo Jung. There is the real anxiety of being downsized and made redundant, of losing one's job, of becoming a nothing. The selectors, who are unwittingly caught up in this anxiety, select someone who, they feel, will be sure, certain, and offer vision (or some such phrase), by promising to 'put some backbone' into the business. The immature narcissists are remarkably clear in their perspective for they have no doubts – because they split-off any doubts and ambivalence.

Once selected, they make a draconian decision, which will be some form of rationalisation of the business. They set attainable goals. This works fine for a time, but fails ultimately because their original interpretation of the business-in-its-environment gradually ceases to be in touch with reality. They can no longer generate working hypotheses that can keep up with the changing reality of the business.

The business operates, at first, on a collusive basis. The followers need the certainty of the leader to enable them to defend, even to deny, the anxiety they hold. Gradually they become aware that they are living and working in a business environment that is characterised by a totalitarian state of mind. Thinking which will disrupt this is not allowed, and to pursue this thinking is a sure way to find oneself looking for another appointment. The totalitarian state of mind lasts as long as the followers in the business can keep themselves out of touch with their inner worlds of objects, keeping themselves blinkered, in thrall to their anxiety. Once the followers rescue their ego functioning capacities, a revelation of the true state of the business occurs. As a result the leader has to leave, well endowed with pension funds, to look for another position, where he/she will repeat the same process.

The immature narcissist is always exercising a degree of power and authority over his object relations. He/she tries to recreate a closed society, as Karl Popper identified it. As he put it:

> ...civilization has not yet fully recovered from the shock of its birth – the transition from the tribal or 'closed society', with its submission to magical forces, to the 'open society' which sets free the critical powers of man. (Popper, 1945, p.1)

The closed society operates on kinship in terms of symbolic meaning, or social image, or inherited social rank. Who marries whom becomes very important.

In an open society, people strive to rise socially, based on meritocracy. This is the basis of democracy.

Narcissists are against civilisation (and all it represents), against thinking that would lead to an open society, because they know that their chances of survival are enhanced in a closed society. For them, the survival of the individual is more important than the survival of the group. A closed society is a tribal society based on family and kinship. A meritocracy is based on contest mobility, which limits the use of family ties and kinship. Narcissists hate contest mobility for they know that survival depends on creating a system of nepotism and cronyism, i.e. the exercise of power.

But, most important of all, narcissists are against thinking. They hate it. And, more important, they hate it so much that they destroy the capacity for thinking. In other words, they take on psychotic-like qualities. This means that the unthought known and dreaming have to be discarded and other forms of thinking (being and becoming) are diminished.

To conclude: in group relations education we have the continual puzzle of trying to focus on Sphinx while being aware of the Oedipal factors that each participant brings to bear on the situation. We do this by concentrating on the nature and quality of the thinking in which the group/system engages.

We also have to recognise the struggle between the egocentric (narcissistic) impulses and the socio-centric impulses (the social-ism), which is a dilemma every participant faces. They are caught in the forces of love and hate. We are always, in our role as group takers, mobilising Sphinx in a social-istic fashion. Oedipus is held in mind. By this is meant the nature and quality of thinking. This invokes the processes whereby participants come to know in a subjective way why they are pursuing narcissistic preoccupations, and why these are militating against the pursuance of common human ends and spontaneities that transcend individuals. The way into this is to conceptualise the unthought known and dreaming. This we do by making available our countertransference feelings and thinking through working hypotheses.

Bion firmly holds the view that:

> ...the experience of counter-transference appears...[to] enable the analyst to differentiate the occasion when he is the object of a projective identification from the occasion when he is not. The analyst feels he is being manipulated so as to be playing a part, no matter how difficult to recognize, in somebody else's phantasy – or he would do if it were not for what in recollection I can only call a temporary loss of insight, a sense of experiencing strong feelings and at the same time a belief that their existence is quite adequately justified by the objective situation without recourse to recondite

explanation of their causation. From the analyst's point of view, the experience consists of two closely related phases: in the first there is a feeling that whatever else one has done, one has certainly not given a correct interpretation; in the second there is a sense of being a particular kind of person in a particular emotional situation. I believe ability to shake oneself out of the numbing feeling of reality that is a concomitant of this state is the prime requisite of the analyst in the group; if he can do this he is in a position to give what I believe is the correct interpretation, and thereby see its connection with the previous interpretation, the validity of which he has been caused to doubt (Bion 1961, pp.149–150).

By being able to work with the transference and countertransference feelings, I submit that we are able to work with the futility (unthought known) that every person experiences at some point in their lives. Futility and tragedy are closely linked. And the connection between them we can often see in dreaming.

The acceptance of tragedy and seeing the interaction between the forces of destiny and those of fate is the mature position. This means, I believe, seeing narcissists as always generating tragedy around them with the people they relate to. The social-ists, on the other hand, are aware of the transcendent forces at work in their environment, and able to see that in groups and social systems they are entering into the perennial issues and problems that face every human being, as they have from time immemorial. This can be summarised as: 'Why are we here?' and 'What is the purpose of our being here?'

I used to see group relations as being about the opportunity to learn about groups, to learn about the unconscious processes at work. But now I see group relations education as being about learning and internalising a methodology for understanding the interplay between the finite and the infinite, the conscious and the unconscious, i.e. thinking. This methodology needs to be re-affirmed, relived, and re-established in every working conference.

As part of this methodology, I see the experience of re-thinking the bases of narcissist impulses, tolerating the thought processes that split the ego in infancy, and the discovery of the emotional impulses of social-ism as being the triumph of a group relations education. This is how we learn of the myth of Sphinx, i.e. about thinking, scientific method and how we arrive at knowledge. Once we can grapple with this we enter into the domain of mature human beings, able to face the meaning of futility and tragedy and to make meaning for a creative life.

References

Bion, W. R. (1961) *Experiences In Groups*. London: Tavistock Publications.

Bion, W. R. (1962) *Learning from Experience*. London: Maresfield Reprints.

Bion, W. R. (1970) *Attention and Interpretation*. London: Tavistock Publications.

Bion, W. R. (1992) *Cogitations*. London: Karnac Books.

Bollas, C. (1987) *The Shadow of the Object*. London: Free Association Books.

Davies, P. and Gribbin J. (1991) *The Matter Myth*. London: Viking.

Fairbairn, W. R. D. (1952) *Psychoanalytic Studies of the Personality*. London: Tavistock Publications.

Lawrence, W. G. (1985) *Management Development… Some Ideals, Images and Realities*. Washington DC: A. K. Rice Institute.

Lawrence, W. G., Bain A. and Gould L. (1996) 'The fifth basic assumption.' *Free Associations, Vol. 6*, Part 1, No. 37.

Lawrence, W. G. (1998) (Ed) *Social Dreaming at Work*. Karnac Books: London.

Lawrence, W. G. (1999) 'Das Denken im Spiegel der Organisationen. Das Endliche und das Unendliche – Das Bewußte und das Undewußte.' *Freie Assoziation* 2 Jahrgang, Heft 3/99.

Popper, K. (1945) *The Open Society and its Enemies* (1966 edn.). London: Routledge.

Soros, G. (1998) *The Crisis of Global Capitalism*. London: Little, Brown and Company.

Sutherland, J. D. (1989) *Fairbairn's Journey into the Interior*. London: Free Association Books.

Winnicott, D. W. (1971) *Playing and Reality*. London: Tavistock Publications.

Part III

Bion as Pioneer in Thinking, Learning and Transmitting Knowledge

8

Transcending the Caesura:
The Road Towards Insight

From *Experiences in Groups* to *A Memoir of the Future*

Lia Pistiner de Cortiñas

P.A.:   Seductive possibilities, concealed in the wide range of options available, will ultimately compel the growth of a capacity for discrimination – or catastrophe.

Robin: Why catastrophe?

P.A.:   Because unless the human animal learns to become expert in discrimination, he will be in imminent danger of the wrong choice.

Alice: Nuclear war, for example.

P.A.:   There are no labels attached to most options; there is no substitute for the growth of wisdom. Wisdom or oblivion – take your choice. From the warfare there is no release. (Bion, *A Memoir of the Future*, p.576 Volume 3)

I. Introduction

The ideas Bion developed in group research were brought together in his mind with his observations as a psychoanalyst, in a symbiotic container –

contained relation, resulting in developments of great depth, that are awaiting further evolution.

His style of writing, unsaturated, open, presents the reader with the challenge of going through the experience of not understanding, of doubts, mysteries and uncertainties; and stumbling across the impossibility of enclosing his ideas in neat pigeonholes of understanding.

My attempt in this paper is to outline some of Bion's open-ended issues.

The first of these issues is his suggestion that a science of relationships (not of the related objects) has to be developed, to further research in psychoanalysis and in social functioning, in groups, institutions, etc. This science has its peculiarities: its object of investigation is animated and not sensorial, it belongs to the psychic domain, and changes while being investigated. It also modifies the researcher who is taking part in the observation; therefore methods have to be developed that will adjust to these specific problems.

Thus the second issue refers to the methods Bion suggested for the investigation of the relationship: binocular vision, oscillation and alternating use of different vertices, observation and correlation of what is observed from multiple vertices, reversible perspective, are some of the names he gave to these methods. So the macroscopic vertex of group observation can be correlated to and complemented with the microscopic vertex of psychoanalytic investigation.

The third issue, which will be the focus of this paper, will deal with what Bion has called the developmental conflict when addressing the problem of evolution and mental growth.

In *Attention and Interpretation* his model of mental growth is the achievement of an evolution in the direction of respect for truth and concern for life. The problem of mental growth transcends the formulation of making conscious the unconscious or Kleinian integration.

> ...personality does not seem to develop as it would if it were a piece of elastic being stretched out... (Bion 1977b, p.47)

Growth takes place by layers, like the skins of the onion. Between each layer there are caesuras that have to be traversed to promote a meeting, a dialogue between the different parts. A method to make possible an encounter has to be found. Its aim is to try a reflexive dialogue where each part could listen to the other: either between the primitive, prenatal, protomental aspects and the more sophisticated, post-natal ones, or between the BA-group functioning and the work–group functioning, or between the primitive mind and the separated one, etc.

The problem in traversing the caesura towards mental growth is not only that of the neotenicity[1] of the infant, (Bianchedi, Pistiner de Cortiñas *et al.* 1999) that needs the mother's alpha function to grow and develop, but also the neotenicity of the species, that in order to achieve maturity has to develop discernment and 'becoming' responsible.

The development of methods of scientific approach, even rudimentary ones, is essential, since human beings also produce with great intelligence instruments for an active un-knowing.[2]

I want to include the terms 'caesura' and 'vertices' in this introduction because I think they will help understand some of the issues I am trying to deal with in this paper.

Caesuras and vertices

In his paper 'Caesura', by means of the metaphor of the caesura of birth, separating intra-uterine from postnatal life, Bion (1977b) approaches the fascinating and difficult investigation of the still embryonic or rudimentary mind of our species whose evolution can lead as much to genius as to psychosis.

Bion extended the term that he borrowed from Freud to a complex notion of gap, fissure, space, bridge, having the function both of separating and communicating.

Caesura can also be thought of as a 'trans' zone (Sor and Sennet de Gazzano 1988), an area of transition, that has to be traversed by those elements that are in a transformational state.

Caesura is a zone that separates two regions of the personality (primitive mind/separate mind), two modes of functioning (BA and work group) and traversing this zone threatens catastrophic change because this is where the different aspects can meet, and this meeting causes turbulence. Catastrophic change is a dweller of this zone and also an indispensable factor to develop capacity for insight, which is the only way to understand mental growth.

The title of this paper refers to the implications of traversing caesuras, from BA-group functioning to work-group functioning, not in one direction but in both, to promote dialogue and controversy. 'Controversy is the growing-point from which development springs, but it must be a genuine confrontation and not an impotent beating of the air by opponents whose differences of view never meet' (Bion 1970, p.55).

For a scientific approach to the facts it is necessary to define the vertex from where observations and statements are formulated. When this vertex is made explicit then it is possible to establish a relation between the different vertices. A fruitful dialogue requires that caesuras be permeable.

II. Individual and group: Two observational vertices – a science of relationships

When Freud discovered transference, after he had already begun to understand the nature of unconscious processes, he laid the grounds for a science of relationships. Bion, in the course of his work, was able to bring together,[3] his experiences in groups with his research in psychoanalysis to further the development of this science. 'A science of relationships has yet to be established and one would look to find some discipline analogous to mathematics to represent relationship of one element in the psychic personality with another.' (Bion 1970, p. 64)

Bion suggested that there was a link between his work with groups and his work with individual patients. The subtitle in *Attention and Interpretation*: 'A scientific approach to insight in psycho-analysis and groups', implies a common ground for both of them. I think that the nature of this link lay in his method of work: a scientific approach to insight through attention disciplined by negative capability, and interpretation of the emotional experience.

At the heart of this approach is this receptive and disciplined attention to the present and presented emotional experience.[4] At-one-ment with 'O', with the emotional experience evolved from 'O' is the ground of in-sight.

We usually tend to situate the emotional experience within the individual, as if it were coincidental with his anatomical aspects. Bion draws attention to the fact that the emotional experience seldom remains within the limits of a purely individual space. Psychoanalysis itself is rather more the investigation of the emotional experience of the working pair, of what is taking place between them.

The group setting allows for the observation of different constellations of emotional experiences and different mechanisms for dealing with these constellations. Working analytically with groups, or organisations, implies turning attention to the emotional experience presented in those settings as the means for understanding, formulating and interpreting the relatedness in the group or the organisation. The understanding of this relatedness is what allows the discovery of the emotional experiences and the meaning of what working and being in the group or the organisation turns out to be.

The method Bion proposed for understanding relatedness was the investigation of the caesura:

There is much more continuity between autonomically appropriate quanta and the waves of conscious thought and feeling than the impressive caesura of transference and counter-transference would have us believe. So...? Investigate the caesura; not the analyst; not the analysand; not the unconscious; not the conscious; not sanity; not insanity. But the caesura, the link, the synapse, the (counter-trans)-ference, the transitive-intransitive mood. (Bion 1977b, p. 56)

A Memoir of the Future is written in the style of a dialogue between different characters, including Bion and 'Myself', Tyrannosaurus and Stegosaurus, 'Captain Bion' and 'P. A.', Sherlock Holmes and Moriarty, 'PS' and 'D' (the positions), the scientist, the priest, the devil, prenatal states, EM (mature), somites, the boy of 14, the man of 40, the man of 80, the heart, etc. Different characters attempt various forms of dialogue; some of them show that communication has been achieved, others give evidence of its failures.

This 'psychoanalytic science-fiction novel' is also part of Bion's search for a science of relationships, showing the kind of caesuras that hinder dialogue and insight, and those that facilitate it. A discussion and reflection, by means of a dialogue, between different modes of functioning would help to develop a capacity of discernment, contrasting with rivalry, which is a serious obstacle. This book, at times disturbing, shows in dramatic form the difficulties and possibilities of dialogue.

The first part of this trilogy[5] called 'The dream' starts with a 'dream/indigestion' and with an attempt of observation from two different vertices (from the arse to the tonsils and from the tonsils to the arse-hole).

Waking up leads to awareness of an invasion and the pages of a Bible scattered all around. Do these represent catastrophic change and the invasion of thoughts without a thinker? Does the Bible allude to the institutionalisation of a BA mode of functioning?

Rosemary, the maid, is leaving. Alice, her mistress, dismisses her without any concern for what is going to happen to her. The submissive maid pleads with her until, because of the invasion, she becomes aware of Alice's fear. A chain of events takes place and suddenly they lead to a homosexual or sexual and sadomasochistic relationship between the two women.

There is an automatic reversal of roles that remains all through the book: Rosemary, who seems to represent the primitive aspects of the mind, vital and with some life experience but also cruel, will become the 'mistress' and Alice, who represents the 'educated' aspect, in my view educated for emotional disconnection and hypocrisy, will become the submissive maid. At times Alice seems to acquire wisdom, and so does Rosemary. This is how Bion represents the meeting between the primitive and 'civilised' parts. The invasion seems also to represent a threat of change that could end in catastrophe.

Characters vary in their manifestations, displaying different aspects of themselves. A kind of language is presented as primitive but vital: as some words used by Rosemary are considered 'rude' but convey authentic meaning, exposing the language of Alice and Roland, her employers up till then, as an educated, 'civilised' language but hypocritical, used for lying, a language used as substitution for thought, and not for communication. In other manifestations the primitive emerges transformed into violent and destructive action: Alice is thrown out from her bedroom by Rosemary and ends up in the servants' room where she is raped by Tom, the 'brute' and until then submissive servant.

That is to say, what first emerges when traversing the caesuras is the threat of catastrophic change with its features of subverting the system, violence and invariance that pass transformed into the new system. In this case a form representing the invariance is the relationship of mistress and servant, or sado-masochism: Rosemary and Alice change places but the essence of the relationship does not change.

There are attempts of establishing dialogues, language of achievement emerges as an instrument through poets, musicians, etc., which to this day has not achieved the aim of being used by mankind for developing insight.

Gratitude shows up in the last book, *The Dawn of Oblivion* as a factor of transformation in the relationship: The 80-year-old man owes gratitude to his 'Somite 3', like the tree to its seeds. Will Psyche and Soma be able to establish a dialogue at some stage where Psyche will be receptive to pain and not only to gratification, and Soma might be receptive to the meaning of words and not only to the noise?

Some characters are changing and ambiguous and their moves are unpredictable. The most mysterious one is 'Man': is he an invader? Does he come from the Future? Does he carry a bar of chocolate or an automatic gun in his holster? Will he marry Rosemary, the primitive part, and kill Roland? Anyway his attitudes are arrogant and threatening through the book.

Meanwhile Bion, Myself, Sherlock Holmes and Moriarty, the P. A., the Priest, the scientist, etc., try a dialogue, where others, like the Devil, take part. Another unique character is Du: he can be 'do' (action) and also 'Du' the German for 'thou' (Bion quotes Martin Buber's 'I and Thou' in *Caesura*.) Once more dialoguing is difficult and depends from which vertex and which side of the caesura it is seen. 'Du' can be action that substitutes thinking, or action as prelude to thinking or a thought transformed into action.

A Memoir of the Future is a name with polysemia and I believe that it is also this quality that Bion thought useful for a science of relationships: as a pre-conceptual, non-saturated science open to new 'realisations'. I think it is a science that has to investigate continuity through caesuras, and growth through the discontinuity of catastrophic change.

I would now like to point out briefly some of the factors for the development of the 'science of relationships':

(a) tolerance towards recognising turbulence

(b) tolerance for the observed turbulence to be thought of and considered in words

(c) tolerance towards the decision: to the selected fact as the articulator of the observation

(d) tolerance towards uncertainty – negative capability (Keats) as a factor, or, as Freud wrote, to cast a beam of darkness on the dark spot, to avoid being dazzled by the light of what is already known, of what is saturated

(e) tolerance towards co-operation.

III. Emotional development

'The infancy of the species coexists with its more developed functioning, both scientific and not scientific.' (Pistiner de Cortiñas, 1999)

The emotional experience is ineffable, but traversing caesuras towards mental growth requires transformation and formulation: transformations from K to O (at-one-ment) to intuit the emotional experience that is evolving and transformations from O to K to formulate them.

Bion distinguishes at-one-ment', to become one with oneself, that is the road to insight, from 'atonement', which means expiation, sacrifice, and is related to the operation of the primitive 'super'-ego $\otimes e\tau$, that with –K operations obstructs the scientific discrimination between true or false.[6]

On the other hand, the road of private and public communication has to be cleared of the primitive tendencies towards evacuation, of action as a substitute for thinking, and turned into the field of transformations where thought is the prelude to action. The automatic functioning of BA, the emotional primitive forces, is inescapable. It is not enough for the work group and/or the thinking operations of the personality to develop devices for establishing contact with external reality. Psychoanalysis with its microscopic lens focused on relationship has made valuable contributions and has developed instruments such as the need to think and become aware of the transference–countertransference phenomena.

Growth cannot take place without taking into account primitive emotional functioning. In the same direction, it is also an urgent problem for developing research into the interaction between the production of instruments through technological skills and the development of emotional growth towards wisdom.

IV. The challenge of investigating the caesura

Working with groups provides an opportunity to observe the interaction between the emotional situation that is seemingly restricted to the individual and the way it spreads out and affects other members of the group.

One of the disadvantages of the group situation is that the anatomy of the participants may seem so dominant that one tends to assume that the personality is likewise delimited by the physical appearance.

Sometimes those 'dramatic or impressive' caesuras of being in the presence of several persons makes it difficult to observe that the personality does not end in the anatomy of an individual. So the relational field, generated by the underlying BA and protomental functioning through the invisible net of crossed projective identifications, is obscured.[7]

Based on his experiences in groups and his subsequent psychoanalytic investigation of the psychotic and non-psychotic parts of the personality, Bion acquired a profound understanding of the problems in the relational field generated by projective identification.

A model to think about this and be able to become aware of a peculiar communicational network could be a group of mushrooms: the observer sees the mushrooms separated one from the other and scattered over a great area: if an infra-red picture were taken, we would see, instead of the mushrooms, the network that unites them.

Caesuras can act as opaque screens, barriers against communication, so an urgent need is the development of articulating caesuras. A model for this articulation is Picasso's painting both sides of a plate of glass which leads to the persistence of a barrier, which at the same time is permeable and allows communication.

Bion described a contact barrier as the permeable structure that allows differentiation and contact between conscious and unconscious functioning. I think that this contact barrier acts as an articulating caesura, that makes thinking (private communication) and public communication possible.

In the domain of psychic reality (non-sensuous) we should enlarge our field and explore the infra- and ultra-sensuous spectrum. So there is also a need to construct sufficiently large and resistant screens, like radio telescopes to be able to receive also the 'interference'.[8] Changing the vertex is important: once someone heard the interference instead of hearing the music and thus radio astronomy was born (Bion 1977b, 1989).

If tolerance to catastrophic change is developed and the relation is investigated, then a broad spectrum of events in the personality and in the group is laid open for investigation:

- between mental states awake and asleep
- between pre- and post-natal mental states
- between group mentality and the individual.

Bion suggests studying the total personality; and he visualises the latter as if it were a group of different aspects within one personality. And he also suggests considering the 'total group', with its different operating modalities, which become, in the last part of his work, the relation between the mystic, the group and the Establishment.

Each caesura, when traversed, implies that the previously achieved equipment is disarticulated. If it cannot be disarticulated, this equipment acts as ballast in the turbulence and hinders a new creative articulation.

Intense saturated preconceptions (different from unsaturated preconceptions) of a group with no disposition to confront a crisis by contacting new facts, generate obstacles for this process of articulation and disarticulation in a growing spiral.

Messianic, saturated expectations take the place of preconceptions, stimulating such intense feelings that the group can become resistant to any emotion whatsoever, for fear of turbulence. No task in the group is exempt from this problem.

An omnipotent, omniscient leader, as a means for problem solving, is part of the BA-group functioning. For the work group there is no messianic leader, or in any case the leader is the idea or the task, and the problem-solving method includes contact with facts, with reality and with the passage of time. BA functioning does not get on well with preconceptions since it cannot tolerate the anxieties generated by development and whatever is undetermined and unsaturated. The predominance of this kind of functioning entails the risk of creating a caesura that might also become an impermeable barrier to the extent of reaching the degree of prohibition. This barrier is erected to protect or preserve a previous, archaic mode of resolution. It sets up caesuras between present, past and future, that by becoming impermeable, become also an impediment for further development.

Instead, sometimes, illuminating ideas become permeable caesuras and if a symbiotic container–contained relationship between the idea and the group exists then it can lead to development. Once the illuminating idea has been accepted and established, if the members of the group are able to see the problem, then they seek the solution. But again, if the solution does not remain with an unsaturated part, it turns irretrievably into a closed situation.

There is no solution for ever: the solution to a problem always reveals a field of problems undiscovered hitherto. This means that the development of personality in a psychoanalysis as well as that of a task in a work group is dependent on the possibility of tolerating the anxieties raised by the open-ended search, and of the building of a mature container to contain anxieties that arise because of the features inherent to the investigation.

Decisions on what method is used to deal with mental pain are made in the community, in the family, in the group, in the individual. Decisions are reactivated as emotional turbulence. The proposal of psychoanalysis is the treatment of this turbulence through thinking and discussion. This implies a considerable process of maturation and 'maturation involves *being* responsible' (Bion 1965, p.155).

Caesuras as inaccessible barriers might bring about catastrophe both for the individual and for the group if circumstances should stimulate development and pressure to traverse it. If a latent turbulence is activated by an external or internal event, and if the barrier between different modes of functioning becomes inaccessible (through evasion of pain) instead of being a contact zone, then the barrier can be broken and provoke a sudden catastrophe: psychosomatic, somatopsychotic, a psychotic breakdown, a social breakdown, etc.

V. Primitive/evolved, encounter and turbulence

His experience as an officer in a tank unit in the First World War, and as an army psychiatrist in the Second World War left a deep impression on Bion. In his paper 'The Grid' he says:

I do not believe, and nor does anyone else who has had close contact with men in battle conditions, prisoners of war or civilians in similar stress, that the feelings of men and women either as individuals or as members of a group have changed: they are dormant. Often they are covered by a veneer of civilisation which however, does not conceal though it might disguise the forces beneath. (Bion 1977b, p.23, 1989)

…there may well be some analogue in the personality to the capillary blood system which in ordinary conditions is dormant but in extraordinary conditions may dilate in surgical shock. The analogy would be such hyperstimulation of the individual or of the individual 'groupishness' that his capacity for conscious, sophisticated behaviour seeps away into his 'unconscious'. (*ibid.* p.24)

Omnipotence – omniscience – god, together with the symmetrical elements, helplessness – incomprehension – agnosticism, are the abstract statements of the basic group. (*ibid.* p.29)

So an issue present since Bion's early work and onwards is the coexistence within one and the same personality, and within a group, of different modes of functioning, separated sometimes by impenetrable caesuras, and its implications for the insight of psychological problems.

Bion conjectured that those prenatal forces that press the neotenic creature to get rid of his 'sensations/ideas/emotions' are still active, and thus archaic thoughts that have remained inaccessible can erupt in this passage of caesuras, with the risk that instead of a transformation with contained catastrophic experiences, the emotional turmoil can lead to a catastrophe. When transformations occur in –K, this change is close in different degrees, but always very near, to a real catastrophe (Pistiner de Cortiñas 1999).

The mind is still a very premature, rudimentary and powerful development that can evolve towards psychosis, creativity or destruction. Man has developed thought and language as instruments, and also produced technological development. All these very powerful instruments can be used in dissimilar ways: at the service of destruction or at the service of concern for life and truth. A disturbing question arises: where will this development lead when what is still in an embryonic state in a neotenic creature develops?

If we take the infant as a model, developing its potential does not only imply growth towards life. Destructive potentialities also exist in it: a baby with potentially murderous, predatory aspects lacks the appropriate physical development to translate this impulse into action. Alternatively the capacity for transformation in hallucinosis is greater in the neotenic state because it has still not developed enough reality principle and maturity for discrimination. The terrors of the baby are more intense because he has no 'names' to bind the constant conjunction and thus help him to discriminate and stop the terrifying explosion.

Growth, continuing with the model of the baby, can take place creatively, if terror meets with receptive and detoxifying parental functions that lessen the dread, giving it a name, giving it a meaning.

Failures of this function are substituted by what seems to be a moral conscience. Bion has described it as the 'super'-ego, which appears endowed at the same time with destructive potential as murderous 'super'-ego and inhibitor of growth capacities.[9] The individual, the group, has to become able to discern between mental growth and 'division and multiplication – cancerous, not qualitative increase' (Bion 1970, p.127).

Growth directed towards development of wisdom involves decisions and making choices of methods to deal with mental pain: evasion or modification. The choice of avoiding pain leads the personality and the group to develop the wrong methods to solve problems, which can lead to destruction. Thus an equipment for denial of reality develops instead of an equipment for discernment and growth.

Any institution, group or instrument can be enlisted for one purpose or the other:

> For the apparatus of denial, endopsychic and social, is formidable indeed if it is to be effective as it is in fact... Nor can his labours cease at the borders of his own personality: as the scientist has to seek the aid of groups, institutions, elaborate apparatus, and social support as well as maintain his mental acumen, so the individual oriented to frustration evasion has to enlist the aid of, or actually initiate, social institutions to help in the task of denial of reality. The actual social institutions need not differ: those used by the scientifically orientated and by frustration-evaders can be the same but used differently. It is obvious that a psychotic will use the institution of marriage, the family and state differently from the frustration-modifier. (Bion 1992, pp.99–100)

In this statement one can follow Bion's articulation of his experience with groups and his psychoanalytic practice with patients with psychotic functioning. From the latter he learned that the psychotic part of the personality has enough reality principle and uses it to preserve his 'apparatus to evade reality and frustration', using the institutions for this purpose and enlisting them in his cause.

So the coexistence in the individual or in the group of more primitive and more developed functioning generates emotional problems that are not only concerned with performing a specific task. The emotional turbulence has also to be solved. Different forms of thinking about the problem of this coexistence have emerged all along the history of thought, but all unsatisfactory until now.

As we know, in *Experiences in Groups* (1961) Bion had the opportunity to observe and describe two modalities of group functioning: the BA group and the work group. He then introduced the idea of specialised work groups as those who are in charge of dealing with the emotions of the BA, trying to avoid a transformation into action. How does the specialised work group perform this task to find a way to neutralise the BA group's emotions preventing them from translating into action, and at the same time perform the task of containing a new idea?

Bion's description of how this twofold task is carried out by the known specialised groups (church, army and aristocracy) is very interesting: to prevent the translation of the BA emotions into action, but providing at the same time an outlet, the specialised work groups, for example the church, will adjure the group to thank God when presented with the achievement of a task. Thus there is an outlet for their longing for 'awe and reverence', or the search for omnipotent and omniscient leaders. At the same time the specialised work group tries to avoid that the BA-group functioning should become incarnated in a leader, because this translation into action would be highly dangerous.

The BA group functioning has a very limited repertoire, pervaded by basic emotions hostile to contact with time or any other event or idea that stimulates development. The threat is the new and unknown idea that promotes change and growth. If the work group is able to contain the BA-group functioning, the task can be done, although not without difficulties.

As well as discovering transference, Freud also discovered and conceptualised as something unwavering in human beings man's instinctual basis and the conflicts that arise when he becomes 'human', 'civilised'. In *Civilisation and its Discontents* (1930) he was quite pessimistic about the future of the relation between drives and culture. On the contrary, Bion depicts a more hopeful perspective in *Experiences in Groups*:

> I attribute great force and influence to the work group, which, through its
> concern with reality, is compelled to employ the methods of science in no

matter how rudimentary a form; I think one of the striking things about a group is that, despite the influence of the basic assumptions, and sometimes in harmony with them, it is the work group that triumphs in the long run. (Bion 1961, p.135)

He maintained that the individual is a group animal, at war with the group as well as with those aspects of his personality that constitute his 'groupishness'. Bion thought that this war was not limited to a conflict with 'civilisation' (Freud) and that other issues existed which had to be examined. He introduced the idea of groupishness, the 'political animal' condition and the group mentality as an inherent factor of human beings. This becomes manifest in a group but it does not cease to exist in an isolated individual.

Bion used splitting and projective identification, the mechanisms described by Melanie Klein, as instruments for his observation of groups. His experience as a psychoanalyst with very disturbed patients was articulated with what he had already observed in groups to conceptualise that the personality can be fragmented and those fragments be evacuated, not only at an omnipotent phantasy level. This evacuation is performed through realistic projective identification which produces real effects. Contagious functioning produced by projective identification can be observed in groups and it should not be forgotten that no relationship is immune to the erosion brought about by the externalization of internal relations. The ability with which people manipulate others to play the roles in the drama of their phantasy life, or in Bion's terms, their 'waking dreams', is only surpassed by the enthusiasm by which those people are ready to take part or to play those roles.

Bion made a great contribution to the concept of countertransference in psychoanalysis, partly as a result of his observation of group functioning, which L. Grinberg used for the concept of projective counter-identification:

> Now the experience of counter-transference appears to me to have a quite distinct quality that should enable the analyst to differentiate the occasion when he is the object of a projective identification from the occasion when he is not. The analyst feels he is being manipulated so as to be playing a part no matter how difficult to recognize, in somebody else's phantasy – or he should do it if it was not for what in recollection I can only call a temporary loss of insight, a sense of experiencing strong feelings and at the same time a belief that their existence is quite adequately justified by the objective situation... I believe ability to shake oneself out of the numbing feeling of reality that is concomitant of this state, is the prime requisite of the analyst in the group...in a group treatment many interpretations, and amongst them the most important, have to be made on the strength of the analyst's own

emotional reactions. It is my belief that these reactions are dependent on the fact that the analyst in the group is at the receiving end of what Melanie Klein has called projective identification, and that mechanism plays a very important role in groups. (Bion 1961 p.149)

These experiences with groups and with psychotic patients led to the expansion of the development of the technical instruments that Bion brought forward in *Attention and Interpretation* (1970), suggesting the discipline of 'without memory, desire and understanding'.

The concept of counter-transference, broadened along these lines, can be applied advantageously outside the consulting-room, to indicate when pressure from a group induces a person to lose, albeit temporarily, his insight with regard to his emotional state.

Will this contribution help to develop methods that will apprehend, contain and transform primitive functioning creatively as an equivalent of an alpha function?

If we take into account neotenicity (born immaturely) not only of the baby, but of the species, we face a vital question: which would be the counterpart of the reverie function of the mother in the work group, or which could be the specialised working group that could perform this task (alpha function) of transformation?

This work group has to be able to carry out a twofold function: the specific work-group function, and the containment and insight of primitive emotions, preventing the danger of translating into action, which would lead to catastrophe. The problem of containment, insight and transformation of the primitive is very intricate, and undoubtedly neither the tasks demanded by the adaptation to the outside world, nor the offering of a way out in the mode of the 'classic' specialised work groups, are sufficient to solve it. Psychoanalysis and research in groups have made their contributions but there is still a lot of work to do.

VI. Mystic, group, mental growth and catastrophic change

Bion's development in the course of his work led him first to formulate the problems posed by learning from emotional experience and subsequently to consider the different facets of what he called mental growth. The conflict that emerges through this new conceptualisation is described as the one between *knowing about and becoming*, between thought and substitutive action and between faith and lies. The heading, under the title *Transformations*, is

'From learning to growth'. The underlying model is that of an expanding universe.

The terms genius, mystic, Messiah and group emerge in reference to the problem of developing insight in this task of growth. Also the term 'Establishment'. The genius and the Messiah can be easily invested with the features of the leader of the BA group and thus become an obstruction for growth.

Bion uses the term 'genius' again in *The Grid* when he refers to the problem of the liar, and in *Attention and Interpretation* when he says that many times genius has been said to be akin to madness. Bion suggests that a genius is required to deal with psychotic mechanisms adequately.

With much humour and irony he describes in *The Grid* that when he had to begin to write papers, give conferences, etc., he found himself regretting not having been born a liar. He immediately realized that he was deploring the lack of the one characteristic which is in fact inborn, though it had to wait, as always, for the genius to reach its full capacity. 'In this case the genius, or group genius, who invented speech released the liar from his bondage' (Bion 1977b, p.20, 1989).

Any primitive prenatal characteristic has to wait for the genius to develop its full capacity, but this characteristic can be creative or destructive and also the genius can lead towards growth or towards destruction.

The term 'mystic', can be understood as the mystic idea: the unknown idea, the idea still not developed. The mystic (implying the transformations in O: at-one-ment) is necessary to contact the idea, but also the group is necessary and the transformations in K (disposition to discover and formulate the discovery) so that the idea can be used by common people who are not geniuses. The mystic makes direct contact with the Godhead (the unconscious in psychoanalysis). This contact needs a disciplined opacity towards the senses, memory, desire and understanding.

Bion introduces the term 'Establishment' as a bridge spanned between the mystic and the group. The group needs the mystic, the mystic's idea revitalises, nourishes the group. The mystic also needs the group to prevent the idea from producing a disintegrating effect in him (megalomania?).

The function of the Establishment in the direction of growth, is to perform the task of taking the mystic's innovative idea and transforming it so that it becomes tolerable for the group. This transformation allows also for the group to make use of the creative idea.

The messianic idea is an unknown idea that is hated and feared at the same time. Frequently the group (in BA functioning) tries to deal with the idea through projection and materialisation. Thus the idea is 'embodied' in a person: it is no longer an idea but something much less frightening, a person or a thing.

Punning once again with a lot of humour and irony, Bion says that physical persons can be detained, either by idealisation (and proving that they are not real) or by realisation (and proving that they are not ideal). But it still is difficult to determine the rules of psychic growth.

In the relation between the mystic and the group an emotional pattern can be observed that will be repeated in the course of history although it adopts different forms. Bion suggest that we have to learn about that pattern in order to be able to find creative ways of dealing with the coexistence not only of primitive and sophisticated functioning, but also with its destructive and creative manifestations. In the development of Bion's ideas related to the dynamics and functioning of groups, the bipolar model proposed initially (BA group and work group) becomes transformed into the relation between the mystic, the group and the Establishment. The investigation of this relationship as a container–contained relationship, which can be symbiotic, commensal or parasitic, offers a new instrument for the research of problems in the relation between primitive functioning and work-group functioning.

The container–contained relationship can be envisaged with two different models:

> 1. The military model: one force containing another, keeping the other one in check. This is a model for thinking about two modes of functioning, BA group and work group, psychotic part and non-psychotic part of the personality, like two forces where one tries to obstruct the progress of the other. There cannot be growth in this model, nor development towards growth. It is a model of rivalry: there can be truces, balance, usually unstable, temporary compromises, but it leads neither to change nor transformation towards growth. Its major success could be to obstruct the 'enemy's' progress, its worst option is to annihilate it. In my opinion this is the model that Bion puts forward when he describes the kind of transference operating in the relationship when there is a predominance of the psychotic part of the personality: it can be transformed from planar to lineal and *vice versa*, but it lacks the depth of the container–contained relationship that I will now describe.

> 2. A relationship on the model of a container with receptive qualities and a content with a penetrating quality. Significantly Bion uses for this model the masculine and feminine signs ($\lozenge\,\sigma$) that have the characteristics of an abstraction but also contain the common matrix of the emotional

experience they emerge from. This model also emerges as a way of conceptualising the relation between the projective identification of the baby, a
content with a capacity of penetration, and the container–receptive quality
of the mother's reverie. This is also his model of the origin of thinking.

When there is a *symbiotic* container–contained relationship (two who get
together to mutual advantage and/or for the benefit of a third party)
projective identification is used in a communicative way and is detoxified and
transformed into meaning, thus it can become a preconception open to new
meanings. In terms of groups, it is the Establishment in a symbiotic relation
with the messianic idea that carries out the container function, which
detoxifies and attenuates the disruptive quality of the new idea, so that as a
nutrient it can be accessible to the group that lacks the qualities of the genius.
These characteristics of the relationship are growth factors.

In the *commensal* relationship, container–contained live together without
making contact, without establishing a relationship. The caesura is very wide,
thus no conflict ensues. This is what happened with the heliocentric ideas of
Aristarco of Samos, that did not arouse conflict and were forgotten in favour
of the geocentric ones. Galileo's ideas did provoke conflict and were finally
accepted. Is controversy, conflict, the tension of conflict necessary, if the possibility of transformation towards growth is to exist?

The *parasitic* relationship between container and content is a mutually
destructive relationship. Projective identification is explosive, destructive of
the container. The proliferation of splitting might happen, as Bion describes
in *Experiences in Groups*, as a result of aberrant changes. The container is also
destructive for the content.

VII. Emotional growth and catastrophic change

Mental growth is timeless and catastrophic. In order for development to take
place the relation between container and contained has to be symbiotic.

'Catastrophic change' is a term used by Bion to point out a constant conjunction of facts, whose realization can be found in the mind, in the group, in
the psychoanalytic session, in society. The facts that the constant conjunction
refers to can be observed when a new idea appears in any of these areas. The
new idea has a disruptive force that threatens a more or less violent break-up
of the structure and the organisation where it is expressed.

The change towards growth involves the transformation of a structure or
part of it. This transformation cannot occur without moments of disorganisa-
tion, pain and frustration. The already existing organisation has to be

disarticulated, the newly achieved implies a choice, that is to say, tolerance for what has not been achieved and also towards the incertitude about the newly revealed problems undiscovered hitherto. The model container–contained can be used to study these vicissitudes: the new idea can be considered the contained, and the mind, the individual, the society a container, or *vice versa* together with the investigation of the relation and the possible interactions.

I come back now to the problem of the relationship between the mystic, the group and the Establishment. As I already said, the mystic can be either creative or destructive. At best he will be creative, but the nature of his contributions is certain to be destructive of the laws, conventions, culture and therefore coherence of the group.

The Establishment's function is to achieve an adequate containment and representation of the new idea, attenuating its disruptive character and at the same time making it accessible to the non-genius members of the group.

The disruptive force of the mystic will or will not be contained, according also to the means of communication he uses, the vehicle of his message. If projective identification is his means of transmission it will stimulate BA group phenomena. In this sense Bion suggests a language of achievement, which is the one that contains a high degree of negative capability, because of its creative and change-promoting quality of traversing the caesura between the mystic and the group. It is a language that does not operate as a substitute to thinking, it has thinking as a prelude and is at the same time open, unsaturated.

VIII. Language of achievement, caesura and growth

In the relationship between the mystic, the group and the Establishment, the recurring configurations that Bion brings from history are those of a potentially explosive force within a framework that tries to contain it. History also shows that to this day this never has been quite achieved.

Growth depends on a symbiotic container–contained relationship, which supposes the existence of links in the direction of concern towards life and respect for truth, links that Bion named: L (love), H (hate) and K (knowledge). It also ineluctably implies confrontation, crisis and conflict because the concern towards life meets what is potentially destructive in our circumstance of predatory species, and the respect for truth has to deal with the inclination to avoid pain and frustration through deception.

Change towards growth is vital for the individual, for the group, for society. The tendencies towards growth coexist with those that oppose them and even the new 'endowments', the achievements, the 'inventions', such as, for example, language, can be used to oppose or destroy growth.

Besides the destructive factors... 'To dare to be aware of the facts of the universe in which we are existing calls for courage' (Bion 1979, p.248, 1990). Scientific methods, even if rudimentary, are those that tend to modify pain as well as develop the capacity to tolerate unavoidable pain involved in the facts that we call 'chance' and 'decision'. The pain-evading methods are false solutions, because they are deceitful and toxic. The 'basic assumption' in psychoanalysis consists in the use of the psychoanalytical function to amend deceitful solutions.

Psychoanalysis and experience seem to demonstrate that when the work group is engaged only in making contact with problems of external reality, caesuras become very rigid and impenetrable and the primitive mental states (BA) become isolated or have turned automatic, while the proto-mental (autonomic) remain confined, without transformation, to the neuro-physiological, neuro-humoral systems.[10]

We must also take into account the evidence of compromise solutions that keep the system clear of crisis, maintaining thus in operation a set of unobserved primitive beliefs, in parallel to developments where the emphasis is placed on any achievements related to the external world. The latter are often manifestations of 'enforced splitting' (Bion 1962), dissociating material gratification from emotional experience, restricting the relation only to the material, because of survival motives. In my opinion this last configuration predominates in the present, in the aspiration for more and more technological development and materialistic success.

These are false solutions, given that they avoid conflict but cannot protect or prevent succeeding evasions from becoming unbalanced at some stage, and with this comes the feared emergence of disruptive emotions as a catastrophe.

If we take the model of an earthquake-proof construction, we see that it requires equipment with a certain degree of plasticity, of flexibility, to traverse the caesuras towards growth. This raises the question about what equipment is needed to be able to conjugate identity and organisation together with an openness that can maintain a factor of unsaturated preconceptions ready to approach new realizations?

In a way scientists of the hard sciences have acknowledged a certain epistemological modesty, stating that scientific hypotheses have to be refutable (Popper), and also inquiring and trying to answer the question on changes of paradigm (Kuhn). But this has always taken place in the field of reason and in relation to inanimate and sensorial objects.

But what equipment must a work group use in the field of a science of the animated, non-sensorial, human – an equipment that should provide an alpha function, a scientific equipment to make contact and understand both the emotional as well as the external reality? In what way is it possible with scientific equipment to approach the facts of the 'domain' of psychic reality, the emotional experiences, belonging either to the spectrum of 'narcissism or of social-ism' (Bion 1992)? The problem thus stated presents at least two slants:

The first is that the objects of this 'domain' are a-sensorial but they express themselves mainly in very crude terms that stem from the experience of sensuous reality, arising from our animal nature. Thinking and communicating can only have their realisations by means of sensuous forms. This can lead to deceptive devices of communication. There is a need to widen the spectrum towards the infra- and ultra-sensorial, beyond the animal sense experience.

The second aspect is related to something common to all human beings beyond the deceptive separation into races, religions, languages and the temporal distances of different historical epochs, and it refers to the relation between man's group functioning as a herd animal, subject to the emotional turmoil of BA, and the development of the separate mind with as yet very rudimentary instruments.

> Our concern is how this 'domain', usually left to be 'dealt' with by geniuses, is to be managed by ordinary humans. Nietzsche says a group must produce or find a genius; how is it to recognize and preserve it when found? Can Freud's theory of consciousness be extended to the whole human mind and the object of its attention to whatever lies 'beyond'? (Bion 1977a, p.118, 1989)

In the domain of psychic reality the task of the group work mentality is not only containing but also investigating how to achieve insight into primitive functioning. This is the task of the 'separate mind' (Bion 1963) and it stimulates anxieties because it is felt as an experience of detachment from the vital sustenance base. Participation in the primitive BA mentality is felt as vital, even if it leads to catastrophe, while separating from the state of herd animals brings about the realisation of our profound dependence and a feeling of social isolation, loneliness and helplessness.[11]

The conflict between the work group and primitive mentality is fundamental and leads to transformations. No possibility of real growth exists
without this prospect of contact.

The larger the predominance of the BA mentality, the more limited will
the space for thinking be. The coexistence between both modalities of functioning always occurs and is inescapable. It is present in the caveman as well as
in his modern successor, technological man. Furthermore, primitive mentality
in technological man is much more dangerous since it is masked by a sophisticated logic and it is endowed with an overwhelming strength. Only when the
evolved aspects resonate with the primitive ones can we affirm that we are in
the presence of a possibility of real development in the group or the
individual. But the investigation of the meeting in the domain of psychic
reality cannot be done other than with instruments that stimulate both
meeting and turbulence. In psychoanalysis this is obvious: the meeting
between analyst and patient through transference relationship establishes an
inescapable area of disturbance. As anyone who works with groups and
organisations knows, the same is valid for the investigation in groups.[12]

In his search for instruments Bion, true to himself, resorts to more than
one vertex and maintains the need to alternate them. Abstractions, formulations in increasing levels of abstraction (the Grid) without alternation of
vertices, run the risk of becoming, like pure mathematics, an empty manipulation of signs without meaning.

Therefore he suggests also, as a complementary and revitalising alternative vertex, a 'psychic digester', the use of myths, dreams, dream thoughts, the
C row as a verbal picture gallery.

To avoid this becoming only a pictorial, anecdotal illustration, and
therefore an inevitable distortion of the facts it attempts to represent, he
proposes that this 'verbal picture gallery', which emerges from artistic and
cultural functioning, be used as preconceptions, that is to say with an unsaturated quality, like nets to 'fish' the unknown. Its function is that of a receptive,
exploring thinking, similar to the function Freud ascribed to attention in
relation to the outside world and an aspect of Bionian reverie in relation to
psychic reality.

On the other hand, he says in *The Grid*: 'The practising psychoanalyst, the
portrait painter, the musician, the sculptor, all have to 'see' and demonstrate,
so that others may see, the truth which is usually ugly and frightening to the
person to whom the truth is displayed' (Bion 1977b, p.31–32).

But neither psychoanalysis nor investigations in groups have reached a point where truth can be communicated without the presence of the objects which have to be 'demonstrated'.

I think it is interesting to put together the psychoanalyst who has to 'demonstrate' psychic facts in the presence of the 'object' in his practice, with artists who attempt to capture emotional experiences and transform them into some kind of sensuous shape. Great changes in artistic movements have also produced turbulence that astonishes us even today. Why did the Impressionists produce such turbulence when their intent was only a new way to represent the light, a new vertex?

A microscopist cannot be constructing his microscope while he is looking through it, though he may be adjusting his powers of observation to the defects of the instrument (Bion 1977b).

Which are the defects of the instrument used in the investigation of psychoanalysis and groups? Even though the mind of the investigator is the ultimate interpretative instance of any instrument, this fact is much more obvious in the field we are concerned with.

This means that it is the instrument that suffers the turbulence of this encounter and when traversing the caesuras between the BA group and the work group, between the genius, the Establishment and the group, etc. That is why Bion suggests the use of two kinds of instruments (the Grid and myths) to exercise and train the equipment for intuition and observation.

The Grid is to be used outside the session, to exercise the capacity to elaborate imaginative conjectures and relate them with observations done during the psychoanalytic session.

Bion's use of myths as instruments implies using them as an unkown (incognita), as 'radiotelescopes' open to unknown facts or those that have not happened yet, which the different parts of the myth, acting as a receptive net, could help display and illuminate. 'The Oedipus myth may be regarded as an instrument that served Freud in his discovery of psycho-analysis and psycho-analysis as an instrument that enabled Freud to discover the Oedipus complex' (Bion 1963, p. 92). Bion chose several myths (the Garden of Eden, the Tower of Babel, the Death of Palinurus, the burial at the cemetery pit in Ur) and used them as preconceptions in search of clinical realisations.

The oscillation or alternation of vertices demands tolerance of a conjectural level, tolerance because what is illuminated from one vertex casts a shadow that can only be observed from another vertex, and finally tolerance because the pre-conceptual level entails that the point of arrival of the observation of one problem is also the starting point of another.

As an open-ended conclusion of this paper I would like to illustrate some of the ideas using as a pre-conceptual instrument a movie, *2001, a Space Odyssey*, that I suggest can be thought of as a 'memoir of the future' of its director, Stanley Kubrik.

I think that culture generates, especially from the artistic vertex (literature, cinema, theatre, art, etc.) formulations of emotional experiences that interact in different ways with the emotional experiences of different personalities and groups, developing a function that in my opinion is comparable to the reverie function: a detoxifying, digestive, provider-of-meaning function. Such formulations open a space for thinking.

The movie starts with a pack of monkeys acting savagely. Suddenly a monolith appears whose meaning the monkeys don't understand. They start to move around the object with increasing unrest. One of the monkeys takes a large bone and uses it to break other animal bones and skulls. Whilst he is playing he suddenly turns serious as if hit by an intuition.

In the following scene the monkeys are drinking water at a well. A pack of rival monkeys, from which they always had to run away, appears. The monkey with the bone, who understands how to use it as a killing instrument, faces them and kills some of the rivals. In the following scene the bone is thrown into space and the camera follows it. A big leap, and the movie passes to the space age. A spaceship is exploring.

The appearance of the monolith is the reference point of a new, meaningful development, 'catastrophic change' in Bion's words. Another tool, the computer Hal, starts to become aware of itself inside the spaceship headed towards Jupiter. It is a very developed computer from the point of view of the capacity of technological thought, but it has not developed the capacity to tolerate frustration, the capacity for emotional growth. At some stage it makes a mistake when estimating the resistance period of a piece of the ship's equipment, and another computer on earth points this mistake out; Hal cannot tolerate making a mistake and develops an overwhelming fury, which he expresses by killing astronauts.

In the first scenes of the film what is represented is the moment of evolution when the hominid traverses the caesura of birth from an 'embryonic mind' with intuition and capacity to play (banging bones and skulls) and with a potential of fight and flight, to a thinking mind capable of discovering instruments and using them. In the following sequence this capacity provides the up-to-then defenceless animal with the possibility of protection, and this, the bone, becomes a weapon, not only to defend himself but to kill. The discovery and the capacity of technological thinking are immediately used in the service of primitive fight and flight functioning. The images of the spaceship show the enormous development of technological thought represented by the computer Hal. What has not developed is the capacity of frustration tolerance. Intolerance to frustration impedes traversing the caesura that leads from the monkey's cunning to the wisdom of learning from experience: articulating emotions and thoughts to provide meaning. This is the caesura between a rudimentary consciousness harnessed to the sensuous, and a consciousness that has the capacity of becoming aware of ideas and feelings.

Some of the difficulties when traversing these caesuras are described with humour in *A Memoir of the Future* such as the problem of 'sucking' an erection, referring in one layer of multiple meanings to the passage of man from a four-legged animal to a being that stands on two legs.

In his last conferences, published in *Clinical Seminars and Four Papers* (1987) Bion puts forward the possibility for psychoanalysis to traverse this caesura between a primitive prenatal mind and a 'civilised' postnatal mind in both directions, so that they can make contact. The primitive mind contains potential for creative developments that can be suffocated by the postnatal, 'civilised' mind. It also contains potentially destructive primitive terror and impulses that can also be disguised by technological development. As infants we knew of these primitive emotions, but had no words to name them; by the time we learned language, we had already forgotten those experiences.

The attempt to traverse the caesura unavoidably stimulates emotional turbulence but it is imperative for the fate of humanity, since what is at stake is what is going to predominate in us: the shrewdness of a monkey in possession of a super-developed technology or the wisdom of learning through becoming aware of emotional experience. Psychoanalysis and investigation in groups can throw some insight on it and make a contribution in the direction of traversing that caesura towards becoming aware and illuminating the unconscious emotional forces.

In the film one can see in the flaws of the computer Hal that this self-awareness requires a high dose of frustration tolerance. If this fails: Happy holocaust! says Bion at the end of *A Memoir of the Future* and Hal kills the astronauts who are attempting the adventure of exploring.

Bion (1992) suggests that there is no need for the unknown psychological factor in the growth and decay of civilisations to remain unknown. Distracting attention from these problems is dangerous, since problems have a way of reappearing through deterioration and becoming explosive.

These problems have been dealt with by different disciplines that concern themselves with individual or group relationships. Philosophers, priests, law-givers, political scientists, statesmen, etc., have all been concerned but all have failed to produce anything but ephemeral solutions.

The existence and operation of unconscious emotional impulses in the community has not been recognised, so leaders in these disciplines return again and again to a superficial and therefore sterile approach towards human relationships. The challenge that humanity confronts today is not that of an increase in technological advancement, but the attention and investigation of the unconscious emotional impulses that operate in the individual and especially in groups and society.

The urgent problem is the development of research into the interrelation between the production of technological instruments by means of techniques, a kind of 'simian' skill, and the development of emotional growth, which means maturation and 'becoming' responsible. It seems that to this day technological skills are leading the race.

Bion's observation, 'Society has not yet been driven to seek treatment of its psychological disorders by psychological means because it has not achieved sufficient insight to appreciate the nature of its distress' (Bion 1961, p.14) is still a challenge for psychoanalysts and group researchers.

References

Bianchedi E., Pistiner de Cortiñas, L. *et al.* (1999), Bion Conocido/ Desconocido, Buenos Aires: Ed. Lugar.

Bion, W. R. (1961) *Experiences in Groups*. London: Tavistock Publications.

Bion, W. R. (1962) *Learning from Experience*. London: Heinemann.

Bion, W. R. (1963) *Elements of Psychoanalysis*. London: Heinemann.

Bion, W. R. (1965) *Transformations*. London: Heinemann.

Bion, W. R. (1967) *Second Thoughts*. London: Heinemann.

Bion, W. R. (1970; 1990) *Attention and Interpretation*. London: Heinemann.

Bion, W. R. (1975) *A Memoir of the Future. Book One: The Dream*. Brazil: Imago. (London: Karnac Books, 1990.)

Bion, W. R. (1977a) *A Memoir of the Future. Book Two: The Past Presented*. Brazil, Imago.

Bion, W. R. (1977b) *Two Papers: The Grid and Caesura*. Brazil, Imago. (London: Karnac Books, 1989.)

Bion, W. R. (1979) *A Memoir of the Future, Book Three: The Dawn of Oblivion.* Strathclyde: Clunie Press. (London: Karnac Books, 1990.)

Bion, W. R. (1987) *Clinical Seminars and Four Papers.* Oxford: Fleetwood Press.

Bion, W. R. (1992) *Cogitations.* London: Karnac Books.

Freud, S. (1930) *Civilization and its Discontents.* Standard Edition XXI. London: Hogarth Press.

Keats J. (1952) *Letters.* (ed. M. B. Forman, 4th edition) London: Oxford University Press.

Pistiner de Cortiñas, L. (1999) 'El Nacimiento psíquico de la experiencia emocional.' In E. Bianchedi and L. Pistiner de Cortiñas *et al. Bion conocido/desconocido.* Buenos Aires: Ed. Lugar.

Pistiner de Cortiñas, L. (1999) 'Psique/ Soma: diálogos y cesuras.' In E. Bianchedi and L. P. de Cortiñas *et al.* (1999).

Sor, D. and Sennet de Gazzano, M. R. (1988) *Cambio Catastrófico,* Buenos Aires: Ed. Kargieman.

Endnotes

1. Compared with other species the human infant is born very immature (as if born prematurely) . This implies at the same time that he is extremely dependant for his physical and psychological survival on the care and reverie of his parents, but also this neotenicity opens up many opportunities for further evolution.

2. '...the theories in which I have used the signs K and – K can be seen to represent realization in groups. In K the group increases by the introduction of new ideas or people. In – K the new idea (or person) is stripped of its value, and the group in turn feels devaluated by the new idea' (Bion 1962, p.99).

3. 'I am impressed, as a practising psychoanalyst, by the fact that the psychoanalytic approach, through the individual, and the approach these papers describe, through the group, are dealing with different facets of the same phenomena' (Bion 1961, p.8).

4. The second book of *A Memoir of the Future* is *The Past Presented.* There the reader is 'presented' with attempts of discussions between the scientist, the priest, the philosopher, the psychoanalyst, the devil, etc., on issues that are shared by all of them, although under different names: unconscious emotional forces.

5. *A Memoir of the Future* is one of the last books written by Bion. The second part of this trilogy is called *The Past Presented.* I think the title refers to the emotional experiences present and presented in a group that is trying to function as a 'work group', and its failures. The third volume, *The Dawn of Oblivion,* introduces the prenatal aspects of the mind . As 'Em – mature', the first character introduced in this volume puts it: 'This book is a psycho-embryonic attempt to write an embryo-scientific account of a journey from birth to death overwhelmed by premature knowledge, experience, glory and self-intoxicating self satisfaction...' (Bion 1975, 1990 p.429).

6. Bion used ♀♂ as signs to denote container and contained. He added the sign: – (minus) before those symbols, as he did with –K, –L, –H, when he wants to refer to emotions denuded of their quality of emotions, for example –H (minus H) is not the same as H (hate). – (♀♂) he uses to denote a 'Super' ego that has the quality of

denuding. It is a relationship based on envy and rivalry between container and contained.

7.   'Taking what I may call a macroscopic vertex I do not see the same things as I do from a microscopic vertex. In what I would call a macroscopic formulation the difference is easily explained by the fact that a group is not an individual or vice versa, but... The microscopic vertex – ... reveals something which does not correspond to the anatomy or physiology of the individual or the group of human individuals' (Bion 1990, 1975 p.182).

8.   We are not only prejudiced in favour of our consciously known functioning but from that vertex we are also blind to our 'protomental or pre-natal' manifestations. Often they are felt as 'interference', so there is also an urgent need to develop instruments to transcend the caesura and be able to apprehend this kind of functioning (Pistiner de Cortiñas 1999).

9.   'The supposition that inhibitions should be decreased seems to be based on a view of the individual analogous to a view of the group in which democracy is a bad form of government but none less the best' (Bion 1970, p.127).

10.   A transformation of the autonomic into automatic might take place: when proto-mental, prenatal states traversing the caesura become an automatic, defensive functioning, like the one in BA groups.

11.   Detachment can only be achieved at the cost of painful feelings of loneliness and abandonment experienced (1) by the primitive animal mental inheritance from which detachment is effected (2) by the aspects of the personality that succeed in detaching themselves from the object of scrutiny which is felt to be indistinguishable from the source of its viability. The apparently abandoned object of scrutiny is the primitive mind and the primitive social capacity of the individual as a political or group animal. The 'detached' personality is in a sense new to its job and has to turn to tasks which differ from those to which its components are more usually adapted, namely scrutiny of the environment excluding the self. Part of the price paid is in feelings of insecurity (Bion 1963, p.16).

12.   A sample of this turbulence was the storm stirred up in a group of lawyers with whom we were investigating some problems concerning the need to establish a setting for their work, to be able to contain the emotional turbulence inherent to the issues that had to be dealt with legally. We could understand, after the storm, that in the group the same emotional problem presented itself as they had to deal with in the practice of their profession. Clients asked for legal advice and that the lawyer should be able to find a legal solution to their problems, and at the same time often invaded, in an intrusive way with their anxieties, even the private life of the professional, calling on weekends, etc. The need to establish a setting for containing the emotional turbulence became more obvious.

9

'So you Want to Write a Fugue?'

Wilfred R. Bion with Glenn Gould

Jacquelyne P. Colombier

Contents

Theme

Part I: The Voice Horizontally And Vertically

1   'Oral Tone Poems': A New Type of Listener
    'A deliberate lack of linear contact' and a
    multichannel listening
    The entry of voices
    The condition of solitude
    North as a metaphor

2   Bion's Looking and Auditory Mirroring Phase
    A non-identified looking-glass phase
    The reader as equalizer
    A Memoir of the Future **in a contrapuntal key**
    1   Visual elements
    2   Non-verbal parts
    3   The voices

Part II: The Beauty Link

    ± **B** and the listening room
    The Third Principle

Theme

This paper started with a vision: I saw *A Memoir of the Future* covered with musical notes. I ventured to carry on with it through a reading of *A Memoir of the Future* in a contrapuntal key and to support the conviction that a *heard* version would be congruent with Bion's claim for 'rebellion' (Bion 1991, p.578).

Bion was very explicit about what the form had to be: it had to be different from that of the narrative of a book, to 'discourage the familiarity of a group with the printed words', a printed (visual) communication ruled by conventions which are part of representation (Bion 1991, p.87).

In producing 'unfamiliarity' with established formal conditions of thoughts, *A Memoir of the Future* is Bion's 'distinctiveness' (Bion 2000, p.135), a breaking through the conflict he contributed to, the conflict between narcissism and social-ism.

In his introduction to *A Memoir of the Future* Bion stresses the changes, some 'not so obvious', the changes of rhythm, on which he relies to bring the readers 'to *hear* when they *see* the pattern formed on the paper' (Bion 1991, p.87).

To detect the rules of the changes of rhythm in *A Memoir* Bion suggests a musical reference, 'as would the key of a musical composition written without the statement of the key signature'. He even gives a dynamic indication: *'Prelude and fugue'* – and that is a Bach signature.

If a musical form can be basically appropriate to Bion's horizontal and vertical Grid,[1] the contrapuntal is the one. Just as well; the unceasing motion, constantly shifting, with its possibility of recursion continually altering, can best fit with Bion's psychoanalytic responsibility for *psychoanalytic* time.

The title 'So you want to write a fugue?'[2] unites Gould with Bion, and Bion to the contrapuntists. If *A Memoir of the Future* is a book, it is a book to be listened to, with the tentative subtitle: 'Contrapuntal piece for three voices and *basso continuo'*.

To associate Gould with Bion is not so adventurous. If one takes into account the important points they share,[3] what is amazing, on the contrary, is that they never met.

Both Gould and Bion were aware of the conditions they needed to achieve their work and dared to brave the conflict with established environments.

Gould was a 'mystic' artist in the Bionian sense, that is a man of music whose artistic activity[4] merges into creation, who had the courage to make choices[5] in order to safeguard the integrity of creative acts and to live along his convictions; Bion 'fugued' from London to Los Angeles, aged 70. He chose to encounter a caesura, less afraid of exposing himself to new and possibly dangerous conditions than of staying with a secure and highly esteemed position.

Both Bion and Gould were untiring minds. They raised to an exceptional level the debate between mental activity and sensuous, physical experiences.

It is an outstanding feature of Gould that he praised thinking the reality of music over the tactile power of the performance.[6] As B. W. Powe wrote: 'Gould made exploration itself his method. He was a supremely self-conscious artist who made awareness part of his subject'.[7] In so doing he came closer to the ultimate mystery of music, to '*music itself*'; Bion's theory of thinking strained at the relationship with senses and went as far as possible in the endeavour to overcome the inadequacy of language, so far as to include an 'atelier' in the consulting room, inviting the psychoanalyst to get closer to 'aesthetic elements of beauty'.[8]

Gould ended *The Solitude Trilogy*[9] at the time Bion started writing *A Memoir of the Future*. These two controversial works are unique and therefore both qualified, too restrictively, as 'experimental', because both are creative events of huge magnitude, with new and far-reaching significance.

Gould had a visionary awareness of the main cultural change introduced by the techniques of communication.[10] The form he invented is a hybrid one, made of documentary, drama, and music, based on montage from taped interviews and sound effects. The *Contrapuntal Radio Documentaries* (CRD) represented the most resolute way to carry on with his composition work through the human voice and to achieve his understanding of the consequences of technologies in the making of a 'new listener'.

The Solitude Trilogy is also an anthropological documentary relevant for individuals and collective psychology. It describes the condition of solitude *per se* and, interestingly, its category of 'apartness' challenges Bion's idea of individual valency to combine with 'groupishness' (Bion 2000, p.168).

Just as Gould's innovative work was, Bion's *A Memoir of the Future*[11] was received with embarrassment: what sort of work did it belong to? 'The Trilogy is an exciting and disturbing work, impossible to categorize', writes Francesca Bion.[12] In fact, *A Memoir of the Future* is written is a way never done before, in the *specific* time of psychoanalysis.

Bion's aim with *A Memoir* was a 'description of psychoanalysis' (Bion 1991, p.86) which brought the difficulty akin to the long-lasting problem of publication of psychoanalytical sessions. The conventional publication of the narrative of a psychoanalysis could never resolve the fact that what is heard in the consulting room becomes visual, read by eye in its printed edition. In *A Memoir of the Future* Bion rebels against 'conformity with his training' and resorts to a communication of psychoanalytic experience coherent with the experience itself.

Though he was very clear about his aim, commentators of *A Memoir* took inopportune trends along autobiographic, artistically oriented readings which delayed its acknowledgement as a lay and scientific psychoanalytical text.

The fact that biographical events are present in *A Memoir of the Future* does not make it automatically an autobiographical project, as Bion himself warned: '...To me, that the book bore witness to its mental origins might be an unwelcome irrelevance, a feature additional to the main component of my wish to communicate and your wish to receive'.[13] Nor was its merit on the artistic side.

Parthenope Bion Talamo fought against *A Memoir* being 'dismissed as being simply an elderly gentleman's frolic in the realms of literary production' and insisted it be taken as 'a serious psychoanalytic text' with 'clinical relevance'. She did not go deeper into this, though, because she based her comments on her experience as a translator. From that point of view, she suggested *A Memoir* be read in a group, in order 'to get the more fun' out of it but also because 'the group can comfort and give backing to the individual who may be quite intensely disturbed by his own beta-elements as they fight to come up despite resistances' (Bion Talamo 1997, pp.236–7, 239). But this 'choral reading' remained on the theatrical model.

Francesca Bion rightly labelled *A Memoir* a 'self-analytical' work and I will extend her statement to the point of making my working hypothesis that its clinical and theoretical relevance holds to mirroring facts and theorisation in a way hitherto unformulated.

To introduce musical reference of a contrapuntal nature is neither to introduce music as alternative to literature, nor to reintroduce an artistic perspective, it is to introduce mirroring mechanisms and auditory mirroring experiences fitting with the split between ear and eye on which *A Memoir* depends. Thus, it will raise the question of Bion's looking-glass version.

The meeting of Gould and Bion also opens up controversies within the traditions of psychoanalysis and between them, individual and collective traditions.

Emphasis has been put more on the visual side of the mirror comparison made by Freud in describing the psychoanalytic attitude (the psychoanalyst must remain inscrutable for the patient, as a reflecting surface) than on the auditory side ('play the psychic instrument', use of one's unconscious 'as an instrument', be like a telephone receiver[14]), no less stated by Freud and no less meaningful. It seems that the 'sonorous experience' was acknowledged in the psychoanalytic field long after valuing the sonority, the resonance of the words, had become a psychoanalytic tradition.

It seems, in fact, that mirroring effects were more easily heard in the group situation (Pines 1984, 1998), a place where Freud's decision of transfer from seeing to hearing has not been fulfilled. But Gould's *CRD* might reveal a blind spot in the so-called group situation.

It never happens, even in a group, that two people can speak at the same time; conventional politeness allows only one by one. Just the same, notes taken from group sessions force a *linear* review of auditory experience. At a time where the therapeutic field itself comes under electronic influence,[15] Gould's experience of sound in space, his method of listening to more than one conversation, to more than one vocal impression, could be of great interest.

Last but not least, Gould claimed solitude as the necessary condition for ecstasy experience – for the artist and for the listener – ecstasy defined as union with an unnameable object of which Beauty is a possible name.

Gould had experience of the relationship between the artist and mass phenomena (such as the audience, the applause) and his conviction was that music leads to a contemplation state impossible to reach 'among 2999 people around you' or more.[16] Hence he claimed that the link of ego to other egos (such as a gathering at a concert performance) is a superficial one while the most intimate is the one-to-one link of recorded music.

The mission of the artist in the electronic age is not to take advantage of technology as a technical power but to bind it to aesthetic decisions correlative to a moral attitude. Gould dedicated himself to that responsibility.

When death interrupted him, Bion was coming to Beauty as a psychoanalytic dimension of the object in the psychoanalytic listening room, another one-to-one and solitary situation. This paper will end in raising the question: must we add a Beauty ($\pm$ **B**) link to Bion's H, L, K links?

To shed light on that very question requires a musical artist. So let J. S. Bach and Glenn Gould enter.

Part I

The Voice Horizontally and Vertically

'The prerequisite of contrapuntal art, more conspicuous in Bach than any other composer, is an ability to conceive *a priori* of melodic identities which when transposed, inverted, made retrograde, or transformed rhythmically will yet exhibit, in conjunction with the original subject matter, some entirely new but completely harmonious profile' (Gould in *GGR* p.240). No one but Gould could explain better. I shall just underline that the contrapuntal repetition, though based on a process of acoustic mirroring effects, is not a *symmetric* recursion.

The contrapuntal writing combines in tremendously complex form sameness and unfamiliarity. Each listening, far from exhausting complexity, reveals its abstract structure as the constitutive factor of transformations, developing variations, recurring motives in praise of self-reference of the (principal) subject.

The effects of so many ruthless permutations on the listener may create enjoyment but also anxiety. More or less, one has to make a choice, either to follow one voice at a time or listen to the global effect of all the voices and combinations without trying to untangle one from the other. As a matter of fact, one way is exclusive of the other and the choice is often more improvisatory than mastered, at least for a lay listener and before he has learnt to listen.

In the following pages I shall present how Gould and Bion have treated the voice horizontally and vertically to serve their respective projects.

Just as in Bach's contrapuntal works, the listening/reading can be repeated over and over; it is never the same and the pleasure keeps on with the same feeling of adventure and discovery as the first time.

1. 'Oral Tone Poems'
A New Type of Listener

Gould suspected that 'the sense of space, the sense of area is something all too easily taken for granted when most people listen to sound' (Gould, 'Radio as music' in *GGR*, p.382). He was also preoccupied with sensory deprivations spread by the media, particularly the techniques of radio which he found 'strikingly obvious and shockingly neglected' (Gould 1992, p.107). Convinced that technology could provide editorial potentiality for using the sense of space, he made the project to combine information and work of art and created the conditions of a 'real listening experience'.

If he knew what he wanted – for radio documentaries to go beyond the presentation of historical facts and events, beyond geographic description, and associate a 'drama-like conjunction within the documentary' (docudramas) – Gould did not know how he was going to proceed. Almost fortuitously he found how to achieve his idea: the Canadian Broadcasting Corporation's (CBC) requirement of a certain duration of time freed him to apply his knowledge of contrapuntal musical structure to verbal material and the human voice.

He organized the acoustic environment so that the listener would not be immersed in a sonorous chaos. Use of the new technology of stereophony was introduced from the second part of the trilogy (*The Latecomers*, 1967), adding a supplement of exciting difficulties and possibilities with space localization of left and right.

Gould himself made and tape-recorded the interviews but the montage required technical collaboration. It is reported that the montage was enormously time-consuming.[17] The fascinating result is a great lesson of technology in the service of musical and human sensitivity and a new form of 'radio as music' (Paysant 1978, Chapter IX).

'A deliberate lack of linear contact' and a multichannel listening

Gould's first rule was to: 'Keep all the elements in a state of constant flux, interplay, nervous agitation...so that one is buoyed aloft by the structure and never at any moment has time to sit back and say "Oh well, that's going to be the bridge to Act Two'" (*GGR*, p.330). Lacking the possibility to 'predict a caesura', the listener 'gradually grows into a different sort of awareness' through 'forbidding memories of linearity' (*GGR*, p.380).

It would be totally misleading to equate linear independence with some aleatory project. On the contrary, it relies on a thoughtful discipline: '…If not necessarily leading to a fugue in every incident…every voice leads its own rather splendid life and adheres to certain parameters of harmonic discipline. I kept a very close ear to how the voices came together and in what manner they splashed off each other, both in the actual sound and in the meaning in what was being said' (*GGR*, p.457).

Techniques were used to differentiate simultaneous motives and characters and to put them in interplay action. Besides the razorblade on tape:

1. Non-verbal parts, sound effects, music; some are brief and some more permanent, acting as a *basso continuo*: the train in *The Idea of North*, the sea in *The Latecomers*, the scansion of the Reverend's sermon in *The Quiet in the Land*. The *basso continuo* has an extraordinary presence, almost haunting. It supports the voices and the silences, as in *The Latecomers* where the rolling of the sea makes the silence of the human voice *heard*.

2. Filters were placed, in varying degrees, to emphasize character differentiation. In fact, the listener gets awareness and pleasure in male and female contrasting tones all the more since the female voices are less numerous.[18]

3. To construct the 'sonorous frame' Gould borrowed editing processes from the cinema.[19] As a director edits a film with moving back and forth of camera angles, mixing of perspectives, he moved a sound source from one place to another ('pan-potting'), using distance, proximity, perspective, fading effects.

All the resources of the visual registering were employed to reinforce the auditory one, contributing to maximise the contrapuntal effects of the listening to a 'polypersonne', i.e. several voices, without accumulating confusion. (This is why Gould's *CRD* are so close to Bion's trilogy and would have to be used in its auditory and visual edition.)

In fact, linear independence overcomes the weakness of a one-by-one narrator, and the playing with the time sense allows the listener to hear one voice and yet receive simultaneous messages. The form thus produced is not centred, it is 'integral structure'.

Highly sophisticated precision of time, by the second, co-ordinated to manipulation of space, is in the service of exceptional clarity.[20] Everything is done for the listener so that he can *learn* to listen, on both sides[21] simultaneously, to both the sonorous registering and the meaning of what is said.[22] Plus the beauty, plus people's truth.

The entry of voices

The moment of entry of the voices is under constraint in fugal forms, whatever their numbers may be. Five voices in *The Idea of North*, thirteen in *Latecomers*, nine in *The Quiet in the Land*, with incessant combinations of solo, duet, trio going in interplay. The tremendous skill of the *CRD* holds to the fact that the voices are never mixed by chance and though several lines can overlap, the meaning, the singularity are preserved. In fact, Gould's work enlightens the moment when one takes the floor and reminds us how daring that is.

It is amazing how, from different interviews with people who never met, Gould brought them together in a common space so that the individuality of each voice is heard in the resonance of the others, as interactions of people talking together. The effect is not of a mere superposition of several lines but of an integrating structure where voices may enter in collision, one having precedence over the other, where the sonority of the words crosses over so that the 'texture, the tapestry of the words themselves differentiate the characters'. Here is one example of how voice and words cross over: 'A girl enters first and speaks very quietly…and after a time she says: "And the further north we went, the more monotonous it became". By this time we have become aware of a gentleman who has started to speak and who upon the word "further" says "farther"'.[23]

The virtuosity of the mixing is never detached from a sense of the beauty of the human voice in articulate speech, recorded with as much care as for singing voices. The beauty, though, cannot help individual and collective tragedies.

The condition of solitude

Comments about the *CRD* focus almost exclusively on the technical exploit rather than on their contents. The fact that the characters are 'fictitious', i.e. made of a collage of interviews, does not lessen, though, either the value of the documentaries or their drama aspect. Characters are 'fictitious' in the sense that they are disengaged from action and movement but not from thoughts. I find that, as the surviving evidence of bygone realities, the *CRD* are not only documentaries on the North and its inhabitants, but also on human sufferings, at a level and in a way as worthwhile as the way in which psychoanalysis enables us to hear the individual on the couch.

As any artist composing a work, Gould indulged in projective identification with its topic. He had to 'hermit against his own milieu' (*GGR*, p.339). With such a compass oriented on his own emotional reality, he could best achieve true documentaries on the North[24] and make heard others' sufferings: the distressed people in Arctic isolation and coercive environment (*The Idea of North*); poignant sufferings because of the loss of vital collective links, divorce between younger and older generations, the dying of a whole way of life for the Newfoundlanders (*The Latecomers*)[25]; the isolated, messianic community of the Mennonites, facing the threats of disintegration of group identity, the fundamental conflict between being 'in the world and not of the world' for the survival of their values and beliefs (*The Quiet in the Land*).

The price of the conflict with the Establishment, here, is paid not by the 'mystic' only but by anyone emotionally alive who feels his heart broken, without remedy, when nothing is left but 'adaptation'. In fact, it seems there is no end to pain for people who felt in charge of human links, of Beauty, of spirituality, obliged to exchange their human struggles against adversity of nature for functional ease, ugliness, tourism exposure, etc., i.e. loss of their soul. In *The Latecomers*, the sea voices this loss on equal terms with the speaking subjects.

The conflict between the cost of non-conformity and collective power and authority do not equate, though, with any latitudinal factor. Gould meant the North to be an opportunity to examine conditions of solitude as such.[26]

North as a metaphor

Most of the time people do not allow themselves to live in solitude, and lose contact with solitude as a condition. Interestingly, Gould suggested that a sort of balance needs to be made between collective time and time spent with one's self.

The North is metaphorical of a state of isolation needed to assume the process of differentiating the 'I' from groupishness, the process of conquering one's inner space and mobility over allowance for conformity. Hence it can be representative of the conflict between the artist and collective formations.

On several occasions Gould has denounced 'the syndrome of the group'. He found group psychology inappropriate, even injurious, to creation and to self-respect when one is forced to collective consensus.[27] His own experience as a public performer made him very aware of the contagious potentiality of the relationship of a crowd to an artist. To the question: what do crowds want? Gould's answer is: fusion.

Gould has narrated the moment when he himself in 1958, aged 26, indulged in no-conformity, realizing 'that the collected wisdom of my peers and elders to the effect that technology represents a compromising, dehumanising intrusion into art is nonsense' (Gould 1992, p.18). With this independent and bold statement Gould began his personal 'love affair' with recording technology (Bazzana 1997, Chapter 10). From that day on he resorted to what he named 'the solidarity of the ego', the sake of the artist regardless of 'groupishness'. This claim does not intend to widen a grandiose self; on the contrary, it gets rid of mass psychology's seductions, idealized competitiveness, flattering illusions, overestimation and cult of originality.[28]

If apartness is vital for the creative process on the 'mystic' side, Gould insisted that the other partner, the listener, be offered a similar experience. Paradoxically, it is through separation from the ego that a link is established which takes greatest care of the other. The communion of 'the ego of the artist with other egos' cannot fail to detract from the apprehension of emotional reality, of ecstasy, which is one's very own intimate experience.

The artist for whom this ethical attitude is relevant in the conflict between 'aesthetic narcissism' and 'groupishness' makes a sacrifice in terms of 'ego'. He must keep himself in the background as much as possible so that the other, the listener, can come in contact with the interiority of music, with 'Beauty' and not with the ego of the performer.

The recording technology offers a shelter for the artist choosing 'aesthetic narcissism', i.e. altogether 'outself' oriented and entirely bound to the intimate pleasure of creation. It offers a link which does not depend on a drive to gather, more or less under influences of local, hierarchical, establishment settings.[29]

This conflict between distinctiveness and conformity, Bion acted out with another trilogy of solitude, *A Memoir of the Future*.

2. Bion's Looking and Auditory Mirroring Phase

Bion had to 'manufacture the apparatus' to proceed with in order to construct *A Memoir of the Future.* Contrary to Gould, Bion had to rely on a printed, i.e. visual, edition. He had to invent the way of producing 'unfamiliarity' with the visual, to decide when and how to create an ongoing tension between the visual and the auditory registerings. It would be erroneous to take this preoccupation as a trick for occasional writing; it comes from Bion's psychoanalytic practice.

Bion challenged the supremacy of the visual; he gave weight to 'the auditory system with which is linked transformations such as music noise' (Bion 1963, p.95), and he did for the auditory sphere in the psychoanalyst's practice what Freud did for the visual one: consider the importance of 'artificial silence' in order to hear very faint noises (Bion 1989, pp.22–23).

A non-identified looking-glass phase

If it is noticeable that the first time Bion came to recognize a specular image, it was through the rhythm of a jocular scansion (Bion 1993, pp.5, 8–9), it is just as noticeable that though the visual dimension ('binocular vision'; 'reversed perspective'; 'vertices') dominates Bion's conceptual endeavour, he did not develop it into a mirroring theorisation as such.

In his cultural background Bion had at his disposal a major reference, and he does refer to *Alice Through the Looking Glass* as representative of the psychotic 'murder' of the self-image when mirroring coincides in time and space (Bion 1992, p.104). But what would be the *non*-psychotic way? Can Bion's conceptual endeavour do without it or is there a non-identified looking–glass phase underlying Bion's conceptual corpus?

Several times, but rarely, Bion refers to a reflection model, to the reflection in water of non-human objects, i.e. the visual aspect in a horizontal plan. But as this evocation of the surface of the water takes place in the context of the conflict of narcissism and social-ism (Bion 1991, pp.47–8, 68–9, 78–80), one could have expected to find a reference to the myth of Narcissus; but Bion said the psychoanalyst must choose the myths he needs the most and he seems to have had less reason to elucidate the myth of Narcissus than other myths connected to knowledge and learning.

Since *Cogitations* has been published, we can see, though, that he was interested in the case of 'the youth who seeks a mirror in which to observe his beauty'. 'Here' comments Bion, 'learning is associated with the personality of the investigator himself – his need to find a mirror helps him to satisfy curiosity, his *loving* curiosity about himself. The curiosity, one might say, is not disinterested' (Bion 1992, p.237). It is striking that Bion associated Narcissus with the mirror and not with the reflection in water. In fact, the Narcissus myth does not refer so much to self-knowledge as to the identification of the appearance of the body as 'Me'. In fact, death happens in the moment of the gaze coincedent with identification.

But Narcissus is not only the spectator of his reflection, he speaks to it, and so the myth of Narcissus is representative of visual *and* auditory mirroring (Pines 1991). The Echo part must be taken into account in the impossibility of the looking-glass stage, as tragically as for Alice.[30]

Narcissus's appeal is left without answer, in a sort of perfect pitch milieu, in absolute contact with sounds not settled by self-image and so left/right considerations. Echo returns words – but only the ends of them – and sounds indistinctly, i.e. as *beta-elements*. In place of the PS→D threshold, here, only psychic death happens, not because of loving one's self-image but because of the impossibility of involvement of a self-image.

In *A Memoir*, the basic questioning: 'Who is I?', 'When was the birth of me?', 'Who is the me?' has clinical relevance for the looking-glass topic. The mirror, here, is the sheet of paper in space.[31] Like the surface of water it induces visual mirroring. But the author has wanted 'changes' and in particular 'changes in the rhythm' adding the *auditory* mirroring experience. Bion's reader of *A Memoir* is (very much like Gould's solitary listener) committed to 'a real reading experience'.

The reader as equalizer

Emotionally the reader may not overcome the anxiety trapped in Bion's writing with deliberate broken linearity, cut-offs, bifurcation, with inversion and reversal. With so many overlapping changes, some very abrupt, which he cannot keep in memory, the reader is forced to lose understanding, and the unconscious form of anxiety, boredom, can lead him to drop the book.

The reader is left with a sort of impossible task, with a narrative mode not to be grasped sequentially, but grasped progressively in a cumulative way; it is no wonder if the reader feels like jumping out of the frying pan into the fire!

What is to read if not just see, not to submit to senses? To counterbalance the defect of the printed page, to resist a linear reading, to equalize auditory and visual effects.

Bion intended neither to throw the reader into confusion, nor to thwart 'the wish to communicate' (Bion 1991, p.4), nor be pleased by a realisation remaining undisclosed. He claimed *A Memoir* to be 'confusion→clarity oriented' (*ibid.* p.89). In fact, Bion knows that the reader will have to get through the visual to hear and he put signposts, stage indications, expecting 'sound and sight could be linked with creative effects' (*ibid.* p.112).[32]

In analogically applying the contrapuntal key to *A Memoir*, my aim is to make it be *heard* and not only read by eye, to suggest a vertical and horizontal editing combining audio and video, to bring the point of view of a contrapuntal reading within the psychoanalytic perspective I choose to convey: Bion's looking and auditory mirroring phase.

A Memoir of the Future in a contrapuntal key

The contrapuntal mode limits and organizes voices around a particular moment, their entries. Leaving aside subsidiaries and lateral characters, I shall focus on each main subject, its most representative composites as summarised in the box below.[33]

- *Subject:* **I**

Contra-subjects: Bion; Myself; Em

- *Subject:* **Rosemary**

Contra-subjects: Alice; Mother

- *Subject:* **P.A**

Contra-subject: Bion

Basso continuo and non-verbal parts
- 8. 08. 1918
- 'Arf, arf, arf'
- Tabla players
- Gould playing Bach's 'Goldberg Variations'

---

1. Visual elements

Most commentators are trapped in fascination by the numerous talkative personifications in *A Memoir*, but some mute signs are just as meaningful:

(i) *Italics* are a typographic possibility commonly used. But here they do more than catch the eye as a sensory visual element. Italics mark subjective pronouns, personal and possessive, for all the characters and all through the trilogy: their value is to capture a clinical moment of differentiation – I/you; you/us; his/her – which the italics of the negation '*not*' keep on reinforcing. (In Gould's third *CRD* the loud intonation of 'me', 'you', can be heard giving an immediate sonorous effect of differentiation.)

(ii) *Lower and upper cases*: such as 'the reader/Reader' (p.147); 'capital letter please' (p.253); 'Hymn/HIM/him' (p.66). One visual effect is particularly relevant for the psychoanalytic perspective I have chosen: 'wilfred r bion' ... 'rbidefilnorw' (p.87). 'r bion' transposes into 'Robin'. This writing obviously bears a mirroring quality which has to be elaborated beyond its visual evidence.

(iii) *Mute signs* such as □, a sort of hieroglyphic element in articulate speech, 'represents,' writes Bion, '"some thing" that I want to talk about', (p.88). An enigma to be translated in manifest meaning.

2. Non-verbal parts

Indications of sounds, of noises, have been placed by the author (p.10, p.105), with an auditory awareness which Gould would have applauded! Such as 'the silence was so sudden that the words were clearly and shockingly audible' (p.40). In a combined audio-visual edition of *A Memoir* choices would have to be made using the possibility of transformation of sounds and noises into music. It would be interesting to imagine some reversed directions.[34]

'Arf, arf'

The abundance of characters must not obscure the absence in *A Memoir* of a character as meaningful in psychoanalysis as the father, absence counterbalanced by the permanent evocation of the 'Father figure' (p.266) and by two characters, Paul (enters p. 224) and Priest (enters p.305). A childhood version of 'Our father' in 'Arf, arf' sounds (enter p.50) is the other evocation. These sounds, marked with different use of lower and upper case, are associated to different characters in 'The Dream' (and *only* in 'The Dream' sometimes with indications as in musical scores.[35]

The idea that God is a 'father figure' is a major contribution of psycho-analysis, associated to primordial conjunction with Superego. I would suggest an auditory editing sonorizing these 'Arf, arf' sounds without explaining away the belief in God. It could be best inspired by 'The Quiet in the Land', where a hymn, children's voices and choir, the Reverend's sermon 'Oh God, our Father', and a call for prayer establish a church ambience and liturgical solemnity.

Tabla players

If he permanently associates Bach with his feverish interest for mathematical notation (and not the least of Bach's work, *The Art of the Fugue* and the *B minor Mass* – especially in *Cogitations*), then paradoxically, Bion does not say much in his works about Bach's rhythmic vitality nor does he share his emotional listening to this music.[36]

Bion evokes precise rhythms in relation to drums, and he tells us how he was 'stirred' by the rhythmical communications of drums. He gives one personal memory during the war: 'I remember in war being incredibly moved when I heard the distant music of the bagpipes of a Highland division that was to accompany us in the battle' (Bion 1997, p.31). Here, though, I will not follow the author with the sound of military drums. I will choose tabla players, i.e. Indian drums, because of the passage just above where he links musicians, rhythms and a memory: ('when I was very small').[37] 'Bion' makes an allusion to 'Poor Nanny! it was old Ayah, poor old thing…' (p.134) but she does not enter as a speaking subject. The Indian drums would represent the lost object of her voice talking, singing to the 'very small' one.

The basso continuo

8. 08. 1918 is a recurrent date all along the trilogy but the recurrence is masked by the fact that different characters evoke it.

- The author: 'the date in -K is August 7th and 8th' (p.155)
- Captain: 'before August 8th' (p.156)
- Man: August 7/8th (p.159)
- **P.A**: 'August 8, 1918, that was' (p.256); 'I died there' (p.257)
- Roland: August 8, 1918 (p.294)
- 20 years: Ypres (p.453–455)
- **P.A**: August 8th (p.474)

An auditory edition could restore the repetition of the traumatic events through the roaring of a tank, following Gould's use of the train and of the sea in his *CRD*. The effect of a concrete auditory part is not meant to be 'illustrative' but to convey *beta-elements* through noise.

3. The voices

In a contrapuntal key the subject (voice) exposes the motif to be heard several times in different dispositions; even different tempos; it can be followed by a contra-subject (or several), a secondary theme chosen to contrast (at different levels, rhythm, harmony, melody) with the subject. This dynamism built on the scansion – appear–disappear–reappear – is permanent and can be traced. Transposed to *A Memoir* this principle allows us to take it as a whole and not as split in different parts. (Here, of course, the one-volume edition of *The Trilogy* by Karnac Books was most helpful, in fact essential).

But before coming to the three main subjects, something must be said about Bion's qualification of the characters as 'fictitious' if *A Memoir* is to be taken as different from a literary or artistic work, i.e. as a psychoanalytic one.

Psychoanalysis has demonstrated that identification can promote numerous others and that condensations, transpositions are part of the ordinary dream work, so that 'different' elements can represent a unique event or a single person. There is in *A Memoir* a very complex working through of the real/imaginary dimensions. The publication is meant, deliberately, to treat the wake-work in a way as enigmatic as the dream-work. Bion seems to enjoy thinking paradoxically: '. . . the dialogue between me and me might just as well be conducted between me and a fictitious character', (p.113); 'Falstaff, a known artefact, is more "real" in Shakespeare's verbal formulation than countless millions of people' (p.4); a real phantasy is a real fact (p.485); 'idealized figures' are often 'more powerful that real human beings' (p.354). So, as **P.A** says: 'We shall have to consider what *a real* image is' (p.489) – which is the very question of the looking-glass topic.[38]

> • *Subject*: **I**
>
> *Contra-subjects*: Bion; Myself; Em

'I am tired' (p.3) ...'I have been imprisoned, frustrated, dogged by common-sense, reason, memories, desires, and greatest bug-bear of all – understanding and being understood' (p.578). These terrible words have a Lear tonality. We can now translate □ as anticipation of death. At dawn of future death, the past is re-presented.

This sentence reappears (voiced by Roland): 'I *am* tired' (p.275) and the added italics indicate that the feeling cannot any more be put in words.

- '**I**' is composed of 'Bion'[39] duplicated by 'Myself' and may be represented by 'Em', reversing 'Me'. This 'I' needs the myth not hitherto so much used, the self-knowledge myth 'with *loving* curiosity' 'about me and my objects' (p.87). In other words, a Narcissus-like myth:

- 'Bion': enters p.81; disappears p.216; reappears p.552 as contra-subject of **P.A**: '...I myself introduced in the narrative' (p.86). The clever Sherlock enters (p.91) to discover evidence: '...*you* have included yourself. You have even put your name on this book' (p.189). Whether 'Bion' is a convincing portrait is less important than what 'Bion' answers: '...I would find difficult to name the mental world which is now part of what *I* think of me' (p.189).[40]

- *Myself*: enters p.95, does not reappear after *The Dream*. Mirror dreams happen in contexts of loss, mourning, separation (Colombier 2000) and *The Dream*, it seems to me, would rank in that category. The fact that Myself disappears confirms that Myself is a mirror mechanism in a mirror dream. The relation between 'Bion' and 'Myself' goes both ways:[41] sometimes, one is foreign to the other and speaks to the other as to a Not-me: 'You mean I am wrong?' (p.182); 'I don't understand' (p.189); 'That is *not* my point' (p.216); 'Excuse me; but you have got me mixed up with Bion' (p.124). Of course, there is a laughing effect of the two Bions, (p.102) not agreeing with each other; sometimes, on the contrary, specular episodes bring Bion and Myself in sameness: 'So do I' (p.194); '*I* do/*I* do' (pp.94–95).

It would be very appropriate here to hear Gould's *CRD* technique (coincidentally but differentially) 'Bion' and Myself speaking 'two-gether' (cf. Bion 1991, p.222).

- Em (enters p.429) voices unselfconsciousness. Bion's skilful, witty style could be just a literary trick or speculative psychoanalytic imagination, but the 'anticipation' tense brings it into the context of the looking-glass topic – and here I shall make a theoretical pause.

Lacan described the mirror-stage as 'a drama whose internal thrust is precipitated from insufficiency to anticipation', which the infant supports by itself, 'caught up in the lure of spatial identification' (Lacan 1977, p.4). Strangely enough, in his 1949 version, Lacan mentions, in passing, the element of beauty in the context of biological experimentation in the animal realm and not in the context of the human infant, a lack correlated with the lack of the significant other by its side (*ibid.* p.3; Colombier 2000)

Unlike Lacan, P. Schilder – who historically made the first psychoanalytical research on mirror and body images – underlined that the interest of the human figure is the immediate interest in its aesthetic quality (Schilder 1950, p.256).

With 'anticipation' of Em, Bion challenges both versions.

'Would you include sheets of amniotic liquid as a reflection surface?' asks Robin, 'Certainly' answers **P.A** (Bion 1991, p.489). Still, as I underlined previously a reflection[42] is not enough to be formative[43], it needs an *I* who recognizes the image as 'Me'.

It has become trivial now that a mother sees and hears the fœtus. It belongs to her reverie to digest an animate, sonorous, concrete imagery anticipating the baby. 'My earliest experiences were of something touching what I later heard was "me"', (Bion 1991, p.430–1) will say the child. He/she will have to cope with the after-effects of his/her image[44] looked at and 'anticipated' by the other, and this might be the only way to recapture something of an 'inaccessible state of mind' (Bion 1997, p.50). If it depends on the mother's reverie to see beauty in the fœtal image, both will have to overcome the loss of some 'ideal' quality attached to the em-mature image, not so rarely associated with a misreading in gender.

Em's mirror stage in Bion's version relies not only on the significant other but on the other's ± **L** gaze at a time where the anticipation is heavily both physical and virtual. Bion adds that it is 'a bodily anticipation making possible the later *functional* operation of a mind' (Bion 1987, p.324), but something will have to happen to give birth to '*I*', to a thinking mind, as *A Memoir* demonstrates in a masterly manner.

- *Subject:* **Rosemary**

  Contra-subjects: Alice; Mother

Rosemary and Alice are a 'pair'. They enter, at the same moment (p.66).

A Memoir's key says that 'the content of **Rosemary's** dream is represented as being the reciprocal of Alice's experience of conscious waking reality' (p.656).

The reversal is presented on the manifest level as a social one, but on the latent level it brings the point of view of the woman, from both sides, Bion would say: the woman as a mother (Alice) and the woman's erotic side (**Rosemary**).

Bion first used the notion of 'reciprocity' borrowed from a mathematical model (Bion 2000, pp.86–88). At the same time he coined 'the reversible perspective' by E. Rubin's optic illusion where 'one sees a vase while the other sees two faces' (Bion 1963, pp.50, 54). But what if one looks at one's face and views one's *self*? The symmetric profiles facing each other cannot stand both for the appearance of the body and as one's own self-image, i.e. this model lacks libidinous significance.

In *A Memoir* the other is involved in mirror-gaze moments (p.206), the ± **L** link orientates the gaze (p.490) matched with beauty, as when **Rosemary** says: 'I have a lady's watch which Alice gave me. It marks beauty – the kind that's in the eye of the beholder' (p.350). Beauty is seductive and not being as pretty as before is painful (Alice, p.8, p.222).

It seems that the author has transformed his previous models and grounded the looking-glass in libidinous bonds between desiring others, instead of isolated, inanimate and non-human objects. And now it can happen that 'I can't see what she sees in him' (p. 206),[45] symmetry is broken.

Alice and **Rosemary** are a pair but each has a specific feature.

- **Rosemary** is entrusted with the task of speaking in the name of Beauty (pp.203, 340). Like a Sphinx she asks questions: 'Could Beauty help?' (p.130); 'Why leave out Beauty and Art?' (p.376); 'Why are Science and Knowledge unaware of Beauty?' (p.386).[46]

Quite a lot of quotations from artists and artistic works appear in *A Memoir of the Future* but if questions raised by insistent **Rosemary** are to find an answer, the Artist will have to enter, for the question of Beauty needs the Artist as such.

- Alice speaks for motherhood (p.365, pp.446–7), and that gives her reasons to be presented as weeping: crying in her sleep (p.425); near to tears (pp.14, 26); *weeps*, (p.327). This feature conjoins her to Mother as second contra-subject.

- 'Mother' is alluded to – 'I remember my mother saying to me' (p.65); as English mother tongue; not there on the battlefield (p.256); her death, her tears in her dreams (p.377); mother's desire, (p.451) – but she enters as a speaking subject (p.437) among a chronology totally upside down. The fact that she appears as a speaking subject is very important: it puts an end to atemporality which supports what astrophysicists called 'the mother paradox': a human being can voyage in time and go back to the past, but as far as one goes, one cannot prevent one's parents from meeting, i.e. make one's conception impossible and one's birth be absurd. This dogmatic limit has been named 'the mother paradox', also named the matricide or parricide line (Thuan 1998, p.252). As far as one gets back to past life, one cannot cut one's genealogical tree. Since **P.A** was invented, psychoanalysts call it the primal scene.

> - *Subject*: **P.A**
>
> *Contra-subject*: Bion

- **P.A** enters (p.223) with a pun[47] and **P.A** is the last of the characters to speak (p.576). Here, in his self-analytical enterprise, **P.A** says: '…I do not like looking glass, sheets of water, novels, psychoanalysis'. Poor **P.A**, so why did you become a psychoanalyst then? '…[We] I have wanted in psychoanalysis to nourish an instrument, analogous to a mirror of the physical world, which would make it possible for each of us humans to see himself' (p.320). But does **P.A** want to know *himself*? So many times **P.A** sees himself as not **P.A**, so many 'ifs': 'If we could speak the language of mathematics…if we could talk the language of religion…' (p.230); 'If I were an artist I would try to formulate it in terms of painting or music' (p.295); 'If I had a Shakespearean or a Victor Hugo vocabulary' (p.466), etc. The more he multiplies the vertices, the more **P.A** makes a self-portrait of what he is *not* (p.534).

'O' is the common ground of religion, arts, sciences, psychoanalysis, but what matters is when **P.A** says: 'I am careful to choose what I know and what I believe and, to the best of my capacity, not to mix them up' (p.304), 'I differ' (p.351). And because **P.A** differs, **P.A** knows that the life of real human beings is not spaceless nor timeless and that we cannot see ourselves 'from both sides of the screen'[48], we cannot see our back nor even 'both sides of a hand' (p.465).

M. C. Escher went even further than Picasso, quoted by Bion: in *Mains dessinant* the right hand draws the left one, and reciprocally. Except the fact that *one* hand is not on the picture: Escher's! Composers do not have this advantage, they cannot cheat that way.

P.A should listen to Jean Sébastien Bach instead of indulging in historical argument and claiming: '…*that* I am told is out of date' (pp.231–2): Bach was outdated even in his own times![49] *This* Bach has composed mirror-fugues of which lines get turned upside down to go in the opposite direction, rotated, and, as hands are symmetrical, a second player is necessary to perform them.[50]

So, **P.A** has to separate from a wish for totality i.e. to believe **P.A** could see from all the different vertices through their representative characters.[51] Therefore **P.A** calls back 'Bion'.

- 'Bion': enters (p.552) and says he has nothing more to say on groups for he did not go on with groups: 'I had more pressing problems which could be adequately dealt with only by Psycho-Analysis', answers Bion, problems with Em. More important, really, than discussing P. Schilder's statement that there is 'no collective body-image' but 'a collection of the various images of bodies' (Schilder 1950, pp.273–4)? Would that not be helpful in dealing with the question of the 'collective' of 'all antenatal souls' vs. full term foetus?

When discussing the psychoanalytical approach to groups Bion had said: 'It is possible to hope that the capacity of the artist, though useful, may not be essential to the psycho-analyst. Indeed, it may be a disadvantage in so far as the artist's capacity may enable him to provide, as Plato feared, *a substitute* for truth' (Bion 1993, p.2). 'Bion' is at one with **P.A**'s difference, some problems can be dealt adequately *only* by psychoanalysis: '…with the passage of time I am convinced that there is no substitute for Psycho-Analysis' (Bion 1989, p.22). For **P.A** also, the price of distinctiveness is solitude.

Part II

The Beauty Link

Freud started his psychoanalytic inquiry of aesthetics with the question 'What makes us laugh?' Things would have taken another path had he started by 'What makes us weep?'. More than any other art, music is the art that makes us weep, without knowing why, the art where ravishment tears one's heart out. But Freud did not surrender to music and developed a conception of art as a slight 'narcosis', a tranquilliser socially acceptable. He expected, though, Beauty to be a safeguard condition for civilization, a driving force of the impulse to survive.

In *Civilization and its Discontents* Freud opposed Beauty, as non-utilitarian, to usefulness, in an extending technological environment. He anticipated that 'Future ages will bring with them new and probably unimaginably great advances in the field of auxiliary visual and auditory organs. With tools recordings visual and auditory man will perfect his own organs, materialising a power of recollection, his memory he already possessed' (Freud 1963, p.28–29).

Freud lacks words to define the 'unimaginable' which goes 'beyond limits of visibility and recollection'. All he can say is that it does not respect the 'unattainable' which even fairy-tale wishes respect. He strongly concludes that man's self-image is becoming 'Godlike' while this magnificence only means that man is becoming a kind of 'prosthetic God' (*ibid.* pp. 27–8). Though he rightly anticipated the power of the new technology, Freud did not infer its immediate consequence on mass psychology – in, for example, the role of radio in World War War II.

It took quite a long time to overcome Freud's 'applied psychoanalysis' orientation and his belief that 'psychoanalysis, unfortunately, has scarcely anything to say about beauty'. Freud could not, though, limit its field, 'the beauty of human forms and gestures, of natural objects and landscapes and of artistic and even scientific creations' (*ibid.* p.19). This program is fulfilled in *A Memoir of the Future.*

But what Freud achieves with two principles of mental functioning, Bion needs three 'principles of living': 'First, feeling; second, anticipatory thinking; third, feeling plus thinking plus Thinking;' (Bion 1987, p.329). Should this third principle not have led to some revisions? Been included in the L, H, K links? Now that psychoanalysis has something to say about Beauty?

Bion himself wished the psychoanalyst would know what sort of 'artist' he is and somehow consider his consulting room more as an 'atelier'. But, at the same time, he confessed he could not tell what an 'artist' is: 'I prefer you to go beyond the word and see what I am trying to convey to you by this inadequate word'.[52]

Bion left the question unfinished, on a borderline, wishing that a chance be given to the psychoanalyst of *feeling* (my italics) that 'beautiful' things can happen on the part of both analyst and patient (cf. Bion 1992, p.238). But when he expects the aesthetic element to make 'a very difficult situation tolerable',[53] not only does he break with Freud's criteria (non-utilitarian) but he leaves unanswered the problem of an aesthetic element that would stir more than assuage the situation. (Even so, the choice Bion suggested: 'Do you choose a Shakespeare play or do you come to an alleged "scientific" paper by me?' is not a fair one! (Bion 1987, p.330))

± B and the listening room

Bion rightly emphasized the attacks against the 'mystic' but the difficulty does not come exclusively from outside and from institutional authorities. There are also attacks of Beauty itself on our own 'established ego-structure' as D. Meltzer (1988, p.277) pointed out: he suggests that our own 'established ego-structure' exposed to the attack of Beauty will re-form the vertices of L, H, K. But he himself was aware that the aesthetic conflict is of a kind to drive us back to the group, to flight from one's own self risk, giving preference to adaptation, to compromise, to conventional normality rather than emotional turbulence and growth (Meltzer 1988, pp.180–4). So, why and how would the 'ego-structure *re-form* (my italics) the vertices of L, H, K in response to the recognition of Beauty?

One major aim in *The Apprehension of Beauty* was, Meltzer wrote, 'to establish the term "passion" as a specific response to aesthetic objects: as a *qualitatively* distinct consortium of L, H, and K which is therefore subject to very specific forms of attack by negative links' (*ibid.* p.135).

The choice of this term does not seem to me so convincing. This term was first used by Bion (1963): 'By "passions" I mean all that is comprised in L, H, K…by passion I mean one of the dimensions which L, H, K must possess if it is to be recognized as an element that is present' (Bion 1963, pp.4, 12–13). As long as for Meltzer the response is '*qualitatively*' distinct, why should Beauty only complete already existing links, under another and a not specific name? Why could not Beauty initiate a link of its own, a $\pm$ **B** link ?

Whatever the answer will be, the element of Beauty is a fact, specific, constantly conjoined in psychoanalysis between the myth of Narcissus, the looking gaze moment, the aesthetic conflict, and the psychoanalyst in the listening room.

The apprehension of Beauty is not only joy but pain, but hatred and 'the aesthetic conflict' has to be recovered (cf. Meltzer 1988, Chapter 8). Analysis contains the potentiality of a catastrophic change *coincident* with a change of involvement in the 'object', sometimes leading to an artistic practice, sometimes to the giving up of an artistic practice with a threshold (not much studied hitherto) to a K link, i.e. a crossing to a psychoanalytic practice. This potentiality and its landmark make becoming a psychoanalyst (**P.A**) different from any profession.

Until psychoanalysis had something to say about Beauty, the attack against psychoanalysis was identified as 'resistance'. But as long as **P.A** can be a container for an object related to Beauty, **P.A** will share with the Artist the attacks, singular and collective, of defensive reactions which must be recognized as a feature of a Beauty link.

The third principle

Music is the art whose object disappears, almost at the same moment it appears, which brings it very close to the presence/absence scansion. Not only is the fugal form not 'outdated' as **P.A** imagined, but it is one of 'the most durable creative devices in the history of formal thought and one of the most venerable practices of musical man…fugue arouses some primeval curiosity which seeks to uncover in the relations of statement and answer, of challenge and response, of call and of echo, the secret of those still, desert places which hold the clues to man's destiny but which predate all recollections of his creative imagination' (Gould in *GGR*, p.234, p.241).

Thus, the basic cell of the contrapuntal writing is akin to a fundamental link, the link which unites the appeal and the answer. Even wordless, music achieves it through rhythm. Hence attacks against it as its container.

In an electronic age Beauty will still be a driving force of the impulse to survive but we know it will not be a substitute for Thinking (cf. Bion 1991, p.161). **P.A**'s choice is final: '...there is no substitute for the growth of wisdom. Wisdom or oblivion' (*ibid.* p. 576).[54]

But there is also no substitute for artists. Gould made clear that technology can be used in service of Beauty and emotional growth only by ethical individual awareness and choices. And he made his.

The haunting subject in Gould's and Bion's trilogies is the price of non-conformity and of thinking. Both Gould's and Bion's trilogies belong to the contrapuntal fugue tradition in formal thought.

A Memoir of the Future is constructed on a mirror reversal A/Q–Q/A and Bion noted it 'Prelude and fugue'. But such a mirroring process seems to me closer to the *Goldberg Variations*, music wherein 'the theme is not terminal but radial, the variations circumferential, not rectilinear', a work 'which observes neither end nor beginning' and where the return to the Aria suggests 'perpetuity'.[55] Closer then to Bion's definition of the psychoanalytic 'Principle of perpetuity': '...that the unpleasant emotions and events do not re-occur' and that the pleasant ones go 'on without cessation' (Bion 1991, p.170).

'**I** have been imprisoned, frustrated, dogged by common-sense, reason, memories, desires, and greatest bug-bear of all – understanding and being understood... **I** am tired'.

The legend says that Bach composed the *Goldberg Variations* to soothe and rejoice someone with trouble in sleeping, that state leading to the Dream. So, play on, Glenn Gould.

Acknowledgements

To Malcolm Pines and Robert Lipgar for the opportunity they gave me and for their assistance to establish the manuscript in 'conversational English'; to Francesca Bion for her support and kind willingness to answer my questions; to Thérèse Salviat for providing documents and sharing personal memories about Glenn Gould; to Lorne Tulk for giving information; and for *F minor*, the Internet mailing list devoted to Glenn Gould, and the Bion 97 Internet Mailing list for the stimulating climate of their discussions.

References

Bazzana, K, (1997) *Glenn Gould. The performer in work.* Oxford: Clarendon Press.

Bion, F. 'Life is full of surprises.' In P. Bion Talamo (1997) *The Clinical Relevance of A Memoir of the Future. Journal of Melanie Klein and Objects Relative 15,* 2, p.236–37, 239.

Bion, W. R. (1963) *Elements of Psycho-Analysis.* London: Heinemann.

Bion, W. R. (1978) Seminar held in Paris, July 10th 1978.

Bion, W. R. (1987) *Clinical Seminars and Four Papers.* Oxford: Fleetwood Press.

Bion, W. R. (1989) *Two Papers: The Grid and the Caesura.* London: Karnac Books.

Bion, W. R. (1991) *A Memoir of the Future.* London, Karnac Books.

Bion, W. R. (1991a) *Transformations.* London: Karnac Books.

Bion, W. R. (1992) *Cogitations.* London: Karnac Books.

Bion, W. R. (1993) *Second Thoughts.* London: Karnac Books.

Bion, W. R. (1993a) *Attention and Interpretation.* London: Karnac Books.

Bion, W. R. (1994) *Clinical Seminars and other Works,* London, Karnac Books.

Bion, W. R. (1997) *Taming Wild Thoughts.* London: Karnac Books.

Bion, W. R. (2000) *Experiences in Groups and other Papers.* London and New York, Routledge.

Colombier, J.P. (2000) 'Des rêves un peu spéciaux. Les rêves avec scène au miroir.' *Le Mouvement Psychanalytique III,* no. 2.

Freud, S. (1963) *Civilization and its Discontent.* The Hogarth Press, London.

Gould, G. (1992) *Selected letters.* Oxford University Press, Toronto.

Lacan, J. (1977) *Écrits.* Tavistock Publications.

Meltzer, D. (1988) *The Apprehension of Beauty.* The Clunie Press.

Page, Tim (ed) (1987) *The Glenn Gould Reader.* London: Faber and Faber.

Paysant, G. (1978) *Glenn Gould, Music and Mind.* Toronto: Key Porter Books.

Pines, M. (1984) 'Reflections on Mirroring.' *International Review of Psychoanalysis II,* 1, 27–42.

Pines, M. (1991) 'Narcissus and Echo: Vision and hearing in early development and some applications to individual and group psychotherapy.' Unpublished.

Pines, M. (1998) *Circular Reflections. Selected Papers on Group Analysis and Psychoanalysis.* London: Jessica Kingsley Publishers.

Roberts, J. (ed) (1999) *The Art of Glenn Gould. Reflections of a musical genius.* Malcolm Lester Books.

Schilder, P. (1950) *The Image and Appearance of the Human Body.* International Universities Press, New York

Thuan, Trinth Xuan (1998) *Le chaos et l'harminie: La fabrication du réel.* Paris: Fayard.

Endnotes

1.   Bion said that 'the imaginative exercise' of the 'psycho-analytic game' – the Grid – was close to 'the activity of the musician who practises scales and exercises, not directly related to any piece of music but to the elements of which any piece of music is composed', Bion, W. R. (1989) *Elements of Psycho-Analysis,* London: Karnac Books, p.101.

2.   Piece for four voices with piano or string quartet composed by Gould (1963). Text in Page (1987) *The Glenn Gould Reader.* Faber and Faber. Available on CD.

3.   Gould's favourite authors were: T. S. Eliot, H. Pinter, Shakespeare; S. Beckett was Gould's admirer. Bion quoted also Shakespeare, H. Pinter, T. S. Eliot, and S. Beckett was a patient of his.

4.   Gould did a lot of recordings – and not only Bach – as a soloist, in chamber music and as an orchestra conductor; he made transcriptions; he composed music; he produced radio and television programs. He also did a lot of writing, cf. Page (1987) *The Glenn Gould Reader (GGR)* and Roberts, J. (ed) (1999) *The Art of Glenn Gould. Reflections of a Musical Genius.* Gould's playfulness and sense of humour is also legendary, he could make 'hilarious imitations' (Dr Wolfgang von Krankmeister!); he made imaginary interviews and he interviewed even himself! Cf. 'Glenn Gould interviews Glenn Gould about Glenn Gould'. In *GGR*, p.313.

5.   In 1964, aged 32, covered with honour and preceded by fame, he renounced his career as a public piano player.

6.   In his comments to Brahms Piano Concerto No. 1 at Carnegie Hall, Leonard Bernstein called Gould 'a thinking performer'.

7.   'Return to Glenn Gould', Internet, 'The Glenn Gould Archive'. http://www.gould.nlc-bnc.ca/

8.   Seminar held in Paris, 10 July 1978. Cf. http://www.sicap.it/merciai/bion/en/links.htm

9.   Three parts compose The Solitude Trilogy. Each program expresses isolation: within the self, The Idea of North (1967), based on a train ride Gould took aboard the Muskeg Express going North for 1000 miles to Fort Churchill; within people living in Newfoundland, The Latecomers (1969); within a messianic group, the Manitoba Mennonites community, at Red River, The Quiet in the Land (1973).

      I have used the CD 1992 edition. CD-ROM editions recently appeared but not of The Solitude Trilogy as such.

10.   Gould, Glenn. (1987) 'R. Strauss and the electronic future' in GGR.

11.   *A Memoir of the Future* is made up of three books – *The Dream,* 1975; *The Past Presented,* 1977; *The Dawn of Oblivion,* 1979 – first published separately. Only in 1991 was a one-volume edition formed as the trilogy by Karnac Books, London.

12.   'Life is full of surprises' Bion, F. (1997).

13.   'This book so far printed can be regarded as an artificial and elaborate construct. I myself, here introduced into the narrative, can be regarded as a construct, artificially composed with the aid of such artistic and scientific material as I can command and manipulate to form a representation of an author, whose name appears on the book and now, for the second time, as a character in a work of fiction' (Bion 1991, p.4).

      Bion Talamo, P. (1997) 'The clinical relevance of *A Memoir of the Future', Journal of Klein and Object Relations 15,* 2, p.236–237, 239.

14.   Nowadays, the telephone is very different from the one Freud used, it makes it possible to receive several calls at the same time: we are now under the multimedia technology, that is, a combination of visual, tactile and auditory experiences.

15. The fact that the preservative aspects of recording are now put in the service of psychoanalysis means audiotapes, video, CD-ROM, etc., might not be purely 'technical' and produce after-effects.

16. Cf. Interview in Mach, Elyse, (1980) *Great Pianists Speak for Themselves*, New York, Dodd, Mead. Cf. also, an 'arena of 12,000 people', letter of 8 July 1958 (Gould 1992, p.15).

17. 'It took hundreds of hours of studio and editing time, but Glenn did it. Conceptually and aesthetically, he did it alone. But as a technical breakthrough and as a labour of love he did it with and through the indefatigable Lorne Tulk', reported Janet Somerville (1992), in *The Gould Radio-documentaries: Some Birth-memories*. Technical supervision for *The Idea of North* and *The Latecomers* was by Lorne Tulk; for *The Quiet in the Land*, technical supervision was by Donald Logan, assisted in Toronto by John Jessop, and in Winnnipeg by Stan Evanishen.

18. They seem to me very plain and soft, particularly in *The Idea of North* and *The Latecomers*.

19. Gould wrote that in cinematic terms 'Bach was a director who thought in terms of cuts rather than dissolves' (*GGR*, p.22). Gould was a movie fan. He adapted and composed music for films: *Slaughterhouse Five* (1972), *The Terminal Man* (1974) and *The Wars* (1983). On Gould's idea of 'acoustic choreography' and his technique treating microphones the way a film director treats a camera, cf. Bazzana (1997), pp.246–247.

20. In that respect, *The Quiet in the Land* is a masterpiece with its nine voices, different levels of speech, the choir singing, the traffic and bar sounds, the music (J. Joplin; Bach). One understands why Gould said it was his favourite; its complexity approaches Bach's compositions.

21. To be compared with Bion's binocular vision but in the auditory sphere.

22. Very akin to the psychoanalytic way of listening.

23. 'Another example of correspondences: thirty days/eleven years, (*GGR*, p.379).

24. Gould was born in Canada. From childhood, Gould's own place of solitude was Uptergrove, the family summer residence at the head of Lake Simcoe.

25. At the time of *The Latecomers* Newfoundland was fighting a government decision to force the fiercely independent Newfoundland population to leave its isolation and relocate in larger centres in the name of access to 'modern' conditions of living.

26. In *The Idea of North* one of the characters meditates on William James's idea that there is 'no moral equivalent of war...apparently very few of us can afford to be FOR something. All of us can afford to be AGAINST something... There was a time when humans used to combine against Mother Nature...our number one enemy is Human Nature'. At that moment, the *basso continuo* shifts from the train to the end of Sibelius' 5th symphony, and though both are emotional the shift itself is meaningful.

27. 'Let's ban the applauses': on Gould's unrelenting opposition to competition, see *GRR* 'Advice to a graduation'; 'We who are about to be disqualified salute you!'

28.   'In the effort of the concert performer to "conquer" the audience (and the music), in the audience's appetite for feats of skill performed in a live situation with risks of uncertainty and even disaster, Gould sensed manifestations of the competitive spirit at once offensive and injurious to music. "At live concerts, I feel demeaned, like a vaudevillian"' (Bazzana, 1997, p.121).

29.   There is a radical difference between an artist making records and an artist who considers the technology of recording *as part of the artistic creation.*

30.   I needed this myth for a cure (in parallel time with this paper) of a little boy, aged four, echo of all speech. This little child could not say 'je' (I) and instead said 'il', the French 'il' referring altogether to 'he' (he is coming/il vient)' and to 'it' ('it rains'/il pleut)'. He called himself by his Christian name, as if speaking of another. The turning moment of the cure happened when he started to throw plasticine against the wall, more and more violently, with growing jubilation. The noise against the wall constructed a barrier, a screen, a resistance from where he could get a sense of being in space and contained in space. From then on, 'the other side' took meaning and he could turn back towards me when I called him by name.

31.   'A book is printed in pages with certain rules of typography disposed in order from left to right and goes from the top of the page' (Bion 1991, p.88–89).

32.   Cf. 'If I suppose he hears what I say to him, but in fact he is seeing my words sailing through the air...' (Bion 1991, p.118); 'If I want to communicate a song to a group of people familiar with the printed word but unfamiliar with sung poems or patterns formed by print of paper, it would obscure comprehension of music I want them to *hear* when they *see* the pattern formed on the paper' (*ibid.* p.87).

33.   Unavoidably, the exposition of the frame has to be done separately, printed linearity imposing its constraint. After trying several possibilities, I finally resorted to presenting the frame *before* the characters, though the obvious difficulty and merit of *A Memoir of the Future* come from the entanglement of form, characters and contents. Hoping the 'creative effects' of sound and sight will await in the reader's mind the entries of the characters and last all along, I do not intend to be exhaustive but to catch the essential point.

34.   Man (enters p.104) is a very talkative character but the feature which identifies Man is just one repeated sentence: 'Shall I shoot him?'. A technical device should be found for the auditory representation of Man, i.e. the drive in speech. It would have to consider the passage where Bion brings together emotional forces active in the time of Tacitus and those beta-elements carried away within the words, like those of the (recorded) voice of Hitler's speeches (British Broadcasting Corporation). 'Emotional forces *still* active' (Bion, 1989, p.23).

35.   Robin (ARF ARF; AAARF! ARRF! p.50); Alice (Softly – Arf, arf, p.67); Roland (*softly in the distance – arf, arf, arf!* p.79) ; 'Myself',(*Faint sound* (Arf, arf, arf, p.97); Memory ('Arf, arf, ARF', p.62); Voice ('ARF, ARF, ARF', p.71, 74; 'Arf, arf, arf', p.106); Mycroft, ('Arf, arf p.120.)

36.   Francesca Bion confirmed Bion's interest in music: 'Bion always regretted not having learnt to play the piano...our Bach recordings are numerous and I think if would be impossible to say that Bion had a marked preference for any one work – except, of course, the one he was listing to at a specific moment. They all moved and intrigued him. We have Donald's Tovey's companion to *"The Art of Fugue"*

which fascinated him; its mathematic complexity appeals to his way of thinking' (personal communication). At the time Francesca Bion showed me Bion's copy of D. L. Tovey's book, I did not know that Gould's knowledge of Bach had been compared to Tovey's, which made full circle! Gould himself was a reader of Tovey's, as can be seen in different papers (cf. *GGR*).

37.   Possibly also because of my own experience of being 'incredibly' moved by drums to the point of bursting into irresistible tears anywhere I could find myself, even in public, I remember how disturbing it was, just a wild, brutal fact I could not link. Until it finally got associated with the BBC beat (*Ici Londres*) which was heard on the radio in France during WWII 'when I was very small', my own psychic battle in loneliness.

38.   The linking of Bion's conception of real and imaginary with mirroring problematics through a comparison with Lacan's theses developed during this paper, and will be published in another paper, forthcoming in *Le Mouvement Psychanalytique. Revue des revues freudiennes*, Volume IV, 2001, bilingual French–English version.

39.   Roland and Robin could be called 'variations' of 'Bion'.

40.   Cf. '...the term "fictional character" is itself an inadequate phrase. Here I have just written "myself" as if I wanted to give it a status different from me. I could call "Bion" a second-class citizen compared with "Myself". I indicate without definition that the opinions expressed by me, even if fiction, are worthy of being treated with respect' (p.95).

41.   The duplication of Bion's self-image by 'Myself' can even be understood as a quotation of Bion's work on the phantasy of having a twin, cf. 'The imaginary twin' in Bion (1993).

42.   The 'beautiful' element has been related to the 'aesthetic conflict' by D. Meltzer. It cannot take place for Narcissus because the gaze of the mother sees the beauty of her baby as deprivation of hers. She dedicates her child to Beauty mirroring, shut in *her* beauty which Echo's tentativeness to initiate articulate exchange will fail to break.

43.   For the little patient I referred to, to say 'je' (I) was possible before he could speak of himself as 'moi' (me). It took time for the possessive pronoun 'mon/ma' (my) to be connected to a part of his body. But nothing took as much time as to be able to address himself to me as 'Tu' (you) and place 'me' in that relationship to the other.

44.   An auditory edition of *A Memoir* tuning Girl and Boy voices would materialize the caesura of birth and gender identiy.

45.   Just like a symmetrical reversal between Rosemary and Alice 'So you do me/So do you me' (p.205).

46.   Bion often quotes Poincaré's linkage between Beauty and mathematical formulation, but he does not dig much into how Science could be linked with Beauty for more than one private experience of one scientist.

47.   See/CC. Reinforced by (Tom): I/eye!

48.   In the fifties, at the Tavistock, the one sided mirror – a concrete mirror – was used in situations including more than one patient, small groups, according to S. Resnik's account: 'J'ai eu la chance d'assister à Londres, à la Tavistock Clinic, en

1958, à l'époque du Dr Sutherland, au travail de psychothérapie de groupe de gens qui travaillaient à l'époque avec Bion à travers une glace sans tain' (one-sided mirror). *Revue de psychothérapie psychanalytique de groupe*, Erès, No 5–6, 1986, p.60.

49.   Of course, it is Alice who says it! *A Memoir*, p.465 (cf. p.436).

50.   J. S. Bach was 'the most independent artistic mind' capable 'to stand outside the collective historical process' (G. Gould, 'Bach the nonconformist' in Roberts, 1999). Gould's opposition to any idea of musical progress was an 'ultimate argument of individuality'; he rejected the concept of a *Zeitgeist*, writes K. Bazzana, that could validate or invalidate an artist product. He was especially vociferous in condemning 'the tyranny of stylistic collectivity…and he himself was never concerned about being or appearing "contemporaneous"' (Bazzana 1997, p.69).

51.   A mirror-fugue is a contrapuntal setting, in which the entire setting can be inverted (cf. *The Art of Fugue*).

52.   Cf. **P.A**: 'This my lack and your misfortune in so far as you want me to talk a language *you* can "understand", and I want you to meet me at least half-way by talking a language *I* can understand' (Bion 1991, p.231).

53.   Seminar held in Paris, 10 July 1978.
      Cf. http://www.sicap.it/merciai/bion/en/links.htm

54.   For differentiating knowledge and wisdom, see Bion 1991, p. 497.

55.   Cf. Bion 1991, p.135, and Gould in *GGR*, pp.22–28. Also, D. F. Tovey (1944), 'The "Goldberg" variations', in *Essays in Musical Analysis: Chamber Music*. Oxford University Press.

10

Preconception and Realisation

A Constant Conjunction of Theory and Measurement

Steven R. Brown

Introduction

In Bion's (1963) notation, a preconception is 'a state of expectation…adapted to receive a restricted range of phenomena' (p.23). It is the mind spring-loaded to meet certain sense impressions halfway, and therefore has affinities with *apperceptiveness* (a prior readiness to perceive) upon which the projective techniques depend. The infant's expectation of the breast is referred to as an early illustration, to which might be added the adult's anticipation that politicians are dishonest, that global warming portends danger, or that provocations will lead to violence. A *realisation* is a concrete event or manifestation – e.g. a political scandal, a devastating hurricane, the outbreak of ethnic hostilities – that serves to breathe life into a preconception, to validate it and thereby transform it into a *conception*. What before was a potentiality is now readily conceivable. (As the churchman exclaimed when asked if he believed in baptism, 'Believe? Why, I've seen it!') In this connection, Bion frequently referred the reader to Semple and Kneebone's *Algebraic Projective Geometry* (1952) in which the authors state that three-dimensional Euclidean geometry 'has as one of its realizations the structure of ordinary space' (p.4).

Wilfred Bion appears to have been deeply interested in science and mathematics – his *Cogitations* (Bion 1992) in particular contains many such allusions, e.g. to quantum mechanics and probability – and in this regard I

wish to suggest that his mathematical preconceptions find at least a partial
realisation in another British innovation which in many respects can be traced
to the same Kleinian roots that stimulated much of his own work, but in other
respects to a quite different tradition. I am referring to the work of William
Stephenson (1902–1989), which is known in some circles by the term 'Q
methodology', and also 'operant subjectivity' (Smith 2000, pp.319–343) and
which was a development of the Spearman School of factor analysis in the
1920s and '30s. Charles Spearman (1863–1945) was interested in revealing
the workings of the mind so as to liberate its creative potential, just as the
physicists of the time were interested in liberating the power inside the atom,
and he was aided in this endeavour by the statistical method of factor analysis
which he had invented during the first decade of the century. Mental capacity
manifests itself in virtually all tasks, from tying shoelaces and remembering
names to reciting poems and solving math problems, and by administering a
battery of tests measuring these capacities and then factor analysing them, the
members of the London School believed that the general factor common to
all abilities (called g) could be revealed. That these ideas are not of mere
historical interest is indicated in Arthur Jensen's recent *The g Factor* (1998),
which is dedicated to Spearman's memory.

Fifty years ago, another book was published that was also dedicated to
Spearman's memory – William Stephenson's *The Study of Behavior: Q-technique
and Its Methodology* (1953). Stephenson was Spearman's last assistant at the
University of London and became director of Oxford's Institute of Experimental Psychology before eventually emigrating to the United States in 1948,
where he was on the psychology faculties at the Universities of Chicago,
California (Berkeley) and Washington before assuming the position of Distinguished Professor of Advertising Research at the University of Missouri
School of Journalism. Originally trained as a physicist (PhD 1927, University
of Durham), Stephenson received his doctorate in psychology in 1929, and it
was during his early days as a psychologist that he was nominated by Ernest
Jones to undergo a psychoanalysis with Melanie Klein. Although published
eight years before Bion's *Experiences in Groups* (1961), Stephenson's book
refers to Bion's early papers on groups which originally appeared in the late
1940s and early '50s in the journal *Human Relations*, and he was involved in
two doctoral dissertations at the University of Chicago (Rosenthal 1952;
Stock 1952) in which the Q-technique procedure which he had invented was
used to help make 'explicit some of Bion's theorising about group dynamics'
(Stephenson 1953, p.236). These early efforts to explicate Bion's theory

utilising Q methodology culminated with Stock and Thelen's *Emotional Dynamics and Group Culture* (1958) (cf. Thelen 1985), and it was almost 25 years later before another effort was made within psychology (Armelius 1980; Armelius and Armelius 1985), although applications by political scientists appeared in the interim (Baas and Brown 1973; Brown and Ellithorp 1970). More recently, Lipgar (1989, 1992, 1998, 2000) has joined the two in a sustained and promising research programme that includes the incorporation of Q technique into the design of Tavistock group relations conferences.

Although Spearman referred to Stephenson as 'the foremost creative statistician in the psychology of our time' (Stephenson 1953, dust jacket), the latter departed from his mentor in many ways. Rather than correlate and factor analyse tests, which remains the overwhelmingly dominant application even today, Stephenson factored participants' subjective reactions. In his earliest published illustration, for example, he instructed experimental subjects to rank-order a set of variously-colored cards from pleasing to displeasing, the factorisation of which indicated types of aesthetic preference (Stephenson 1935). Hence, rather than search for primary abilities (such as g) conceived as objective features of the individual, Stephenson turned factor analysis 'inward' (in a manner of speaking) as a method for revealing the structure and dynamics of the person's *subjectivity* – of wishes, feelings, values, and all such normally embraced as part of 'inner life' or 'private experience' – and it was this receptivity to understanding the world from the individual's standpoint that led to widespread acceptance of his ideas and procedures by psychologists of a more humanistic bent who often eschewed science (narrowly defined) and its over-valuing of objectivity. Stephenson's ideas are an unusual blend of his training as both physicist and psychologist, and his analysis with Melanie Klein cannot but have enriched his appreciation of the centrality of personal experience.

Those unfamiliar with Stephenson's Q technique and method will benefit from a demonstration, but before proceeding it is important to note that Stephenson the Physicist was fully aware of the distinction between method and procedure on the one hand and theory and substance on the other, and his interests were in the latter; however, he was also aware that without telescopes, particle accelerators, and other devices that extend the scientist's perception, a theory deprived of contact with reality will feed on itself, narcissistically, and eventually become wan from malnutrition.[1] Stephenson was sometimes accused of being obsessed with his Q-sort method, but his motivation was no more method-oriented than that of the astronomer who habitually relies on a telescope, or the psychoanalyst who repeatedly applies the leveraging power of free association, not out of fascination with telescopes or free association as such but because of those events in the world that their application renders ostensible and that would otherwise remain obscure. Q methodology was not erected as an altar for 'the worship of the bitch-goddess objectivity,' as Reik (1948, p.147) might have elegantly char-acterised it, but as a means for enabling individuals to represent their own points of view so that these perspectives could be examined and pondered 'in the absence of the objects,' as Bion (1965, p.39) cogently expressed it.

An illustrative case: Political leadership and followership

A case presented more than 30 years ago contains most of the pertinent ingre-dients for purposes of illustration. The study, by Brown and Ellithorp (1970), was of the US public's reaction to a political challenge of an unpopular American president at the height of the Vietnam War. Senator Eugene McCarthy had contested President Lyndon Johnson (John F. Kennedy's successor) in the Democratic Party primary election in New Hampshire and had almost won, thereby demonstrating that Johnson's wartime policies did not have popular support even within his own party. McCarthy's showing gave hope to the anti-war movement, but the party leadership was successful in denying him the Democratic nomination at the 1968 Chicago convention, which was itself marred by televised demonstrations and street violence. Blocked from normal routes to legitimate power and defeated for the nomination by Hubert Humphrey, McCarthy's following had begun to disin-tegrate at the time of the study, some splitting off to support the next-best candidate, others joining an independent write-in campaign, and others lapsing into disgruntled apathy.

As is well known, Bion (1961) posits the existence of at least three group cultures. In a group dominated by the basic assumption of *dependency* (*ba*D), members adopt an emotional state characterised by an actively compliant stance vis-à-vis a central figure coupled with a general disregard of other followers. The central figure in this instance was of course McCarthy, and comments drawn from depth interviews with some of his former supporters were easily recognisable as dependent in this sense, e.g. 'I think that a man like McCarthy, even though he had failed, would have made the country proud. He was a man I could follow.' The basic assumption of *fight–flight* (*ba*F) denotes a posture, often indiscriminately adopted, of either attack or withdrawal, as in the following remarks by two interviewees:

> Maybe we weren't defeated after all. Maybe McCarthy did his job: He got rid of LBJ (Lyndon B. Johnson) didn't he? Besides, it's not over yet by any means. [*fight*]

> I don't think about McCarthy anymore. I was shocked by the result of the convention, and now I have no intention of participating further. [flight]

And by the term *pairing (ba*P), Bion is referring to a group presupposition that the members have assembled in order to break down into smaller ensembles, and that these pairs become the bearers of messianic anticipation and hopefulness on behalf of the group, as when an interviewee comments that 'the McCarthy phenomenon has allowed me to hope that changes will be made, and I am confident that by 1972 someone will emerge to provide the leadership we need.'

Table 1. Factorial design of Bion's theory		
Main effects	**Levels**	**n**
A. basic assumption	(a) dependency (b) fight/flight (c) pairing	3
B. valence	(d) positive (e) negative	2

$N = mAB = (10)(3)(2) = 60$ statements

As a way to model the volume of communication on any topic, Stephenson relied upon the principles of modern experimental design (Fisher 1935), another British innovation. Table 1 represents the main ingredients of Bion's theory of group culture in the form of a factorial design with $3 \times 2 = 6$ cells (*ad* dependency, *ae* counter-dependency, *bd* fight, *be* flight, *cd* pairing, and *ce* counter-pairing), and statements from the discourse during that period fit easily into one or the other of those categories. $m = 10$ statements were then selected from each cell, the *Q sample* (of $N = 60$) being a miniaturised version of the main issues in contention. A relatively small set of followers and former followers of Senator McCarthy were then sought out and requested to represent their own points of view in the form of a *Q sort*, by rank-ordering the statements from agree $(+5)$ to disagree (-5). It is unnecessary at this point to lapse into further technical detail, other than to say that the various perspectives (expressed in the form of Q sorts) were statistically analysed in such a way as to reveal types of reaction, of which there were five.[2]

Before turning to the findings, it is important to note points of confluence between Bion and Stephenson. Basic assumptions in Bion's sense are presuppositions made by individuals and are typically expressed in verbal form, as when a participant in one of the original groups asserts that 'Dr. Bion is the only one who is ever listened to here, and he never says anything helpful' (Bion 1961, p.41), which Bion then uses, along with other comments, as evidence of one kind or another, e.g. about the presence of *ba*D, *ba*P, or other phenomena. (As Bion [1965, p.38] once remarked, 'The medium in which the psycho-analyst works is verbalized thoughts.') Similarly in Q methodology, individuals express various sentiments (in this case about McCarthy's challenge to President Johnson) and from this concourse of communicability is drawn a representative sampling, with Bion's theory being used as a way to facilitate the sampling. That is, it is this set of 60 statements of 'verbalized thoughts' (Q sample), provisionally structured according to Bion's theory, that provides the medium through which participants then express their views in Q-sort form, which is analogous to the free expressions in Bion's group. In both cases, verbalisations are from the person's subjective perspective (Stephenson), or vertex (Bion 1965, pp.91–92). And just as individuals have the capacity for 'instantaneous involuntary combination,' or valency, at an emotional level (Bion 1961, p.153), so does the factor analysis of Q sorts demonstrate the capacity for perspectives to cluster involuntarily (i.e. without intent to cluster). Whether or not participants are in direct interaction with one another when they perform their Q sorts is irrelevant, just as their actual presence in a group is not a prerequisite for the occurrence of group dynamics. Bringing people physically together is a convenience that facilitates demonstration and, as Bion says, enables him to 'give an interpretation without having to shout it' (*ibid.* p.132). Beyond that, 'no individual, however isolated in time and space, should be regarded as…lacking in active manifestations of group psychology'(*ibid.* p.169).

The fact that the Q sample was structured in terms of Bion's group theory gives rise to a lively expectation that there will be some connection between the theory and participants' responses (as condensed through factor analysis), and the analysis did in fact reveal response patterns which closely approximated what is known theoretically about the group cultures of dependency, pairing and fight, but two other patterns, which were just as real empirically, were less aligned with theory. Space precludes going into detail, but even a limited display of two of the patterns should strengthen conviction concerning the reciprocal relationship between Bion's group cultures and the evidential leverage which Q methodology provides.

Recall from Note 2 that the statistical analysis eventuates in a pattern of statements associated with factor scores ranging from +5 (most agree) to –5 (most disagree), and expressing the composite response of a number of individuals displaying valency for the same viewpoint. For the first group of participants, the characteristics of pairing are conspicuous in their composite scores, as revealed in the following statements with which they most strongly agreed and disagreed:

> *Most agree*: Even at the Democratic convention, right up through the voting of the states, I hoped and prayed that McCarthy would get the nomination... The McCarthy phenomenon has allowed me to hope that changes will be made. I am confident that by 1972 someone will emerge to provide the leadership we need... McCarthy was an intellectual. The average person did not understand him. To understand him you have to be educated – above average.

> *Most disagree*: I suppose I was fairly unresponsive to friendly gestures from other persons in the McCarthy group, but I was generally too involved with the 'cause' to waste time socialising... I didn't have much time for those who were interested in McCarthy because it was 'the thing' to do. It wasn't supposed to be fun... The McCarthy movement could have attracted more support if its members hadn't acted like they were part of an exclusive club.

The most salient feature of pairing is hope, which can 'be taken by itself as evidence that the pairing group is in existence, even when other evidence appears to be lacking' (Bion 1961, p.151), and hope is highly visible among those statements with which this group of participants most agree – hope that McCarthy would win the nomination and that a messiah would emerge by the time of the next election. Also present is the tell-tale aristocratic bias expressed in the belief that McCarthy and (by implication) his followers were above average. The sexual overtones typically associated with pairing are more apparent in the statements with which these individuals disagree, which indicate that they were responsive to friendly gestures by others in the movement and that their involvement was the 'in' thing to do. Also in evidence is a denial that the McCarthyites acted like an exclusive club, which runs counter to the aristocratic bias manifested by the same individuals in their choice of statements with which to agree. In keeping with the pairing motif, it is worth noting that two of the individuals in this group (a female and a male) were the president and vice president of the local McCarthy group and at the time were romantically involved.

The pairing group can be contrasted with another that existed alongside it in the same work group, but was dominated by the basic assumption of fight, as is apparent in the following statements with which this group agreed and disagreed:

> *Most agree*: Maybe we weren't defeated after all. Maybe McCarthy did his job: He got rid of LBJ didn't he? Besides, it's not over yet by any means... I was glad McCarthy didn't endorse anyone at the convention. I figured, if he was going to buck the system, he should go all the way... I supported McCarthy because he bucked the political system. He knew the strength of the Johnson Machine, but chose to go ahead regardless of the consequences... I liked McCarthy's attitude after the convention. Humphrey acted like it was a kid's game where everyone shakes hands after it's over. McCarthy realised it wasn't a game, that the issues still existed.

> *Most disagree*: I don't think about McCarthy anymore. I was shocked by the result of the convention, and now I have no intention of participating further... Frankly, I'm tired of the whole mess – Republicans, Democrats, even McCarthy and politics in general. When these things come up, I would just as soon change the subject... When McCarthy endorsed Humphrey, it was his recognition that you can't beat the system. I don't blame him; I think he's probably right.

It is worth highlighting the flight character of the statements with which this group of individuals disagreed – flight, that is, in the sense of emotional disengagement – hence the fight/flight nature of this group culture. This group of individuals (who, incidentally, were all males) is arrayed for battle, disdainful of compromise, and unwilling as yet to concede defeat and to experience the despair that would ensue; indeed, the overtly aggressive attitude may exist in part as a barrier to despair and to its accompanying sense of helplessness (see Duncan 1980).

Space precludes going into detail about the dependency group which was in evidence,[3] but it is of considerable methodological interest to note that two other groups emerged which were unanticipated:

1. The first, which initially supported McCarthy, appeared even more interested in a Democratic Party victory and was willing to support its party's nominee when McCarthy lost the nomination, and it was this pragmatism and cooperative attitude which led to the conclusion that this group, although not free of emotional life, came closest to Bion's work group.

2. The members of the fifth and final group had, at the time of their interviews, adopted the view that 'you can't beat the system' and were in the process of retreating into disgruntled and hope-dashed inactivity. This stance of angry withdrawal could be interpreted as a manifestation of baF (flight), but Bion, who generously agreed to comment on a pre-publication draft of the original study (see Brown and Ellithorp 1970, p.361), suggested that the factor might represent an attitude of hatred toward thoughtful observation itself (which is not incompatible with flight), and that the group's manifest depression might have two roots: failure of the liberal-scientific attitude to prevail and at the same time a failure to destroy the liberal-scientific attitude.[4] The methodological point, however, is that whereas the measurement procedures were organised around the basic assumptions (as shown in Table 1), this did not preclude unexpected realisations from manifesting themselves in the factor analysis, thereby liberating the researcher to some extent from 'the obstructive quality of preconceptions' (Bion 1977, p.23), which can have such a deleterious effect on the selection and interpretation of facts.

Intensive analysis of single cases

The previous illustration has the character of a snapshot in that it freeze-frames the attitudes of a group of participants at a specific moment. Data of this kind can be of considerable importance, of course, inasmuch as they provide realisations of theoretical preconceptions related to the wider world beyond Tavistock group-relations conferences. There is a dynamic quality to groups, however, and in order to reveal dynamics it is necessary to incorporate duration so as to permit the observation of fluctuations under changing conditions. One role of measurement is to bring dynamics under its suzereignty, thereby providing a 'taming' function analogous to the Grid (Bion 1977, 1997) – not as a substitute for observation, as Bion (1977, p.39) made clear, but in readiness for it.

The remaining pages provide space for little more than a caricature of a single individual's experiences during the course of a brief group relations exercise. Mr G (as he will be referred to) had a history of conflict with a demanding father and consequent closeness to a consoling mother, and this had inclined him to something of a passive-aggressive style in response to authority of an overbearing kind. At age 23 and in graduate school (and bound ultimately for a successful career in law), G was participating in a small-scale Tavistock group-relations exercise which involved five small-group and two large-group experiences as segments of a broader seminar.

True to his character, G remained generally aloof until the final session, although his fidgets and glares betrayed a simmering withdrawal rather than indifference. Once the consultant arrived and seated himself for the final session, G launched into a barrage of attacks, accusing the consultant of inhibiting the group, of issuing biting criticisms, and of exercising negative leadership, and concluding that the only reason he was speaking up now was because 'this is the last meeting and I don't give a damn'.

As part of the research component of the seminar, G and the other members were provided with a set of adjectives (each typed on a separate card) which they used to provide Q-sort representations of various images of self and others. When describing himself, for instance, G rank-ordered the adjectives from 'most like me' (+5) to 'most unlike me' (−5), and similarly for the other images, some of which related to G's personal life and others to experiences in the group, as shown in Table 2. (G originally provided more than 20 Q sorts, of which the 13 in Table 2 have been selected for purposes of illustration.) Hence, he was instructed prior to the group experience to describe himself, his ideal self (i.e. the kind of person he would like to be), his conscience (how he was taught that he ought to be), and how he felt on that occasion when he recalled being most sorrowful; he was also asked to describe his mother and father, and the person he most hated. Following the first and fifth small groups, G was also instructed to provide his retrospective perceptions of himself in the group, the group as a whole, and the consultant. As in the prior example, the Q sorts were correlated and factor analysed.

Table 2 contains the kind of information which Q methodology provides in studies of this kind, which reveals in this instance that G's 13 Q sorts represented variations on three themes (factors I, II, and III) – actually, more than three in as much as factors I and II in particular are markedly polar; i.e. some conceptions (e.g. the self) were described by G in ways virtually the opposite of other conceptions (e.g., the ideal self). The factors can be thought of in terms of Bion's (1965) theory of transformations, where each completed Q sort is the end product of a transformation ($T\beta_G$) of G's feelings and perceptions (O) from his vertex, and where the Q sorting itself is the transformational process ($T\alpha_G$). Whether $T\alpha$ is *rigid* or *projective* (Bion 1965, p.36) depends in large measure on the influence of L, H, and K (Bion 1965, pp.46, 68), i.e. on emotional involvement (of love, hate, and the desire to know or understand).

Table 2. G's operant factors

Conditions		Factors[a]		
		I	II	III
Personal	self	**.72**	−.16	.24
	ideal	**−.79**	.16	.28
	conscience	−.19	.02	**.67**
	father	**−.48**	**−.71**	.04
	mother	−.13	**.81**	.34
	sorrow	**.84**	.00	.19
	hate	.06	**−.87**	−.08
First Group	self	**.84**	.10	−.01
	group	.38	**.71**	.23
	consultant	−.16	**−.74**	−.30
Final Group	self	.11	.15	**.44**
	group	.14	**.86**	.24
	consultant	.05	**−.71**	−.06

[a] Factor loadings in bold face are significant (p < 01).

The factor analysis itself is a rigid transformation of the original Q sorts: The factors are matters of *lateral communication* (Bion 1977, p.29), i.e. of second-order transformations which merely reveal the underlying structure of the Q sorts (and, presumably, of the perceptions which gave rise to them) without affecting O or Tβ. Whereas study participants such as G can typically converse in a reasoned manner about each Q sort that is completed, they are invariably unaware of the structure (such as factors I, II, and III in Table 2) which their Q sortings have produced. This implies that there is a *constant conjunction* (Bion 1965, p.14) between certain of G's images, but that he is aware neither of the conjunctions nor of their constancies.

Before providing an interpretation of the results, it is important to consider the status of the conditions of experimentation listed in Table 2. The terms *ideal* and *conscience* might sound like quaint holdovers from orthodox psychoanalysis, and the conditions *hate* and *sorrow* like rather pallid surrogates for Klein's conceptions of the paranoid–schizoid and depressive positions. These conditions are not intended as *tests* of either Freud or Klein, however, at least not in any crude hypothetico-deductive sense; rather, they serve as prompts for inducing the appearance of those dimensions (I, II, and III) documented in Table 2 but which existed prior to the Q sortings and which could have been induced with a different set of instructions.[5] Terms such as *ideal* and *sorrow* (and even *mother, father,* and *group*) are comparable to elements in an analogy, but as Bion points out, 'confusion can occur because attention is given to the two images used in the analogy, and not, which is the important point, the relationship between them' (Bion 1977, p.32); i.e. what is of importance are not the specific conditions governing the Q sortings, but the factor structures which the Q sortings render legible and which tell us something about the natural history of the 'mind' which produced them.

In Mr G's case, the results in Table 2 indicate that he struggles with a sharp conflict between his actual and ideal self (the Q sorts representing each being virtually the opposite of one another in factor I), and factor scores indicated that G characterised the former as unhappy, insecure, dependent, and timid, and the latter as confident, aggressive, tough, and intellectual. This bipolar structure is reminiscent of Freud's description of the melancholic's conflict 'in which the ideal...relentlessly exhibits its condemnation of the ego in delusions of inferiority and in self-depreciation' (Freud 1922, p.107). The chronic character of G's depressive state is reinforced by the fact that he describes the most sorrowful point in his life in the same way that he describes his everyday self. Factor II captures a polarised family romance, with mother at one pole (characterised in the factor scores as tolerant, warm, sincere, and consistent) and father at the other (uncompromising, domineering, self-righteous, malicious), and it is perhaps the father's domineering nature and attitude toward his son that led to G's internalisation of a self-depreciating ego-ideal.

It is also conceivable that this parental conflict provided the early object relationships that G carried over into the group setting, for at both the first and fifth group meetings, he depicted his small group in the same motherly terms (warm, sincere) and the consultant as if he were father (uncompromising, domineering). G's insurrection at the final group meeting – rationalised by this being 'the last meeting and I don't give a damn' – bears the stamp of the insurgence of the sons in Freud's (1922) just-so story of the primal horde, and it is significant in this regard that G's self – normally associated with factor I – undergoes transformation and reappears in factor III where it shares factor space with his conscience (characterised as ambitious, active, conscientious, confident). It is as if, through projective identification, G were able to liberate himself from all the timidity and insecurity of his melancholic self through a singular act of well-aimed aggression against authority, which, in term of the Grid, would provisionally take its place in cell A6: the extrusion of β elements through action. Had the consultant responded as the threatened father (thereby living out G's projections) or had G been forced to confront the implications of his action, he might have found himself in a position similar to those McCarthy supporters referred to in the previous study, of whom Bion suggested the dilemma: failure of the liberal-scientific attitude to prevail and at the same time a failure to destroy the liberal-scientific attitude. But G rebelled in the group's final hour, thereby precluding examination of the relationship between reality and his phantasies of it, which, after all, is the unsophisticated way in which we expect individuals and groups to utilise time when under the influence of basic assumptions.[6]

Before concluding, a brief comment needs to be made about interpretation. An individual's Q sort is a pattern of statements, which must be understood for the same reason that the same pattern would require understanding were it uttered in psychotherapy. (This also holds true for a Q factor, which is a composite of several Q sorts.) The therapist's primary assets in this venture are *empathy*, which is the ability to project into another's frame of mind, and *receptivity*, which is the ability to provide a hospitable repository for the other person's projections and projective identifications (Salzberger-Wittenberg 1970, pp.136–140). Stephenson (1983, p.74) expressed this as the Sontag Rule (named for essayist Susan Sontag): 'to *see* more, to *hear* more, to *feel* more' before jumping to conclusions, whether about art, literature, patients, or Q factors. And whereas social scientists rarely have therapeutic intent, the skills they require are the same as those of the therapist, if less well-honed.

Concluding remarks

Psychoanalysts are generally wary of the claims of science when applied to the human realm and of efforts to express human experience in mathematical form. In a message posted to the Bion electronic discussion list <Bion97@listserver.sicap.it>, for instance, one contributor recently commented as follows:

> In all this exploration of how psychoanalysis is like and unlike the 'natural sciences,' the one thing that seems always to be disregarded is that subjective experience is ultimately private and unknowable to anyone but the subject, while 'natural' science observations and experiments are *ultimately* public and verifiable. We can all (potentially) read the meter on a geiger counter, but it is impossible to say what 'red' looks like or 'C sharp' sounds like (even though we can agree that a certain 'stimulus' produces red or C sharp, we have no way to compare your *experience* of it with mine). (V. L. Schermer, personal communication, 12 July 2000)

This admonition is oft-times warranted, and Bion, too, was cautious in this regard, as when he said that 'the numbers representing feelings have not evolved so that they can handle the realizations of the domain from which they appear to have sprung' (Bion 1970, p.91). Even so, there was something brutely empirical if not numerical about his position, as evident in the comment quoted previously (Endnote 1) that a psychoanalytic theory 'is no good to me unless it reminds me of something which I can see at any time in the world in which I live' (Bion 1978, p.44), and in the view that 'psycho-analysts should restate the hypotheses of which [a theory] is composed in terms of empirically verifiable data' (Bion 1967, p.110). In fact, there is something concrete and, in a qualified sense, 'behavioristic' about the British School generally, as in the characterisation of projective identification as 'the capacity to express feeling through behavior' (Money-Kyrle 1966, p.228) and as an activity that 'results in modes of behaviour and action which in actuality evoke the desired response from a receptive person' (Salzberger-Wittenberg 1970, p.138).

Stephenson was likewise empirical in this qualified sense. He wished to base his science upon observable events, but this need not exclude subjectivity as long as personal experience – which, as Schermer rightly points out, is 'ultimately private and unknowable to anyone but the subject' – can be rendered manifest through an operation (such as Q sorting) performed by the person whose experience it is. Once a participant's vertex has been transformed into Q-sort form, the numbers become as readable as those on a geiger counter. Moreover, as shown in the studies above, this same subjective operation makes it possible, as Schermer required, 'to compare your experience of it with mine,' and this holds true whether the 'it' consists of experiences of McCarthy, study groups, C sharp, or red.

References

Armelius, K. (1980) 'The task as a determinant of group culture.' In *Umeå Psychological Reports* (University of Umeå, Sweden), No. 156, 12pp.

Armelius, K. and Armelius, B.-Å. (1985) 'Group personality, task and group culture.' In M. Pines (ed) *Bion and Group Psychotherapy*. London: Routledge and Kegan Paul.

Baas, L. R. and Brown, S. R. (1973) 'Generating rules for intensive analysis: The study of transformations.' *Psychiatry, 36*, 2, 172–183.

Bion, W. R. (1961) *Experiences in Groups*. London: Tavistock Publications.

Bion, W. R. (1963) *Elements of Psycho-Analysis*. New York: Basic Books.

Bion, W. R. (1965) *Transformations: Change from Learning to Growth*. New York: Basic Books.

Bion, W. R. (1967) *Second Thoughts: Selected Papers on Psycho-Analysis*. London: Heinemann.

Bion, W. R. (1970) *Attention and Interpretation: A Scientific Approach to Insight in Psycho-Analysis and Groups*. New York: Basic Books.

Bion, W. R. (1977) *Two Papers: The Grid and Caesura*. Rio de Janeiro: Imago Editora.

Bion, W. R. (1978) *Four Discussions with W. R. Bion*. Perthshire: Clunie Press.

Bion, W. R. (1987) *Clinical Seminars: Brasilia and São Paulo, and Four Papers*. (F. Bion, ed) Abingdon: Fleetwood Press.

Bion, W. R. (1992) *Cogitations*. London: Karnac Books.

Bion, W. R. (1997) *Taming Wild Thoughts*. (F. Bion, ed) London: Karnac Books.

Brown, S. R. (1980) *Political Subjectivity: Applications of Q Methodology in Political Science*. New Haven, CT: Yale University Press.

Brown, S. R. (1989) 'A brief note on Harris's characterization of interpretations by the Kleinian School.' *Melanie Klein and Object Relations 7*, 1, 82–88.

Brown, S. R. and Ellithorp, J. D. (1970) 'Emotional experiences in political groups: The case of the McCarthy phenomenon.' *American Political Science Review 64*, 2, 349–366.

Duncan, M. G. (1980) 'Radical activism and the defense against despair.' *Sociological Focus 13*, 3, 255–263.

Fisher, R. A. (1935) *The Design of Experiments*. London: Oliver and Boyd.

Freud, S. (1922) *Group Psychology and the Analysis of the Ego*. (J. Strachey, trans.) London: Hogarth Press.

Jensen, A. R. (1998) *The g Factor: The Science of Mental Ability*. Westport, CT: Praeger.

Lipgar, R. M. (1989) 'View of the small group consultant's role: A Q-methodology study.' In T. W. Hugg, N. M. Carson and R. M. Lipgar (eds) *Changing Group Relations: The Next Twenty-Five Years in America*. (Proceedings of the Ninth Scientific Meeting of the A. K. Rice Institute, New York). Jupiter, FL: A.K. Rice Institute.

Lipgar, R. M. (1992) 'A programme of group relations research: Emphasis on inquiry and the trial of techniques.' *Group Analysis 25*, 3, 365–375.

Lipgar, R. M. (1998) 'Beyond Bion's *Experiences in Groups*: Group relations research and learning.' In P. Bion Talamo, F. Borgogno and S. A. Merciai (eds) *Bion's Legacy to Groups*. London: Karnac Books.

Lipgar, R. M. (2000, October) 'Using Q studies to learn more about learning in A. K. Rice/Tavistock group relations conferences.' Read at a meeting of the International Society for the Scientific Study of Subjectivity, Tulsa, Oklahoma.

Money-Kyrle, R. E. (1966) 'British schools of psychoanalysis: I. Melanie Klein and Kleinian psychoanalytic theory.' In S. Arieti (ed) *American Handbook of Psychiatry* (Vol. 3). New York: Basic Books.

Reik, T. (1948) *Listening with the Third Ear: The Inner Experience of a Psychoanalyst.* New York: Farrar, Straus.

Rosenthal, D. (1952) *Perception of Some Personality Characteristics in Members of a Small Group.* Unpublished doctoral dissertation, University of Chicago.

Salzberger-Wittenberg, I. (1970) *Psycho-analytic Insight and Relationships: A Kleinian Approach.* London: Routledge & Kegan Paul.

Semple, J. G. and Kneebone, G. T. (1952) *Algebraic Projective Geometry.* Oxford: Clarendon Press.

Smith, N. W. (2000) *Current Systems in Psychology: History, Theory, Research, and Applications.* Belmont, CA: Wadsworth/Thomson Learning.

Stephenson, W. (1935) 'Correlating persons instead of tests.' *Character and Personality 4*, 1, 17–24.

Stephenson, W. (1953) *The Study of Behavior: Q-Technique and its Methodology.* Chicago: University of Chicago Press.

Stephenson, W. (1983) 'Against interpretation.' *Operant Subjectivity 6*, 3/4, 73–103, 109–125.

Stephenson, W. (1989) 'Quantum theory of subjectivity.' *Integrative Psychiatry 6*, 3/4, 180–187.

Stock, D. (1952) *The Relationship between the Sociometric Structure of the Group and Certain Personality Characteristics of the Individual.* Unpublished doctoral dissertation, University of Chicago.

Stock, D. and Thelen, H. A. (1958) *Emotional Dynamics and Group Culture: Experimental Studies of Individual and Group Behavior.* Washington, DC: National Training Laboratories; New York University Press.

Thelen, H. A. (1985) 'Research with Bion's concepts.' In M. Pines (ed) *Bion and Group Psychotherapy.* London: Routledge & Kegan Paul.

Endnotes

1. Bion (1978) was perhaps expressing a similar view when he remarked that 'I am sick and tired of hearing psycho-analytic theories – if they don't remind me of real life they are no use to me. An application of a theory about dependence is no good to me unless it reminds me of something which I can see at any time in the world in which I live' (p.44).

2. Specifically, the $n = 34$ Q sorts were intercorrelated (Pearson's r) and factor analysed (principal axes), and the 34×34 correlation matrix was reduced to five factors which were then rotated (varimax) to a position approximating simple structure. Factor scores were then estimated for each of the $N = 60$ statements in each of the $m = 5$ factors. For interpretive purposes, the scores were expressed in the original +5 (agree) to –5 (disagree) format. Additional details are in the original study (Brown and Ellithorp 1970). For further information about Q technique and method generally, see Brown (1980) and Stephenson (1953). On the virtual identity of the mathematics of Q factor analysis and the mathematics of quantum mechanics, consult Stephenson (1989).

3.   This group, composed mainly of women, idealised McCarthy and took little inter-
      est in other group members, as indicated in the statements to which they assigned
      the highest scores: 'I think that a man like McCarthy, even though he had failed,
      would have made the country proud; he was a man I could follow'; 'I really felt re-
      lieved to have someone like him stand up for what I believed,' and 'Although I sup-
      ported McCarthy as a candidate, I didn't bother to take the time to become deeply
      involved with other McCarthyites.'

4.   Bion did not elaborate on the ambiguous concept of 'liberal-scientific attitude,'
      but it could have been his way to try to communicate to a young political scientist
      something of what he and Melanie Klein meant by the epistemophilic instinct, or
      K– i.e. of the desire of these participants to reach an intellectual understanding of
      what was occurring politically and the simultaneous inability of reason (from their
      vertex) to prevail. Political withdrawal is a form of attack on the K-link (i.e. an at-
      tack on the tie that binds the person to the political order), yet participants feel
      compelled to validate the social link by providing a socially acceptable justifica-
      tion for their conduct. Their feeling of frustration is narcissistic, whereas their ra-
      tionalizations are social – hence the conceptualization of the individual as a
      political animal (Bion1967, p.118).

5.   Another way to express this is to say that conditions of instruction have the status
      of probes into reality rather than containers of it (Bion 1970, p.73), hence are de-
      signed to evoke responses which are then subject to interpretation (Brown 1989).

6.   At the conclusion of the group exercise, and as part of the seminar's postmortem of
      it, Mr G was shown the results in Table 2, which were explained and discussed in
      light of Freud's and Bion's theories and the events which had transpired. As if ex-
      posed to a helpful analytic interpretation, G's attitude visibly softened toward the
      person who had served as consultant to the group. This corresponds to Bion's ob-
      servation: 'Every interpretation means that a change takes place – if it is a correct
      interpretation. The puzzling situation which has been made clear by the interpre-
      tation at once disappears...' (Bion 1987, p.13).

The Contributors

Hanna Biran is a clinical psychologist and organisational consultant. She is a lecturer on Group Psychotherapy at the Tel-Aviv University, School of Medicine. She is a Founding Member of the Innovation and Change in Society (ICS) foundation (founded in 1987). Hanna Biran is also a member of the Tel-Aviv Institute of Contemporary Psychoanalysis and a Member of The Israeli Institute of Group Analysis.

Steven R. Brown is Professor of Political Science at Kent State University. He was a Fullbright Lecturer, Researcher and Visiting Professor at Seoul National University, Korea in 1981;Visiting Scholar at the School of Education, University of Leicester, England, 1988–1989 and Executive Director of the International Society of Political Psychology, 1997–1998. He currently edits the journal *Policy Sciences*.

Jacquelyne P. Colombier has a PhD in philosophy and psychology. She is a psychoanalyst and editor of the journal *Le Mouvement Psychanalytique, Revue des Revues Freudiennes* (certified L'Harmattan).

Mark F. Ettin, PhD, CGP, is a clinical psychologist and group psychotherapist. He is on the Continuing Education Faculty at Rutgers University's School of Social Work. He is a Consultant and Member of the AK Rice Institute, USA. He was awarded Group Psychotherapy Foundation's inaugural prize for excellence in Psychodynamic Group Theory in 1996. He is the author of *Foundations and Applications of Group Psychotherapy: A Sphere of Influence* (Jessica Kingsley Publishers, 1999) and co-author of *Group Psychotherapy and Political Reality: A Two-way Mirror* (International Universities Press, 2002).

Robert French is Senior Lecturer in Organisation Studies at Bristol Business School, The University of the West of England and an independent organisational consultant. He co-edited *Rethinking Management Education* with Christopher Grey (Sage, 1996) and *Group Relations, Management, and Organization* with Russ Vince (Oxford University Press, 1999).

James Grotstein is Clinical Professor of Psychiatry at the UCLA School of Medicine and a training and supervising analyst at the Los Angeles Psychoanalytic Institute and the Psychoanalytic Center of California, Los Angeles. He is the author of over two hundred published articles and eight books. His most recently published book is *Who Is the Dreamer Who Dreams the Dream: A Study of Psychic Presences* (Analytic Press, 2000).

W. Gordon Lawrence, MA (Aberd.) Dr. rer. oec. (Bergische) is a former staff member of the Tavistock Institute of Human Relations, London and a visiting professor at Cranfield University. Currently he is a visiting professor at the University of Northumberland, Newcastle, and the New Bulgarian University. He is a managing partner of Symbiont Ventures and the Social Dreaming Institute, London. He publishes extensively and his latest books are *Social Dreaming @ Work* (1998), *Tongued with Fire: Groups in Experience* (2000) and *Experiences in Social Dreaming* (2003); all published by Karnac Books, London.

Robert M. Lipgar PhD, ABPP, is a clinical psychologist in private practice and Clinical Professor in the Department of Psychiatry at The University of Chicago. He is a Fellow in the A.K. Rice Institute for the Study of Social Systems and a Life Fellow in the American Group Psychotherapy Association.

Malcolm Pines is a Founding Member of the Institute of Group Analysis, London, Past President of the International Association of Group Psychotherapy and a former Consultant at Cassel, St George's and Maudsley Hospitals and the Tavistock Clinic. He is Past President of the Group-Analytic Society and Editor of the *International Library of Group Analysis,* author of *Circular Reflections: Selected Papers on Group Analysis and Psychoanalysis* (Jessica Kingsley Publishers, 1998) and co-editor of *Dreams in Group Psychotherapy: Theory and Technique* with Robi Friedman and Claudio Neri (Jessica Kingsley Publishers, 2001).

Lia Pistiner de Cortiñas, PhD, is Professor of the post-graduate courses 'Psychosomatic Disturbances' and 'Introduction to Bion's Ideas' at the Faculty of Psychology of the University of Buenos Aires. She is a lawyer, a psychologist and a training and supervising analyst at the Buenos Aires Psychoanalytic Association (IPA). She is the author of many published articles in Spanish, English and French and has written two books in collaboration. The most recent is *Bion Conocido/Desconocido.*

Jeffrey D. Roth, MD, FAGPA, FASAM, is in private practice of addiction psychiatry and group psychotherapy and a fellow in the AGPA.

Mannie Sher is a Director of the Tavistock Institute and Director of the Institute's Group Relations Programme. Through this role he provides work leaders with opportunities for learning about leadership and authority in organisations. These learning opportunities are underpinned by Mannie's experience over 30 years as an organisational development consultant and his conviction that organisational performance can be better understood by integrating social science action research methodologies with organisational theory and systems psychodynamic paradigms.

Peter Simpson is Principal Lecturer and Director of the Research Unit in Organisation Studies at Bristol Business School, University of the West of England.

Gerhard Wilke is a group analyst in private practice. He specialises in organisational consultancy and large group work and has clients across Europe. Recently, he published a book about his approach to organisational work entitled *How to be a Good Enough GP: Surviving and Thriving in the New Primary Care Organisations* (Radcliff Press, 2000).

Subject Index

and its conductor 70–105
methodology of leadership 29–36
process oscillates between paired
  oppositions 57
Latecomers, The (Gould) 259–62
leadership
  authority of leader 39–40
  basic assumptions 136–7
  group acceptance of authority of
    39–40
  leader serves as role model in culture
    building and articulation process
    57–8
  member–leader interface 43–5
  methodology of large group 29–36
  parental qualities 136
  political, and followership 288–93
  responsibilities and prerogatives of
    35–6
  scapegoat leader 43
learning
  Bion as pioneer in 223–301
  at the edges between knowing and
    non-knowing 182–203
    emotional experiences of the edge
      190–1
    naive vs political: working with
      parallel truths 192–5
    parallels to Bion 186–9
    staying at the edge: necessary
      disposition 195–7
    traditional approaches to accessing
      truth-in-the-moment 184–6
    traditions of this state of mind
      197–9
  and thinking 128–30
L-H-K (love-hate-knowledge) links 12,
  171, 276–7
linking, attacks on 166–7
  and 'alpha function' as opposite
    elements of organizations'
    dynamics 164–81
Lithuania 91

Local Group Psychotherapy Society
  subgroup 49
looking-glass phase, non-identified
  264–6
love 133–5
L(ove) links 12, 14, 166, 171, 241, 251,
  257, 272, 276–7, 294

Mass in B Minor (Bach) 268
Maudsley Hospital, London 79
measurement and theory, constant
  conjunction of 285–301
median group
  clinical exposition of 37–59
    heretical sentiments 42–3
    member–leader interface: group
      protection of integrity 43–5
    power and fragility of membership
      46–7
    who will be forced out? 43–5
    who will save group and what will
      members believe in? 40–1
    who would speak and who will
      listen? 38–40
    will group's differences keep it
      apart and in perpetual conflict
      55–6
  depth of median and Tavistock large
    groups 62–3
  mythic symbols generated by 58–9
  prevalence of whole group and
    subgroup themes 54–6
    class 54
    freedom vs constraint 54
    prejudice 55
    status concerns 54
  setup and what it pulls for 34–5
  cf. Tavistock large group setup 32–3
    comparison of models 59–65
    consulting to a median group
      experience 63–4
median model (de Maré) 40
medicalising social distress 131

Author Index

Agazarian, Y. 47, 65, 66
Alderfer, C. 60, 66
Alibegašvili, G. 202
Alpatov, M. 202
Anthony 54
Anthony, E.J. 36, 66, 138, 144
Appelbaum, D. 201
Arden, M. 200, 203
Aristarco of Samos 242
Armelius, B.-Å. 287, 299
Armelius, K. 287, 299
Armstrong, D.G. 41, 62, 68, 128, 143, 184, 200
Arthur 52, 54

Baas, L.R. 287, 299
Babić, G. 202
Bach, J.S. 254, 257, 258, 266, 268, 274, 278, 280–2, 284
Bain, A. 43, 68, 216, 218, 222
Bakan, D. 200, 203
Balfour, F.H.G. 144
Balint, M. 79, 103
Banet, A. 63, 66
Barker, M. 111
Bate, W.J. 198, 200
Bazzana, K. 263, 279, 281, 282, 284
Beck, A. 54, 66
Beckett, S. 279
Bernstein, L. 280
Bettelheim, B. 86, 103, 200, 203
Beukema, S. 62, 68
Bianchedi, E. 227, 250
Bion, F. 189, 255, 256, 278, 280, 282
Bion, W.R. 7–26, 29–32, 34–8, 40–4, 46, 47, 55, 57–66, 71–80, 85, 88, 95, 102, 103, 109–17, 120, 121, 123, 126, 129–44, 149, 150, 154, 162–6, 180–4, 186, 188–90, 192, 195–200, 202–5, 210–14, 216, 218, 220–2, 225–47, 250–301
Bion Talamo, P. 256, 280
Biran, H. 9, 16, 61, 63, 66, 164–81, 302
Bly, R. 101, 103
Bohm, D. 51, 66
Bohr, N. 83
Bolas, C. 95, 104
Bollas, C. 63, 66, 209–10, 214, 215, 222
Bott Spillius, E. 111
Bowlby, J. 111
Brahms, J. 280
Brent 59
Bridger, H. 111
Brown, D. 73, 104
Brown, S.R. 24, 26, 285–301, 302
Buber, M. 230
Burack, C. 53, 66
Burckhardt, T. 184, 200, 202
Burrow, T. 52
Butler, Dom C. 197, 200

Campbell, J. 200, 202
Cano, D. 61, 66
Carr, A.W. 31, 68
Carrithers, M. 81, 104
Chatzidakis, M. 202
Cohen, B. 60, 66, 67
Cohn, B. 53–4, 66
Colombier, J.P. 21, 24, 253–84, 302
Coltart, N. 200, 203
Cooper, L. 31, 67
Cynthia 52, 55
Cytrynbaum, S. 163

Davies, P. 212, 222
de Bianchedi, E.T. 25, 26
de Maré, P. 29, 32, 34, 36, 39–41, 44, 51, 60, 63, 65, 66, 73–5, 77, 94, 104
Dicks, H. 111
Dood, M. 281
Dorothy 44, 58

316